Islam and Democracy

D1529440

Islam and Democracy

The Failure of Dialogue in Algeria

Frédéric Volpi

Pluto Press

LONDON • STERLING, VIRGINIA

495I8928

First published 2003 by Pluto Press
345 Archway Road, London N6 5AA
and 22883 Quicksilver Drive,
Sterling, VA 20166–2012, USA

www.plutobooks.com

British Library Cataloguing in Publication Data
A catalogue record for this book is available from the British Library

ISBN 0 7453 1977 7 hardback
ISBN 0 7453 1976 9 paperback

Library of Congress Cataloging in Publication Data
Volpi, Frédéric.
  Islam and democracy : the failure of dialogue in Algeria / Frédéric Volpi.
    p. cm.
Includes bibliographical references.
  ISBN 0–7453–1977–7 — ISBN 0–7453–1976–9 (pbk.)
  1. Demonstrations—Algeria. 2. Islam and politics—Algeria. 3. Algeria—Politics and government, 4. Algeria—Social conditions 5. Islamic fundamentalism—Algeria. I. Title.
  JQ3231 .V65 2002
  965.05'3—dc21

                                                        2002005040

10 9 8 7 6 5 4 3 2 1

Designed and produced for Pluto Press by
Chase Publishing Services, Fortescue, Sidmouth EX10 9QG
Typeset from disk by Stanford DTP Services, Towcester
Printed in the European Union by Antony Rowe, Chippenham, England

Contents

Preface and Acknowledgements

The dramatic political changes that have taken place in Algeria since 1988 have baffled even the most seasoned political actors and analysts. The unexpected move toward political liberalisation that the Algerian regime made in 1988 set in motion one of the very first and most thorough processes of democratic transition in the Middle East and North Africa. This process of political liberalisation took an unexpected turn in 1990–91, when a newly created Islamic party, the Islamic Salvation Front or FIS (*Front Islamique du Salut*), took the lead in the local and parliamentary elections. A more dramatic political U-turn took place in early 1992 when the army supported a constitutional coup to prevent the Islamic fundamentalists from reaping the full benefit of their electoral gains and from forming a new government. This military intervention gave the signal for a popular insurrection by the pro-Islamic sections of the population that had contributed to the electoral victory of the FIS. Dramatically, it also set the stage for a radical Islamic guerrilla movement which became, after an initial period of street protest and civil disobedience, the pace-setter for the country's social and political metamorphosis.

The Algerian civil conflict raged most fiercely between 1992 and 1999. It involved a large proportion of the population in a struggle for power that only partially obeyed a political logic. Political violence began with the arbitrary arrests and torture of pro-Islamic demonstrators by the army and the police, and with the revenge killings of civil servants by Islamic guerrillas. Later, these violent tactics were used against people who were not directly involved in the struggle for political power. At first the Islamic guerrillas waged a spectacular campaign of assassination and bombing directed at foreign nationals and assets in a desperate attempt to force foreign governments to drop their support for the Algerian junta. By the mid-1990s the use of terror had spread even to the most apolitical segments of the rural population, as blood feuds, struggles over land ownership and organised crime grew out of the confrontation between the pro-government militias and Islamic guerrilla groups. In 1999, as the main military players agreed upon a strategy to de-escalate the conflict, it remained uncertain how far they had the capability and the willingness to reconstruct the political consensus that existed during the most promising episodes of the democratic transition.

This book investigates the political changes and the transformation of the *ethos* of the Algerian polity that resulted from this confrontation between the Islamic fundamentalists and the state/military elite. The mechanisms of this confrontation are the direct consequence of how people understand their political plight and how they devise social strategies and practices. The following account of the Algerian events proposes therefore, mainly, an analysis of these practices and strategies that emphasises the conflicting logics of these choices and the dilemmas that the participants must face. The high visibility of the phenomenon of political violence in Algeria ensures that the country is also a particularly appropriate case study for reflecting on the dilemmas that are common but less exposed in the other authoritarian polities of the region. Apart from the idiosyncrasies of the Algerian predicament, the process of change in Algeria allows a better understanding of the prospects for brutal or subdued political change – i.e. revolution and democratisation – in the Middle East and North Africa.

This book is the result of four years of doctoral research at the University of Cambridge. I am immensely indebted to the staff and students of the Faculty of Social and Political Sciences for this research. Among the many people who actively supported my work, I wish to thank most particularly John Dunn for his thoughtful advice and encouragements. I am also very grateful to James Piscatori and Bryan Turner for their support. Michael Willis, who had written one of the very first books on the Algerian conflict, and Basim Musallam also provided invaluable help in the early stages of this project. During the many months that I spent in Algeria the staff and students of the Research Centre in Social and Cultural Anthropology, in Oran, have offered much appreciated assistance; I am grateful to them all. Finally but importantly, I wish to thank all the anonymous Algerians who helped me understand the nature of this conflict that totally transformed their country. This book is a witness to their everyday struggle for a better life.

1 Understanding Political Democratisation at the Beginning of the Twenty-first Century

ALGERIA AND THE 'THIRD WAVE' OF DEMOCRATIC TRANSITIONS

From the perspective of the political analyst, as much as from that of concerned citizens, the periods of political upheavals that completely redefine the social practices and institutional framework of a polity provide invaluable opportunities to question common assumptions about the logic of social change and the foundations of political order. The events that began to unfold in Algeria in 1988 and that, at the time of writing in 2002, are far from over, are one such instance of a contemporary upheaval that raises many questions. What might the significance be of this attempt at democratisation in a polity of the Muslim world, in a context where identity politics and cultural divides appear to be increasingly shaping world politics? Do the Algerian events tell us something specific about the future of democratisation, revolution or Islamicisation in the Muslim world? If so, what are the mechanisms that produced such a dramatic sequence of events? How far can one analyse and understand these mechanisms with sufficient accuracy to help in resolving the actual Algerian conundrum, or to warn the polities that might unknowingly be following the Algerian path? Before addressing those issues it is important to understand the connections between the macro and the micro level of analysis, and to indicate how far one can extend locally cogent explanations to the international sphere (or the opposite). Political theorist John Dunn warns that one of the most pressing conceptual and practical problems that confronts both contemporary analysts and actors is precisely to identify stable categories for political causality and political agency.[1]

   In the present situation, the category 'Islam', in so far as it is a distinct political category, obviously means very different things to very different people.[2] It is inherently difficult to define accurately and appropriately the contours and features of this category in such a way that the description satisfies both the conditions of a specific social context and the conceptual requirements of a grand historical and international narrative. From a theoretical perspective it is perfectly possible that the question, 'what are effective means of democratisation of a polity at the beginning of the twenty-first century?' requires a significantly different answer from the question 'what are effective means of democratisation in Algeria today?' When trying to answer the first question, one primarily endeavours to produce a coherent general analytical framework based on the statistically significant features of political causality at the global level. By contrast, when one seeks to explain what precisely happened in a country like Algeria during this last troubled decade, one must necessarily include many statistically marginal factors, which nonetheless had a local significance. If we err on the side of statistical approximations, we obtain the kind of sweeping general-isations that Samuel Huntington utilises to introduce his notion of a clash of civilisations.[3] Conversely, if we err on the side of the anthropology of religion, the investigation may become so particu-laristic that it cannot be used in political analysis.

In the contemporary context, I fear that it is not the failings of an overelaborate account of political change that hinder our under-standing of the situation in Algeria and in the rest of the Muslim world but, on the contrary, an oversimplification of the notion of political development. In the Western tradition, a dubious legacy of the Enlightenment is an idea of political progress-cum-a determin-istic natural process of change passing from an old, obsolete political order to a new, better one.[4] Up to the decolonisation period, the idea that swift revolutionary transformations could radically change people's lives (for the better) thrived, mostly thanks to the efforts and successes of communist movements. Unmistakably the success of the communist revolutionaries at mobilising people and at over-throwing regimes in Asia and Africa in the 1960s and 1970s helped to support the claims of Marxism regarding political change – though it cannot be said to have played a prominent role in retaining the adherence of the newly 'liberated' citizenry to the ideas and practice of socialism.[5] In the late twentieth century, however, after the failure of the archetypal communist regime, the Soviet Union, and the comparative success of 'bourgeois' states, neither the association of revolutions with progressive changes nor that of revolutionaries with well-informed political understanding is easily sustainable. Today, as liberalism has (temporarily?) gained the moral high ground, the revolutionary terminology has been downplayed to the benefit of a new liberal vocabulary based on democratisation. (The publication in the mid-1980s of Guillermo O'Donnell, Phillipe Schmitter and Lawrence Whitehead's *Transitions from Authoritarian Rule* was the watershed for this vocabulary shift.)[6] In this context, as John Esposito and John Voll indicated, even the proponents of political Islam have increasingly adopted this democratic vocabulary to voice their demands and present the process of Islamicisation.[7]

This recent change of terminology means that it is today far more difficult for political analysts to discern the normative bias in the new analyses of democratisation and Islamicisation than it was to pinpoint the practical and conceptual flaws in a well-explored concept and practice, such as revolution. The immediacy of the problem, the limited historical insights and the normative preferences of the analysts, ensure that it is particularly arduous to separate the concrete mechanisms of change from the rhetorical tropes and the ideological gloss. Despite the current optimism concerning the spread of democracy, it is by no means certain that the contemporary liberal understanding of the mechanisms of democratic transitions reflects a less hasty judgement than Marx's presentation of revolutions as the 'locomotives of history'. Indeed, considering the explanation proposed only recently by Francis Fukuyama, who interprets political changes using an Enlightenment-like notion of progress and who emphasises the abstract aspects of democracy and liberalism at the expense of their down-to-earth consequences, it is difficult not to remark how easily the advocates of these views may replicate the mistakes of the utopian socialists.[8] Increasingly, today, substantive accounts of democratisation and democratic consolidation – the analysis of how democratisation leads to the formation of liberal democracies – present the democratic process not just as the initiation of a rule by the demos but as the rule of a knowledgeable and polite civil society guided by a general concern for human rights and political fairness.[9] In this context, it is not be surprising that an experienced analyst of democratic transition like Guillermo O'Donnell should criticise the proponents of this new literature on democratic consolidation on the grounds that their analyses only indicate that new democracies are 'institutionalised in ways that one expects and of which one approves'.[10]

In the contemporary 'New World Order' as much as in the Cold War context, the greatest danger for political analysts and actors is to confuse their own normative preferences with what it may be 'rational' to do, or to mistake contingent political arrangements for the outcomes of the 'rational' choices of political players. Avoiding substantive arguments, Adam Przeworski suggested that, using a 'minimalist' conception of politics, one could determine which institutional outcomes could be obtained with quasi-mechanical regularity – i.e. those that even marginally rational political actors had to recognise were the best possible solutions available in the circumstances. Thus, vis-à-vis the recent democratic transitions in Eastern Europe and Latin America, Przeworski concluded that the democratic arrangements obtained were not the preferred outcomes for many actors, considering their ideological inclinations, but simply the end result of a political stalemate.[11] While this analysis is highly pertinent, it must be noted that some of the assumptions about the actors' interests, wants and systems of valuation that could (safely?) remain implicit in Europe or Latin America may turn out to be more problematic in the Middle East, Asia or Africa. More importantly, however, it must be pointed out that, whether one is dealing specifically with the Muslim world or not, only a solid faith in rationalism permits one to conclude that transitions from authoritarianism produce liberal and democratic solutions *because* these arrangements constitute 'objectively' a better state of affairs. As Michael Taylor indicated, the limitations of rational choice theory are immense when it comes to analysing complex series of collective choices, particularly in contexts where one does not fully understand the agents' 'ultimate ends'.[12]

The difficulty of correctly apprehending democratisation from definitional and logical premises is illustrated by Phillipe Schmitter's carefully worded definition of democratic consolidation as

> the process of transforming the accidental arrangements, prudential norms, and contingent solutions that have emerged during the transition into relations of co-operation and competition that are reliably known, regularly practised, and voluntarily accepted by those persons or collectivities (i.e. politicians and citizens) that participate in democratic governance.[13]

In practice, it is evident that such a description of the process of consolidation can only apply to a community that shares many, if not most, of the analyst's (or reader's) liberal and democratic preferences. Severed from these normative underpinnings, the same terminology and logic could be used to describe the entrenchment of a situation of violent and anarchic political order, just like the one that became established in Algeria in the 1990s. From a definitional point of view, the fact that some political practices may be particularly brutal does not make them less democratic, cooperative, or voluntarily accepted. One of the main difficulties in dealing with a polity of the developing world is that it may be particularly inappropriate to infer causally from what we (liberals and democrats) identify as rational political behaviour – principally because the citizenry of these polities does not habitually share the same normative habits and social skills as the demos of well-established Western democracies.

Structuralist-minded analyses in the vein of Theda Skocpol's *States and Social Revolutions* and (neo-)institutionalist explanations in the vein of Samuel Huntington's *Political Order in Changing Societies* offer a handy solution to those who are daunted by the prospect of a political causality sensitive to re-interpretations of rationality.[14] By analysing the long-term organisational and socio-economic trends inside and outside a polity, these scholars propose to narrow down the number of relevant actors and practices in a specific socio-historical context and to explain the collapse and reconstruction of political order (relatively) independently of most historical agents' views on the situation. Although such analyses of institutional and socio-economic regularities have yielded many interesting insights, it is unfortunately not always the case that a retrospective analysis of regimes which were, in Lenin's phrase, 'unable to live on in the old way', provides useful information on the dynamics and rationale of changes to come. The most thorough understanding of the mechanisms of past transformations can never constitute an exhaustive catalogue of political causality.[15]

Furthermore, it is dubious how far one can really weigh 'objectively' these institutional or socio-economic trends *a priori*. In the contemporary context, Forrest Colburn points out that it would be a hopeless task to compare the socio-economic and political situation of the countries of the Third World in order to detect where the situation is ripe for change, because most of these polities face extremely tense situations or are already on the brink of disaster.[16] This observation is directly relevant to the analysis of the Algerian situation, as no knowledgeable political commentator of the situation in the Middle East and North Africa had identified Algeria as the most likely focal point for democratising and Islamicising efforts in the region before 1988. At that time, all the political, religious and socio-economic indicators showed that Algeria was a very *unremarkable* polity indeed.[17]

Obviously, with the benefit of historical insight, one may now be in a position to re-assess these socio-economic and institutional trends and argue that the conditions were in fact ripe for revolt in Algeria in 1988; just as one might explain that the 1979 Iranian revolution or the collapse of the Soviet Union in 1991 were predictable.[18] In a prospective analysis, however, such structuralist and institutionalist approaches can be more debilitating than helpful, especially for policy-makers, as they confine one's perspectives only to historically tested conditions for change. Furthermore, because they emphasise the preconditions for change, these approaches underestimate the extent to which social and political transformations are affected by what the actors want to achieve, how skilful (or fortunate) they can be, and how imaginatively they can interpret their achievements. Unsurprisingly, the role of ideology and culture is particularly badly handled by these explanations. From this perspective the analyst is not in a position to offer a description of ideology or culture other than that of a deviation from the 'objective' pattern of socio-economic or institutional development.

However, we have learnt from the mistakes of Marxist thinkers, from Gramsci to Althusser, that it is extremely difficult to measure the potential of ideology as a relatively independent causal variable in the 'objective' structure of events without reaching the conclusion that this ideological input always distorts people's choices, and alone shapes the course of events.[19] In this respect, the culturalist twist that Huntington proposed in *The Clash of Civilisations* as an addendum to the institutionalist approach that he had developed earlier must be credited at least with internal consistency. But how far should this ideological or cultural analysis intervene in the explanations of the Algerian events? And how meaningful a notion can it be for a generic explanation of political change?

In the present situation, it would be over-hasty to affirm that the failure (so far) of democratic transition in Algeria, as elsewhere in the Middle East and North Africa, is attributable to the agents' lack of cognitive and normative affinities with the rest of the liberal-democratic world. Furthermore, I believe that a theoretical debate aiming at determining the historical possibility or impossibility of having a liberal democratic political order in an Islamic society should not precede and pre-empt the actual analysis of Algerian political events or the inquiry into the behaviour of the Muslim populations concerned. It is particularly unhelpful to start by saying that these communities have no practical experience or conceptual affinity with liberal democracy and, therefore, cannot reach it on their own – be it because of an absence of civil society (according to Gellner) or because of the authoritarian logic of this religious creed (according to Huntington).[20] Conversely, it would be equally unwise to assume that it is just a matter of time before these polities endorse liberal and democratic ideals as people eventually realise that this is what they need for their individual and collective self-fulfilment. (In this respect, one may regret that so many contributions to debate on the future of civil society in the Muslim World have a tendency to recycle the Third-Worldist arguments that developing societies only have to overcome contingent dilemmas and externally imposed fetters in order to flourish.)[21] Vis-à-vis the democratic transitions in Latin America, O'Donnell and Schmitter showed convincingly that one could not have spelt out *ex ante* the likely outcomes of these events, because part of the process of transition was precisely the collective learning of an appropriately democratic way of solving the polities' predicaments.[22] The main characteristic of those democratic transitions was the exploration in real time of the very possibility of democratic political change. To my mind, this observation strongly suggests that it is probably best to investigate the role of culture and ideology in the Algerian and Muslim context in the light of this agent-centred, open-ended practical endeavour to resolve one's political predicament.

ISLAM AND THE 'WEST': A CLASH OF IDEOLOGIES IN ALGERIA

To understand better the Algerian situation and its global implications, it is important to dissect the mechanisms and the logic of the 'social contracts' that different groups of agents endorsed at different stages of the process of political transition. What did they hope to achieve, normatively and descriptively? How did they determine what was a reasonable price to pay to achieve those objectives? And so on. One ought to be able to judge these strategies without having recourse to the facile argument that the actors who shape these events abide by a completely different concept of 'rationality' and without implying that there is something radically different about the Islamic fundamentalists or the Algerians which makes them incomprehensible to other human beings. If Algeria failed to be the brilliant illustration of a smooth transition to democracy, it is not simply because 'evil' political, religious or military actors ensured that this would not happen, or because the conditions were not 'ripe' for democracy.[23] Undoubtedly, the collective choices of the population, particularly in favour of political Islam, constrained the type of institutional arrangements and practices that could be introduced consensually in the polity. However, a state of affairs in which political reforms are more or less possible or successful due to the presence (or the formation) of a particular popular consensus on political order in a polity is nothing exceptional. The degree to which social and political practices and institutions are representative, democratic or Islamic always depends on the active participation of the people concerned. For all those involved (but obviously more so for the local participants than for external observers), it is therefore essential to identify correctly the causal mechanisms that permit strategically placed players, at home and abroad, to utilise the existing institutional, economic and military resources to impose their preferred political solutions. Equally, it is crucial to understand how the semantic configuration of the political arena ensures that some solutions are better accepted or repeatedly challenged by a majority of people in the polity.

For political analysts as much as for the individuals directly involved in a process that one may call democratisation, Islamicisation, revolution or, less exaltedly, a muddled descent into a violent state of anarchy, the definition of success and of failure is always necessarily an exercise in semantic organisation – it can be more than this but it cannot be less. Today, Islamic fundamentalist ideologues are eager to propose a notion of Islam *qua* Natural Law that parallels the Western theorists' utilisation of democratic governance *qua* rational politics. On both sides of the debate, in explaining global social transformations the actors do not hesitate to present conflicts not as a practical opposition between different social groups but as instances of a battle between 'good' and 'evil' or between 'progress' and 'obscurantism' (an eschatologically construed opposition that was stigmatised by the American President's talks of a 'crusade' and the Islamic fundamentalists' calls to '*jihad*' after the attacks on the Pentagon and the World Trade Center in September 2001). Even if the eschatological dimension of this battle is exaggerated, it remains nonetheless true that what agents do and say is rarely simply a response to immediate practical difficulties, individual or collective. It is also a strategic response involving those ideological representations which are constitutive of the identity of the agents or communities. Such identity-driven confrontations have been at the heart of some of the most important conflicts of the twentieth century and the odds are that they will be with us for quite some time yet. It would not be incongruous to present the clashes occurring today in Algeria and in other parts of the Muslim world as a replay of the struggle between democrats, fascists and communists that shook Europe some time ago (a struggle that in the present case would oppose liberal democrats, secular autocrats (of various affiliations) and Islamic fundamentalists). More than Huntington's clash of civilisations, then, it is perhaps Carl Schmitt's concept of the political – the affirmation of the political community in its opposition to a mythically construed enemy – that best captures from an actor's perspective the rationale of this opposition.[24]

In Schmitt's scheme these mythical referents and the arbitrariness of the political ensure that there can be no process of 'enlightenment' which eventually brings together different political communities. As old myths and old enmities lose their relevance, new myths and new enemies are imagined – the 'Green Peril' replaces the 'Evil Empire'. From this perspective anything like Fukuyama's liberal end to world history, or the idea of an end to Islamism advanced in French circles by Gilles Kepel, is wishful thinking.[25] Regardless of whether one subscribes to Schmitt's notion of a total war between friends and foes, however, it is still crucial to note the practical relevance of political myths in the shaping of everyday attitudes between the members of different political communities. In domestic politics as much as in foreign policy, what constitutes a legitimate political action is never solely defined by reference to a technical and legal framework, nor is it simply derived from a specific doctrine. It is also based on ill-specified fears, hopes and expectations – be they of a 'Great Satan' or of a 'New World Order'.[26] To understand better the strategies of the Algerian Islamic fundamentalists as much as to comprehend the attitude of Western governments toward Algeria and toward the Muslim world, one has to be aware not only of the logic of their political arguments but also of the more ambiguous political myths and normative and aesthetic preferences that form the background of their definitions of friends and foes.

Ideology, in a neutral sense, is a body of more or less coherent concepts, symbols and discursive practices that people deploy to understand and act upon their world. The term does not imply a cognitive or normative judgement on the validity of the views proposed.[27] A political ideology is a polysemic 'text' rendered meaningful in practice in a specific context by a sustained interpretative effort.[28] In this interpretation, political ideas and ideals are defined and articulated in specific frameworks with a view to casting a certain light upon one's material situation and moral position. In practice a political ideology provides rules and principles for prejudging the suitability of political actors and for evaluating the appropriateness of their actions. As sociologists, from Max Weber to Pierre Bourdieu, have indicated, because of the division of labour inherent in all complex political systems, a small number of interpreters can accumulate a political authority that allow them to foist upon the community an artificial unity of interest using the authority invested in their discourse.[29] This political authority is not only the capacity to decide *on* political issues but also the ability to define *what* is (or ought to be) a matter for politics. In the present context this definition of the boundaries of politics is a central feature of the opposition between Liberal and Islamic world views. In its everyday expression a political ideology is infused with a specific teleology by, and is indissociable from, a specific group of interpreters within society. Analytically, however, because the success of political actors may not be directly related to the coherence or usefulness of the views that they advocate, it is important to be able to distinguish between the causally relevant relationships that their conceptual schemes reveal and the unintended consequences of the actions of their ideologues (or their followers). In a Muslim context, in particular, it is crucial to make a distinction between Islamic fundamentalism as the set of political insights and ethical precepts which may (or may not) help people to organise their social world better, and Islamic fundamentalism as a name attributed to the activities of a group of political actors who have had some success in claiming to represent Islamic orthodoxy.

In any political context, the political players who are best able to utilise the prevailing myths about political order and to present attractive theories about social unity can gain an important tactical advantage over their competitors, regardless of how accurate their political understanding actually is. In the democratic transitions in

Latin America, O'Donnell and Schmitter indicated that during these hectic periods of change

> unexpected events (*fortuna*), insufficient information, hurried and audacious choices, confusion about motives and interests, plasticity and even indefinition of political identities, as well as the talents of specific individuals (*virtù*) are frequently decisive in determining outcomes.[30]

In Algeria, the rapid transformations that took place from 1988 onward provided propitious conditions for the diffusion and entrenchment of new and unorthodox political views. If, at first, the skilful propaganda of the Islamic fundamentalists allowed them to score extremely well against their liberal and nationalist opponents, it is doubtful, from a causal perspective, that this capacity to manipulate Islamic symbolism alone explains the expansion and resilience of the fundamentalist movement. It is true that during the 1979 Iranian revolution Ayatollah Khomeini successfully induced many Iranian citizens to change their attitude towards the monarchy, by skilfully exploiting Shi'ite myths and symbols.[31] However, as Algerian Islamic revolutionaries discovered to their cost, likening the military regime to the *taghout* (false god) and invoking the myths of martyrdom provide no guarantee for the success of a revolution, even if a significant number of citizens believed them – in fact, it could even become slightly debilitating after a while. More than the ability of the fundamentalists to manipulate Islamic symbols very precisely, what is crucial for understanding the causal significance of the Islamic movement in the long term is how it generates a lasting popular consensus on Islamicisation. What may be said from even the most casual observation of the situation in Algeria, and throughout the Muslim world, is that Islamic themes appear to be sufficiently compatible with the demos' expectations to be able to produce a recurrent demand for an Islamicised form of democratic governance.[32] This constant pressure is unlikely to be simply the result of the superiority of Islamic concepts of governance – or we may expect that secular leaders would have endorsed these ideas by now. Nor can it be simply attributable to the constant manipulation of unenlightened masses – fundamentalists are not that cunning and people are not that blind.

   In a Muslim context there is a real conceptual difficulty in knowing how far a notion such as Islamic democracy may be just an oxymoron and how far contemporary liberals and democrats are blinded by their own normative and aesthetic preferences. However, the immediate cause of the difficulties of democratisation in Muslim polities is simply the fact that the official institutions of the state participate only minimally in the formation of the political judgements of the citizenry. This impasse over democratisation is the result not of the political cunningness and rhetorical subtlety of the Islamic fundamentalists' discourse, but of the crude understanding and practices of the secular regimes that preside over the destinies of most countries of the Muslim world.[33] Where the state fails to teach its citizens how to formulate coherent political projects, how to debate meaningfully and how to rule through consensus, the citizenry is unlikely to learn any more about democracy than it already knows – and it may even forget that much. To date, despite the setting up of new formal political structures and procedures (parliaments, parties, elections, etc.), the lack of a consensus about what is a legitimate rule still undermines the institutional framework of these polities. In Algeria, as elsewhere in the region, because the institutional system is not designed to provide accurate information to (and about) the population, the powers-that-be are unable to know at all precisely what the population might devise by itself and for itself as an appropriate form of government. The lack of genuine social and political dialogue ensures that both rulers and ruled lack the political skills and practice necessary to seize the democratic opportunity and implement these reforms successfully when they can. What is crucial for the establishment of a functioning political order (of the democratic kind) in Algeria and throughout the Muslim world is the emergence of the kind of social capital that Robert Putnam places at the heart of the workings of Western liberal democracies.[34] It is the formation and evolution of such political and social understanding that constitutes the storyline of the failed Algerian transition to democracy and of the new form of state authoritarianism and Islamic radicalism that was produced.

NEW POLITICAL ACTORS FOR A NEW INTERNATIONAL ORDER

After the Cold War the international political debate has focused increasingly on the role of identity politics in world affairs. In the Muslim world the emerging problem for foreign policy analysis and for security studies is the role of transnational Islamic movements.[35]

Transnational organisations structured around religious or secular ideologies are not a new phenomenon in international politics. However, an understanding of the workings of these Islamic movements and of their relations with nation-states in this age of globalisation has been particularly difficult to obtain, particularly by modification of the typical state-centred models of international relations. 'Realist' accounts such as Huntington's *The Third Wave* or Armstrong's *Revolution and World Order*, which depict the domino effects of regime change, are increasingly losing their relevance for analysing current international developments.[36] It is not surprising that Huntington himself should try to reorient his analysis in *The Clash of Civilisations* by suggesting that, although nation-states remain crucial in the post-Cold War period, cultural affinities now dictate the shape of the international system. (Though Huntington's own account of 'culture' and 'civilisation' is not always particularly helpful for understanding the relations between the 'old' *Realpolitik* views of nation-states and the 'new' transnational outcomes of identity politics.) With the benefit of historical insight, we now realise that an event like the 1979 Iranian revolution constituted a watershed for the internationalisation of political Islam not because the new Islamic republic directly engineered a wave of revolutions throughout the Muslim world but because the revolution justified and legitimised the Islamic fundamentalist discourse as a coherent political discourse. The causal consequences of this discourse when it is put into practice at the transnational level by sub-state players, and how these factors can affect the international community, have been major questions and concerns for the international community from the Gulf War onwards.[37]

Unquestionably contemporary transnational Islamic activism is not organised like the Third Worldist, Arab Socialist or Pan-Arab movements that flourished during the period of decolonisation. Regional players like Iran, Egypt or Saudi Arabia continue to be involved in these internationalist networks, but these countries are following these changes rather than directing them. From a security perspective the relationships of these new Islamic movements with their sponsors are far more ambiguous. It is now theoretically *and* practically more difficult to apprehend how the state institutions of specific countries are responsible for the contemporary development of Islamic radicalism on a world scale. Unlike the situaton in the 1980s, when regimes like Iran, Libya or Syria could be identified as the direct sponsors of international terrorism, today the ruling elites of countries like Saudi Arabia or Pakistan are displaying what could be called 'multiple personality disorder'. In practice, if we consider that someone like Osama bin Laden and an organisation like al-Qaida illustrate the threat posed by international Islamic terrorism at the beginning of the twenty-first century, it is clear that international diplomacy is ill-equipped to deal with this form of political activism. Supporting the al-Qaida organisation are not only identifiable 'rogue' states but also a decentralised financial empire with ramifications in tax havens in Western democracies, as well as family and political networks throughout the Muslim world. The list of radical Islamic groups linked to the al-Qaida network published by the Bush administration after the attacks on the World Trade Center and the Pentagon mentions organisations that come from every corner of the Muslim world – from Algeria to the Philippines, and from Somalia to Uzbekistan.[38] Furthermore, a cursory glance at the nationalities of the hijackers of the planes on 11 September 2001 reveals that these groups were composed mostly of Saudi and Egyptian nationals – two countries which are long-standing allies of the United States in the Muslim world. At this level of analysis it is crucial to separate the particular structure of an organisation such as bin Laden's al-Qaida or the Algerian GIA from the general patterns that characterise contemporary, transnational, radical Islamic movements. It is important to realise that an answer to the question 'how can such transnational organisations function and prosper?' cannot simply be a detailed account of how the personal wealth or organisational skills of particular individuals were crucial for constructing such a network.

In a book published only a year before the terrorist attacks in the United States, Gilles Kepel predicted the decline of the radical form of Islamic fundamentalism embodied by the GIA and al-Qaida, and a democratisation and liberalisation of these Islamic fundamentalist movements.[39] In two brief chapters entitled 'The botched war against the West' and 'Osama bin Laden and America: between terrorism and showbiz', Kepel dismissed the relevance of these recent embodiments of international terrorism as self-defeating and unsustainable. In his opinion the downfall of these organisations was a logical consequence of their failure to topple their domestic enemies and of the need to re-create a popular consensus on their activities. Without doubt, the timing of Kepel's analysis was not the most felicitous, and his critics were often merciless.[40] However, this mistiming does not mean that in the longer term his analysis will not prove accurate and that this type of international Islamic activism will not subside for exactly the reasons indicated. (In the very short term the multinational efforts directed against the al-Qaida network after the attacks on New York and Washington in 2001, like the efforts mustered against the GIA after their bombing campaign in France in 1995, will also weaken these organisations' capabilities and force them to reduce their activities.) Yet, in the medium term this kind of radical internationalist Islamic activism could present a major problem to the international community, one that has two distinct but equally important embodiments: direct security threats against Western democracies and indirect impediments to the process of democratisation and liberalisation in the polities of the Muslim world.

By their spectacular activities, radical Islamic actors are providing some easily marketable, media-friendly material that people – Muslims and non-Muslims – will utilise to reflect on what are the pressing political and religious questions of the day. In the Muslim community it is often not the actions of these actors themselves that directly convince people to change their views on what constitutes an appropriate political and religious engagement but rather the reaction of those who are the victims of these attacks. In this respect it cannot be said that the security clampdowns that formed the core of the response of Western democracies and of the authoritarian regimes of the Muslim world to the attacks of these terrorist organisations always provide the best refutation of the arguments and activities of the radical Islamic fundamentalists. The contradiction between the short-term security objectives of Western democracies and their long-term global developmental goals ensures that what is being done today to prevent another attack in the United States by the al-Qaida network or another GIA-sponsored bombing campaign in France is partially responsible for the political dilemmas that confront the unfortunate citizenry and the ruling elite of Algeria, Afghanistan, Pakistan, etc. These security clampdowns ensure that each time a potential terrorist threat is being removed, these regimes' authoritarian legacy is being reaffirmed. It is not just the subversive activities of the Islamic fundamentalists but also the liberties taken in violation of international conventions, individual liberties and liberal ethics by the states and international institutions fighting 'terrorism' that are at the heart of the problem. These authoritarian synergies operate not only at the state level to form the 'anarchic' society of nation-states that 'realist' analysts of international relations presented as the predicament of the twentieth century, but also at the level of a global civil society, whose migrant communities, religious factions and other lobby groups shape both national politics and the response of international institutions.[41] At the societal level we may perhaps expect that in well-established Western democracies the encroachment of an arbitrary rule over personal and civil liberties during a period of emergency will be kept in check by a vigilant political and civil society. In less well-established democracies and in non-democratic countries, however, this predicament is far more serious. Already in the Muslim world people cannot formulate coherent political projects and cannot make themselves heard because of the lack of political structures designed to allow them to do this. In the context of an increased 'securitarian' rule, the citizens of these polities are unlikely to learn more about democracy, and they may even forget what they do know.[42]

Today in the Muslim world – which includes the Islamic communities established in Western democracies – no Friday prayer would be complete without the mention of one of the many conflicts in which Muslim populations are currently the victims. In this context the lacklustre response of Western democracies to an event like the Algerian democratic transition and civil conflict is presented by Islamic fundamentalists as another proof of the evil Western ambition to maintain the Muslim world in a state of dependency. That Western democracies should remain passive while a democratically elected Islamic party is unceremoniously dismissed by the Algerian military is but one more indication that Western powers collude with the autocratic forces of the Muslim world to deny Muslim citizens their rights. Besides a new set of justifications, however, this confrontation between Islamic fundamentalists and the military apparatus in a country like Algeria also brings to international radical political Islam additional skills and personnel. Domestically and internationally it provides both a latent incentive to engage in the path of the armed *jihad* and a practical know-how in terrorism and guerrilla warfare. From this global perspective it is not altogether surprising that French citizens of Algerian descent should be involved both in the GIA bombing campaign in France in 1995 and in the support networks of the 2001 attacks in the United States.[43] For the international community the real challenge is, therefore, not to counter specific terrorist groups but to conceive dependably effective measures of prevention against those individuals who could engage in a terror campaign because of an imagined connection with other peoples' struggles and suffering. As the French Interior Ministry realised in 1995, if it was relatively easy to monitor Algerian political refugees, it was impossible to monitor equally effectively the French population of Algerian descent or French citizens who converted to Islam.[44] No Western democracy today can keep an eye on all the citizens who could potentially decide to pursue violent political activism because of their real or imagined links with an Arab or Islamic community.

These 'emotional' connections constitute one elusive but real and enduring legacy of events such as the Algerian civil conflict, the Palestinian struggle, the Gulf War, the Afghan tragedy, etc. They add to the difficulty of drawing clear causal connections between specific political and socio-economic developments in the Muslim world and the development of this new type of international activism. In practice, all we can say is that the recent foreign policy choices of Western democracies towards the Muslim world have not been particularly helpful for preventing the radical political interpretation of such symbolic identifications. From the Iranian revolution to the Afghan war, from the Gulf crisis to the Chechen war, and from the failed Algerian democratic transition to the (so far) successful Indonesian transition, the international community has had an unfortunate tendency to create powerful loci of anti-Western opposition where there had been none before. At the time of writing, it is particularly hazardous to predict with precision what might be the medium term consequences of the 2001 'anti-terrorist' foreign policy consensus generated by the attacks on the United States. Is the current support of the Bush administration for the Pakistani military (to undermine the Taliban regime) a repeat of the ill-fated tactical playing of Iraq against Iran in the 1980s? Similarly, is French complacency towards the Algerian military allowing the civil conflict to drag on, thus permanently destabilising the southern flank of the European Union? For immediate security purposes it may make sense for France or the United States to support the Algerian or Pakistani military and to remain lax in their condemnation of these regimes' human rights abuses and democratic deficit. For longer-term democratic and developmental purposes, however, it is certain that such international choices do not help in promoting a more democratic domestic political context or a tolerant international ethos. On the contrary, they facilitate the diffusion and entrenchment of authoritarian political views and practices.[45]

Today the Algerian military may be keeping the situation under control in that country, but this is at the cost of radicalising the political opposition at home and abroad, thereby displacing the security risk geographically and perhaps aggravating it over time. (And it is extremely disquieting that only a year before General Musharaf became the United States' most important regional ally, Larry Diamond should suggest that the military coup that had permitted Musharaf to take power in Pakistan could herald a swing away from democracy.)[46]

Historically it has always been far more difficult to reduce international security risks by facilitating the formation and diffusion of more democratic and tolerant political discourse and practices than by having recourse to gunboat diplomacy. Over a century and a half ago Alexis de Tocqueville remarked in *Democracy in America* that 'unlimited freedom of association is of all forms of liberty the last which a people can sustain. If it does not topple them over to anarchy, it brings them continually to the brink thereof.'[47] Today the transnational dialogue between the Muslim world and Western democracies is no less fraught with danger than the challenges that our emerging democratic system faced in the nineteenth century. To be able to address these issues more effectively at the beginning of the twenty-first century and to avoid some of the current pitfalls of the North–South and East–West dialogue, it is crucial to improve our understanding of the limited successes and the dramatic failures of the Algerian democratic transition, both at the nation-state level and in the context of our emerging global society.

2 Political Ideas and Practices in Historical Perspective

GENEALOGIES OF STATE POWER: COLONIAL EXPERIENCES, POST-COLONIAL DILEMMAS

Like most authoritarian polities of the Middle East and North Africa, Algeria is confronted by the unrelenting problem of how to integrate the citizenry into the institutions of the state. Historically, the polity lacks a solid institutional framework that can effectively connect the demos to the state, and the official system is constantly challenged by informal social institutions that have positioned themselves outside, and in opposition to, the state.[1] In this respect the political predicaments that are now ubiquitous in the Middle East and North Africa have been shaped by the long-term process of 'state building', particularly from the colonial period onward. To identify which options are now open for Algeria and for the other authoritarian polities of the region, it is useful to investigate not only the polity's current difficulties but also the genealogy of these predicaments.[2] In particular, it must be established how all the political actors involved addressed the major task of instituting a reliable division of political power and a system of political allegiance. In this respect, the political strategies devised by the political leadership – be they the French or British colonial administration, or local Arab or Islamic leaders – to win power and remain in power over the years have been indirectly responsible for the current lack of political integration and for the continuing opposition between social groups and ideological currents in these polities.

Between 1830 and 1962 Algeria was the scene of a process of exogenous state formation that was probably the most systematic and drastic in the region.[3] In North Africa this process of state- and nation-building under the supervision of a foreign state apparatus constituted an important levelling factor for communities only united until then by a loose formal political or religious allegiance to the Ottoman sultan.[4] One of the consequences of this external imposition of political order was the emergence of a complex administrative apparatus designed to exclude mass participation from the management of the state institutions. When France conquered Algeria in the mid-nineteenth century, this nascent colonial power sought primarily to establish a system of governance that would benefit both rulers and ruled in accordance with their respective status, and not a system permitting an accurate representation of various indigenous interests in and by the state. In contrast to other parts of the colonial world where Europeans simply implemented a policy of *divide et impera*, Algeria, because of the sheer number of colonialists, underwent a thorough process of social, economic and political transformation.[5] Separate rule and segregation were based on the principle of each according to his/her needs and merits, according to the evaluative system of the coloniser. In addition, France's advocacy of the *mission civilisatrice* made it extremely clear that the local population needed to be 'educated' before the issue of political representation could be raised.

The difficulties that the colonialists faced in the nineteenth century were well summarised in a report by Alexis de Tocqueville, a few years after the conquest of Algiers. For Tocqueville it was obvious that the Algerian population lacked a decent nationalist ideology, based on a rationalist philosophy, which would have made of them a truly civilised nation. In 1841, reporting to the French Parliament on the prospects for France in North Africa, Tocqueville pointed out that the colonialists could not reason or coerce the *indigènes* individually but had to work with tribes, 'which are small nations, completely organised, and which can only be led where their own passions drive them'. He concluded that the main challenge for the French was 'to create and exploit in them a common feeling or a common idea that would permit to keep them all in check and to direct them all in the same direction'.[6] Tocqueville recognised that this was no easy task, as the only features all the tribes had in common at that time were an obstinate Islamic faith and a profound hatred of foreign invaders. A few years later, however, after the final defeat of Algeria's main military power, Emir Abdelkader, Tocqueville was more optimistic concerning the prospects for a flourishing 'civilisation' in Algeria. He told his fellow-parliamentarians that they could expect

not the suppression of the hostile feelings that our dominion inspires but their softening, not for our rule to be appreciated but to appear more and more bearable, not to extinguish the age-old Muslim repugnance for a foreign and Christian power but to show how much this power, despite its reproved origin, can be useful to them.

In short, Tocqueville hoped to overcome the reluctance of the Algerian population by encouraging the kind of materialistic and rationalistic attitude that had emerged in Europe in his time – what Max Weber would later call the 'protestant ethic'. As Tocqueville suggested, 'it would be unwise to believe that we will succeed in forming between us a bond based on a community of ideas and customs, but we can hope to form such a bond on a community of interests'.[7] He, like the intellectual and political elite of nineteenth-century France, was confident that any cultural or religious tradition could be incorporated into a modern republican framework of governance based on the French model. Islam was just another field of application for the new political 'science' and Algeria another building block in the grand cosmopolitan 'civilisation' that France was creating.

From the start, the process of colonisation in the Middle East and North Africa mixed *Realpolitik* and economic calculations with 'noble' moral and philosophical objectives. In part the French and British involvement in countries like Algeria and Egypt in the mid-nineteenth century had been spurred by financial considerations, while their role in the partition of the Ottoman Empire was the result of geopolitical calculations.[8] However, another driving force behind the setting-up of the colonial system was the ambitious claim to know better what the relationship between rulers and ruled ought to be in a civilised society. (To a greater or lesser extent, all European nations engaged in the process of colonisation shared the 'philosophy' of the *mission civilisatrice*.)[9] It was from this epistemological claim that much of the colonisers' entitlement to authority was derived. Influenced by rationalist philosophy and positivist sciences, the European elite adopted a Manichean view of the social world that separated science neatly from superstition, and reason from fallacy. As Edward Said showed well, in colonial settings, these preconceptions helped to divide the system of social relationships into two mutually referential but exclusive subsets: modern, European-like relationships and traditional, indigenous ones.[10] The colonial administration drew clear demarcation lines between modernity and tradition, enshrining as representatives the individuals clearly displaying the characteristics of the one or the other. Thus, in Algeria as in many other colonies, France implemented a policy granting French citizenship to small numbers of 'civilised' indigenous notables ('*les évolués*') who were presented as the future of the indigenous society.[11] Simultaneously, the French (and British) administrations made ample use of local notables, chiefs and sheikhs to buttress their new institutional order. (In this respect, as Jacques Berque pointed out, the colonising powers often preferred 'their' Arabs to remain 'authentic'.)[12] Although the colonialists sometimes misjudged the strength of these traditions, sheer technical superiority generally allowed them to prop up the political leadership that, in their view, most befitted the indigenous population. In the long term, however, the utilisation of idealised representations of 'European' and 'Oriental' cultures proved to be self-defeating for the colonial administration. Because participation in, and exclusion from the colonial political order was judged according to the idealised criteria of the philosophy of 'Reason', most people invariably fell short of the colonisers' expectations, one way or the other. On the colonised side, even when the indigenous elite succeeded in subverting the colonial policies and in reinforcing its position, it fell prey to these idealised models. Even when the colonialists were about to be defeated, the culturally hybrid political leadership that launched the decolonisation struggle could not avoid re-utilising similar representations of society.

In the 1950s and 1960s the indigenous elites that challenged their colonial masters (or their chosen successors) throughout the region were eager to justify their rule as comprehensively and exclusively as their predecessors had done. The rationale of their approach is embodied in the writings of Frantz Fanon, the herald of the Third Worldist doctrine and an active member of the Algerian's National Liberation Front (*Front de Liberation Nationale* – FLN). Despite its perceptive insights, Fanon's account of Third-Worldist politics was often a mere reversal of the dominant Manichean vision of the colonialists (a reversal that was particularly noticeable in his tactical endorsement of traditional Islamic systems to act as a counterweight to colonial imports).[13] Inevitably, as soon as the decolonisation struggle stopped being the kind of ill-defined political endeavour for which all underprivileged groups could unite – what Tocqueville had identified earlier as the hatred of the foreign invader – the new state elite set out to trim down this motley crowd that had united against the French, using their own idealised criteria of political representation. The new leadership dictated its conditions of accountability and discriminated against those citizens who, in their eyes, could not be fully trusted. If not European 'civilisation', then Arab socialism, Pan-Arabism and Third Worldism justified the exclusion from the decision-making processes of social groups that were deemed either too 'traditional' or too 'Westernised'.[14] (Inside the state elite, rivalries were also phrased in the same vocabulary. Thus, in the Algerian FLN the more liberal leaders (Mohammed Boudiaf, Hocine Ait Ahmed) were jailed or exiled just after independence by a more 'revolutionist' left-wing leader (Ahmed Ben Bella); only for the latter to be overthrown a few months later by a more 'orthodox' military leader (Houari Boumediene).)[15] As in colonial times, these choices were not presented simply as better strategies to develop the country, but as moral imperatives. These grand schemes justified the (temporary) persistence of an unequal distribution of rights, wealth and power – hardships that were worth enduring, it was said, because of the example that the country was setting for the rest of the developing world.[16] (More practically, too, these new ideals had the advantage of bypassing traditional ethnic and religious divisions – Berbers versus Arabs in Algeria, Copts versus Muslims in Egypt, Alawis versus Druzes versus Sunnis in Syria, Shi'ites versus Sunnis versus Kurds in Iraq, etc.)

The capacity of the state's repressive apparatus to suppress dissent, and the administration's ability to buy off social aggression, boosted the confidence of the new state elites and supported *de facto* their claims to know better what national progress required.[17] Because political opposition was seen as a deviant form of social expression, harmful to the stability of a new polity, the post-colonial regimes unapologetically revived the repressive techniques deployed by their colonial predecessors to ensure the obedience of their subjects. In the post-colonial situation, however, the issue of the organisation and loyalty of the repressive apparatus proved difficult to handle in a context where the 'hidden hand' of the colonial metropolis no longer kept in check the allegiance of the civil servants. After independence, as a succession of military coups made clear, the mechanisms of succession to office at the head of the complex state organisation built by the European powers reverted to a system based on nepotism and traditional clan competition, rather than employing the democratic tools that the departing colonial powers had (belatedly) tried to set in place. In analytical terms, the dilemmas that faced the new, essentially military, elite that inherited or gained power in most of the Middle East and North Africa resembled what Ibn Khaldun described as the archetypal political predicament of

Arab Empires in the classical Islamic period.[18] (The relevance of Ibn Khaldun in this context is not simply that he wrote the *Muqaddimah* in North Africa but also that the dilemmas of political allegiance often present themselves in similar terms, and his account captures one such dilemma with perceptiveness.)

For Ibn Khaldun the usual process of replacement of the leadership of an Arab city or an empire was a combination of external conquest and internal collapse. Ibn Khaldun's explanation of the cyclical character of the Arab polities is grounded on his analysis of their dual systems of economic production and coercion. In his view, these mechanisms distinguish in the classical polities two apparently antagonistic but in fact mutually dependent subsystems: the industrious trading towns and the warring tribal countryside. Ibn Khaldun argued that, in a tribal situation, the absence of a strong state and a weak political, military and economic division of labour produced communities that tended to be egalitarian and to muster their forces by cohesion rather than by coercion. Because many armed men were permanently needed to defend the tribe in a harsh physical and political environment, the tribal chief could not act too arbitrarily toward his subjects, otherwise these quarrelsome tribesmen would refuse to obey him, leave him, or even try to topple him.[19] In cities, by contrast, the lifestyle that resulted from a specialised mode of economic production induced (and was induced by) a strict division of political and military labour. As citizens were busy making money, the role of the ruler was primarily to arbitrate disputes and to protect the city against invaders. Ibn Khaldun indicated that, in this situation, diligent but timorous townsmen 'were prevented by the influence of force and governmental authority from mutual injustice, save such injustice as comes from the ruler himself'.[20] Significantly, he remarked that for the ruler himself it was far more important to remain legitimate in the eyes of the tribal clan that formed the nucleus of his armed following (his *assabiyya*), than in the eyes of the masses. For Ibn Khaldun, a ruler could not be successful without the support of dedicated followers bound together by feelings of solidarity and an allegiance based on intimate relationships like ties of blood (*assabiyya*).[21] Thus, he attributed the recurrent collapse of cities and empires to the lenient urban lifestyle that progressively eroded this group solidarity and its ability to fight (a decline that was completed in three generations after the conquest of a city or an empire, according to Ibn Khaldun). When a particular clan was unable to muster sufficient forces to defend itself and its empire against fierce tribal groups from the countryside, another conquest took place and another cycle started with a new tribal dynasty in charge.

How far does the contemporary situation in the Middle East and North Africa reflect this Khaldunian dynamic? No doubt the post-colonial regimes of Algeria and of most nation-states in the region are not, strictly speaking, in the hands of a tribal *assabiyya* (though certain Gulf Monarchies, or countries like Libya, may come close to it).[22] However, the modern authoritarian regimes of the Middle East and North Africa have retained from the *assabiyya* system the principles utilised to define the allegiance of the state elite and of the state apparatus. In these modern polities the basic Khaldunian dilemma remains as follows. First, the political elite cannot control the masses without the help of a devoted following with military might. Second, there can be no group loyalty without the attribution of privileges. Third, these privileges cannot but undermine the ability to command the loyalty of this armed following, or its ability to fight. In practice, the more military leaders become involved in affairs of state, the more they loosen their direct and intimate connection with the armed forces (and delegate their authority), and become susceptible to being toppled by new military strongmen that emerge from the lower ranks or from outside the regular army. (A pattern which was well illustrated in Algeria in the 1990s, where successive military strongmen rose to the political leadership only to be overthrown a few years or months later by subordinates who had remained in charge of the military apparatus. Were one to take Ibn Khaldun's three generations model literally, this troubled period in Algerian history would only represent a difficult succession in a single dynasty, as all the military strongmen involved were members of the original FLN–ALN organisation that had led the decolonisation struggle against the French, some 40 years earlier.) In analytical terms, the core of the problem is simply that the organisational principles of the state apparatus are different from those of the state leadership. There is a persistent tension between organising the state apparatus as a political tool for social and economic development and ruling it as a private network of loyalties. (Or, as a well-placed connoisseur of *assabiyya*, Libyan leader Muammar al-Qaddafi, says (perhaps tongue-in-cheek) in his little Green Book, 'the nation-state persists unless its political structure, as a state, is affected by its social structure in the form of tribes, clans and families'.)[23] Thus far, this discrepancy between the rules that govern the state elite and its accession to power, and the rules that organise a modern state apparatus, has undermined all attempts at securing a predictable form of political order. It is to this predicament that all those, both domestic and foreign, concerned with Algerian national and regional politics must today turn their attention as a matter of priority.

HISTORICAL PERSPECTIVES ON ISLAMIC FUNDAMENTALIST IDEOLOGY: A PRAGMATIC ACCOUNT

Apart from power politics, the responses of the Islamic fundamentalists to the colonial and post-colonial order have been dictated by their understanding of what a proper Islamic order required normatively. The ideas and the strategies associated with them which are used by these religious-minded activists to tackle the local social and political problems can be presented as an Islamic fundamentalist ideology. However, because the Islamic fundamentalist movements generally lack well-defined institutional structures, it is difficult to specify at all precisely what may constitute the 'official' corpus of political Islam.[24] In Algeria, during its short period of legal existence, the Islamic Salvation Front (*Front Islamique du Salut* – FIS) was able to construct a system that institutionalised legitimacy and leadership. Once the party was banned, however, it quickly proved tricky to identify which social institutions and political actors best represented the Islamic inclinations of the population, and which discourses best mobilised people politically. As political ideology, the evolution of the Islamic fundamentalism project is best encapsulated not by an analysis of its avowed objectives but by the narrative of its historical genesis. There is a fierce debate in the academic world between scholars who present contemporary Islamic fundamentalism – or contemporary religious fundamentalism in general – principally as an answer to, and a consequence of modernisation in the twentieth century, and those who view it as a variant of the traditional social protests that have commonly used religion as a vehicle for political demands.[25] In my account the choice of a conceptual framework is guided by a very pragmatic concern: to highlight a conceptualisation of political Islam and of the history of ideas that will provide useful tools for understanding the strategic choices and tactical dilemmas of contemporary Islamic fundamentalists. In this respect, therefore, it is best to consider Islamic fundamentalism as barely a century old.

Whether it is voiced by the FIS or not, the project of the Algerian Islamic fundamentalists, like those of the other Islamic movements in the region, has grown by accretion from the ideas about Islam and the state that have emerged since the beginning of the twentieth century. At least two main currents of thoughts have informed the development of this modern Islamic fundamentalist corpus, the Reform/*Salafiyya* movement and the *Qutbist* doctrine. In addition, Islamic fundamentalist political thought has been – and remains – directly or indirectly influenced by the dominant Western political discourse and has passed through different phases of assimilation and rejection of Western political thinking.[26] The issues raised and the solutions offered by the FIS in Algeria in the 1990s were among the latest political reworkings of this religious doctrine in a context where the political debate was/is saturated with notions of democratisation and liberalisation. Their discourse illustrated how Islamic fundamentalism was being reconstructed from what is in some respects a 'contractual' standpoint. To understand fully the 'democratic' tenor of this phase (and its practical implications), however, it is crucial to comprehend how this reaction is articulated on the basis of earlier conceptual models that Islamic fundamentalists developed in response to the 'civilisation-building' schemes proposed by European colonial powers and to the subsequent neo-romantic and nationalistic quests for authenticity (with their authoritarian outcomes).

The rationalist impulse: Abduh, Afghani and the Reform movement

A noteworthy effort at reconceptualising the relationship between religion and politics and between the Islam and the 'West' according to the 'philosophy of Reason' originated at the end of the nineteenth century with the collaboration of Muhammad Abduh and Jamal al-Afghani. While Afghani was a somewhat shadowy character whose religious and political aims are hard to identify, Abduh was a recognised Islamic scholar from the university of Al-Azhar who became Grand Mufti of Egypt.[27] An important Western influence during the formative phase of their project of re-conceptualisation was the French historian François Guizot. (Guizot's *The History of*

Civilisation in Europe had been translated into Arabic in 1876 by a follower of Afghani, and Abduh was so impressed by this work that he started to teach Islamic history during his first official teaching tenure in Egypt using this conceptual framework.)[28] In addition, in the 1880s Afghani and Abduh had a first-hand opportunity to sample the intellectual life of the Parisian *salons* – the former by choice, the latter being in temporarily exile from Egypt because of his involvement in the ill-fated Urabi revolt. From Paris, Abduh and Afghani edited the newsletter *The Firmest Bond* (*Al-Urwa al-Wuthqa*), which was sent to leading figures throughout the Muslim world, and which presented an Islamic reflection on the European debates on science, philosophy, religion and politics. At the core of Abduh and Afghani's arguments was an analysis of the foundations of 'civilisation' and of the reasons for the dominance of the Western world (over the Islamic community). Their conceptualisation of human history and progress recycled Guizot's ideas on the unity of social and individual progress. For Guizot progress rested upon the formation and transmission of an aggregate of civilisation; a civilisational essence whose current historical upshot was 'the Nation'.[29] Guizot had argued that 'Civilisation' only flourished when people were implicated in a rational system of government and when scientific political practices were devised jointly by thinkers and politicians. Abduh and Afghani re-utilised Guizot's perspective and suggested that, for Muslim thinkers, the study of the historical development of nations and civilisations ought to be 'more significant than the study concerning the transmission of traditions' (i.e. Islamic jurisprudence).[30] Looking at the decline of Islamic civilisation from this angle, Abduh and Afghani identified the proximate cause of failure as the lack of 'enlightened' governance and the deeper cause as the divisions between religious thinkers and political leaders. Their diagnosis was that 'the dissolution and weakening of the bonds fastening the Islamic community began when the title of *alim* [religious scholar] became distinct from the title of Caliph'.[31] They concluded that, because no adequate solution to this problem of disunity was offered by the political elite, it was incumbent upon the religious scholars (*ulama*) 'to eliminate the discord generated by the practice of political power'.[32]

Taking the achievements of European civilisation as the model, Abduh subsequently argued that only a rational organisation of society permitted a civilisation to last and, therefore, that the adoption by the Islamic community of the rationalist philosophy used in the Western world was the only means to stop its decline. This was not anathema, Abduh pointed out, because the 'West' and Islam represented not antagonistic forms of social and religious order but variations upon a common theme. He insisted that the Islamic impulse in the rediscovery of the European classical heritage during the Renaissance – hence its lingering influence on the Reformation and the Enlightenment – meant that current Western civilisation was not merely indebted to Islamic civilisation but was also one of its unacknowledged *instances*.[33] In terms of public image this advocacy of a strong historical and philosophical connection between the 'West' and Islam was intended to pacify both a domestic audience generally sceptical of Western concepts and Western thinkers for whom Islam itself appeared incompatible with scientific reasoning. Abduh, like so many Western philosophers of his time – including the champion of rationalism, Herbert Spencer, whom Abduh admired – thought that is was essential to be able to unite science and religion in order to reconstruct a better social order. In the theological field, by insisting on the need for scientific analyses and explanations, Abduh suggested no less than a critical re-evaluation of a large body of Islamic traditions of doubtful origin and/or coherence, which were widely utilised throughout the Muslim world. He estimated that this grand reappraisal of Islamic doctrine would be safe to undertake because only corrupt traditions would be eliminated and scholars would gain a method of analysis that would yield more authoritative interpretations. However, aware that an over-eager pursuit of a rationalist approach could lead to a destructive Pyrrhonism, Abduh indicated that 'this comparison between reason and religion involves some disparagement of the former in matter of faith'. He suggested that

> if there come some things which appear contradictory, reason must believe that the apparent is not the intended sense. It is then free to seek the true sense by reference to the rest of the Prophet's message in whom the ambiguity occurred or to fall back upon God and His omniscience.[34]

Finally but importantly, Abduh made it quite clear that this rationalistic re-interpretation of the Islamic doctrine (*ijtihad*) was a task reserved for learned people. He doubted the optimism of the *Philosophes* regarding the capacity of the masses to be educated through an appeal to Reason. In Abduh's opinion, because ordinary

Muslims were 'caught in the flux of passions' most of the time, it was only proper that the religious commands 'exercise an authority over men's souls superior to that of reason'.[35]

From Reform to *Salafiyya*

During Abduh's and Afghani's lifetime, the Reform movement remained a rather elitist religious pressure group. The implications of the new kind of Islamic hermeneutics which they introduced only became fully clear after their deaths. At the beginning of the twentieth century for the core regions of the Middle East, and sometimes later for the more distant Muslim communities, the corpus of Islamic traditions began to be re-organised according to the Reform movement's rationalistic precepts. In Egypt, under the aegis of Rashid Rida, Abduh's most influential disciple, the Reform movement took a more conservative turn and gave rise to the *Salafiyya* (the way of the ancestors). This rephrasing of the reformist doctrine took place so rapidly, after decades of lacklustre innovations, that by the time the Islamic reformers began seriously to organise themselves according to the Reform's teaching in Algeria, the *Salafiyya* was already exploring new avenues for Islam.[36] In the 1920s in Algeria Ben Badis, the leader of the local Reform movement, still considered that the colonial administration was an ally against obscurantism because of the 'enlightened' philosophy that it possessed. In 1922, in the first edition of the Algerian reformers' newspaper, *El-Muntaqid*, Ben Badis even declared that the Algerians were 'weak and insufficiently evolved', and that they needed to be 'under the protection of a strong and civilised nation that can help them to progress on the road to civilisation and development'.[37] (In fairness to Ben Badis, it must be said that his first editorial went to extremes in order to mollify the French censors.) At the same time, in Egypt, Rida was busy reconstructing a specifically Islamic model for an 'enlightened' society, based on texts and traditions dating back to the Prophet's time and the period of the four 'rightly guided' Caliphs – the 'Golden Age' of Islam.[38] Rida, who had observed closely the collapse of the modernising Ottoman Empire (and the rise of the secular Turkish republic and the abolition of the Caliphate), began suggesting that a reform of Muslim polities according to a European model was inappropriate. He argued that the ideal model for development in the Muslim world ought to be the 'Golden Age' of Islam: a period that illustrated how the superior knowledge that resulted from an accurate understanding of the Islamic doctrine had permitted the expansion of the Islamic Empire. Since rational interpretation was not time-constrained, these traditions constituted for Rida the standard by which to judge subsequent Islamic practices and interpretations.

In practice, the success of the *Salafiyya* is attributable to the popularisation of its themes by the social and political movement founded in 1928 by Hassan al Banna – the Muslim Brotherhood.[39] After Rida's death in 1935, the associative network of the Muslim Brotherhood propagated this rationalist–fundamentalist approach to Islam among the growing numbers of middle- and working-class Muslims who had received an education in the Westernised Egyptian schooling system. (By propagating the notion of scientific causality through the schooling system, the state apparatus had helped reduce the standing of the explanations of the world disseminated by traditional religious systems.)[40] The originality of the Muslim Brotherhood's brand of Islamic activism – or 'Islamic fundamentalism' as we may call it since the Muslim Brotherhood was one of the first movements to self-reflectively acknowledge its political status – was that it turned into a mass phenomenon a practice of Islam that until then had been confined to a small number of Islamic scholars. Unwittingly, Abduh's and Rida's reforms had favoured the emergence of authoritative interpretations of the sacred texts by religious leaders not subordinated to the traditional *ulama*. As soon as these new Islamic leaders succeeded in forcing upon the other interpreters of the Islamic creed a set of epistemological principles that defined valid Islamic discourses and practices, the state itself came under pressure. Because Rida's interpretation had given so much importance to the ideas and practices of the early Islamic period (when there were fewer distinctions between religious and political leadership), the social and political implications of religious reform bore down heavily upon a state elite that had failed to show impeccably Islamic credentials. By the mid-1930s, even in 'backward' Algeria, the French administration was obliged to deny independent imams access to the mosques, as well as limiting the number of Islamic schools and censoring newspapers written in Arabic in order to counter a growing Islamic Reform movement that had become more and more politicised over the years.[41]

Political activism and Vitalist principles: the *Qutbist* revolt

The metamorphosis of the Reform/*Salafiyya* revival into a radical movement of political opposition has been shaped and facilitated by the decolonisation struggle and the formation of independent Muslim states. Whether the Islamic current was co-opted by the nationalist movement, as in Algeria, or whether it clashed with it, as in Egypt, the attempt to reform society using the state system set up by the colonial powers profoundly transformed the Islamic movement. In Algeria, from the 1940s to the 1970s, the Islamic reformers resigned themselves to working with the FLN to Arabicise and Islamicise society. The Algerian Reform/*Salafist* movement, which began losing its dynamism after the death of Ben Badis in 1940, integrated the FLN in 1956 after the start of the war of independence. Following the country's independence in 1962, the half-hearted attempt by the former head of the Islamic reformers to re-create a distinct Islamic pole only resulted in the nomination of his son, Taleb Ibrahimi, to the post of Education Minister. Subsequently, following the transfer of Taleb Ibrahimi to the post of Information Minister in 1970, the main vector of diffusion of Islamic ideas was the state-funded journal *Al-Asala*, which strived to combine the anti-Western themes of the Third-Worldist doctrine with Islamic-populist ideas.[42] Elsewhere in the Middle East and North Africa the marriage of nationalism and Islamism was far less successful. In Egypt, in particular, the rupture was brutal in the 1950s between a state elite that promoted an individualist approach to Islam, based on secular political models, and a religious movement that strove to ground the political system on a comprehensive Islamic social code. The confrontation between the Muslim Brotherhood and the Nasserite regime in the 1950s and 1960s was at the root of the radicalisation of the themes of the *Salafiyya*. At that time the main architect of this re-conceptualisation of the political strategy of the Islamic movement was Sayyid Qutb.[43]

A teacher by profession, trained in the Egyptian state education system, Qutb joined the Muslim Brotherhood in 1950, after having spent two years in a teacher-training exchange programme in the United States. Imprisoned in 1954 with several thousand Muslim Brothers as Nasser came to power, Qutb remained in jail until 1964 and wrote most of his works under these conditions. The publication of his best-seller, *Milestones* (*Malim fil-Tariq*), in 1965 changed the face of Islamic fundamentalism in Egypt and beyond, and led to his execution by Nasser's regime.[44] In his works, Qutb strove to provide the socio-cultural revival led by the Muslim Brotherhood with a practical political philosophy. In his view, although the Muslim Brothers had a method of interpretation of the Koran that was the key to a rebirth of the Islamic civilisation, they lacked a political strategy to guide the Faithful in their daily confrontation with a 'non-Islamic' authoritarian state. Like the efforts of Abduh and Afghani, Qutb's tentative reconceptualisation of 'Islamic Civilisation' was indebted to European thought (notably, the neo-romantic and Vitalist conceptions of society that had emerged at the beginning of the twentieth century and that had been politicised by fascist movements in the 1920s and 1930s).[45] Qutb's reading of the fascistic French thinker Alexis Carrel had prompted him to write his own critique of modern civilisation, *Islam and the Problems of Civilisation* – a prelude to the arguments developed in *Milestones*.[46] (Carrel's own best-seller, *Man the Unknown*, was a sharp critique of the Western social order associated with a proposal for rebuilding a new society on 'healthier' grounds that borrowed heavily, but inconsistently, from Henri Bergson's intuitionist moral philosophy.)[47] The Vitalist ideas that had been used in Europe to turn the 'philosophy of Reason' of the nineteenth century on its head inspired Qutb to rephrase in a similar way the political strategy of the Islamic movement.

Marked by the events of the First World War and by the economic crisis of the late 1920s in Europe and America, European thinkers like Bergson and Carrel agreed that the human mind and 'soul' were unable to control fully the new techniques made available by scientific progress. They suggested that scientific progress and moral progress were disjointed and that, ultimately, it was not scientific reasoning (or 'Reason') but some form of mystical insight (or *élan vital*) that regulated the dynamics of civilisations.[48] Faced with the growing technical capacities of the Egyptian state's repressive apparatus and propaganda machinery, Qutb also understood the inadequacy of these material advances for a flourishing Islamic civilisation. Making the same distinction between moral and technical progress, Qutb reached the conclusion that scientific knowledge only constituted a body of second-rate information, useful for certain practical purposes, but far less important than the moral 'laws' that applied specifically to human beings and that regulated social harmony.[49] In his view, morality was superior to, and qualitatively different from reason. It was the basis of progress, and the main condition for living a civilised life. In the light of this observation, Qutb modified Abduh's earlier conclusions concerning the dominance of 'West' and the direction of progress. He agreed that Western and Islamic civilisations grew from the same root, but denied any suggestion that the current embodiments of Western prosperity were mere variations on Islamic values. For Qutb, Western political, moral and religious conceptions of society were corrupted, and the achievements of the 'West' were slowly undermined by the growing social disorder and depravity of Western societies. Denouncing a perverse Western ranking of cultures and civilisations, Qutb claimed that the whole world had become largely devoid of the 'vital values' necessary to its 'healthy development' and that the age of *jahiliyya* (pre-Islamic ignorance) had returned.[50]

Qutb's denunciation of Western societies was a thinly disguised critique of the Muslim polities that had adopted similar social, economic and political models of development. He argued that the type of Islamic religion practised in most of the Islamic world was so far removed from genuine Islam as not even to deserve the name. For those Muslims who could have access to the uncorrupted body of traditions unearthed by the *Salafiyya*, the only solution available was to restart the Islamic civilisation anew. Qutb proposed to guide committed Muslims along this path but, in a characteristically Vitalist style, he warned that 'moral life' and 'moral laws' could not be taught theoretically. While Abduh and Afghani thought that an academic debate was sufficient to establish the correct Islamic practices (which could then be implemented *de haut en bas* by an 'enlightened' religious establishment and state apparatus), Qutb contended that theological knowledge alone did not endow religious scholars with an indisputable authority over other Muslims. He argued that the 'enlightenment' of the masses could only occur when religious scholars were directly involved in day-to-day social activities – hence, any attempt to institutionalise an Islamic hierarchy ran counter to the spirit of Islam.[51] Qutb abandoned the idea of a reform of the Islamic community's leadership that would reunite the political leaders and the *ulama*. In his scheme the indication of a true Islamic knowledge and leadership was that the scholars were involved in active proselytism, directly conversing with other Muslims and leading social change by personal example. He suggested that the leadership of the Islamic movement be organised to reflect personal achievements and that 'the ups and downs through which the movement passes determine the position and activity of every individual in the movement'.[52] Ideally, for Qutb, this committed proselytising effort and an appeal to reason were sufficient to convince each individual of the appropriateness of an Islamic lifestyle. However, he warned that in the present circumstances this might not happen because an unrepresentative and 'un-Islamic' state leadership had devised social policies that actively maintained the masses in a state of ignorance. A similar problem had been encountered earlier on in Europe by 'social reformers' of communist or fascist allegiance, and they had concluded that what stood in the way of the 'education' of the people and of their moral principles were hindrances that had to be removed at all costs.[53] Like his European predecessors, Qutb argued that recourse to violence could be condoned under these circumstances because it was in fact an act of *self-defence*. In this scheme *jihad* becomes a practical necessity to access the unencumbered self and it only targets the social structures that maintain people in a state of ignorance and dependency. In Qutb's view the Islamic movement

> uses the methods of preaching and persuasion for reforming ideas and beliefs, and it uses physical power and *jihad* for abolishing the organisations and authorities of the *jahili* system which prevent people from reforming their ideas and beliefs.[54]

This aspect of the Qutbist doctrine helped to give a revolutionist momentum to the Islamic movement, particularly after the 1967 war in Egypt (and, following the Iranian revolution, in the rest of the Muslim world). Qutb's interpretation not only affirmed that there was a (single) rational interpretation of the Islamic doctrine (which Islamic activists could use to reconstruct an ideal Islamic society), but it also said that the *proof* that the activists were right was their actual success at *overthrowing* 'un-Islamic' institutions. In other words, the evidence of the rationality of their endeavour was proven *a posteriori* by the success of their political action. This political notion facilitated the emergence of radical Islamic groups that conceived the modern state primarily as something to be overthrown. Unavoidably, the peculiar brand of anarchism implicitly advocated by Qutb placed subsequent generations of Islamic fundamentalist thinkers in a difficult position. The uncompromising distinction between *jahiliyya* and Islamic community, which led Qutb to assert that 'there is nothing beyond faith except unbelief, nothing beyond Islam except Jahiliyya, nothing beyond the truth except falsehood', ensured that it was particularly difficult for subsequent generations of Islamic ideologues to specify a firm basis for the internal organisation of their movement and for its relationships with the rest of the non-Islamic world.[55]

3   The Algerian Political Transition: Democratic Symbols and Authoritarian Practices (1988–91)

Whatever hopes the Algerian population might have placed in the FLN and its home-grown Arab Socialist developmental model, two decades after the end of the war of independence, their faith in the ruling elite had seriously diminished. The ideological cement provided by these early revolutionary ideals had been replaced by a more pragmatic attitude. In the 1980s, when confronted with new socio-economic difficulties, the population swiftly turned towards Islamic and liberal models for help. Islamic and liberal-democratic themes were effortlessly brought to the fore because they were already part of a polysemic official discourse. Since independence Islam had been the state religion, and Algeria was officially the 'Democratic and Popular Republic of Algeria'. In this context Islamic and democratic movements merely emphasised, as in the rest of the Middle East and North Africa, the failures in the moral order and in social justice as the main cause of popular alienation. However, before 1988 in Algeria it is impossible to identify with precision a social or political movement with the ideological and organisational potential to challenge the ruling regime. The Berber associative movement, which had manifested itself violently in the 1980 Berber Spring, had been thoroughly repressed and remained confined to the independence-minded Kabyle region. On its own it did not constitute a serious threat to the Algerian regime. For their part the trade unions were firmly under governmental control and the leftist nucleus of opposition to the regime, like the democratic voices, were mostly confined to small circles of intellectuals and to some student groups. Finally, in the case of the Islamic fundamentalist movement, the rare specialists of Islam like François Burgat, who studied its activities in Algeria in the 1980s, downplayed the capacity of this movement to mount a serious political challenge in the country.[1] Islamic associations were generally not made up of advocates of political action, especially against the state, but operated locally and aimed at changing Islamic practices through community work. These associations expected that changes in the political system would naturally follow from the changes they helped to carry out in the social sphere. (Reciprocally, the poor who frequented the 'free' mosques and the 'independent' Islamic associations did not generally consider that the discourses on social reforms propounded by the Islamic fundamentalists transformed their religious activities into a form of political protest.)[2]

With the worsening of the socio-economic crisis in the 1980s, this network of associations in Algeria was increasingly involved in the running of the country's private social welfare and education system. However, it still required a leap of faith to imagine that civil society's micro-social and micro-economic successes would be able to transform completely the situation of the polity. (It may appear counter-intuitive to talk of civil society when the associative networks that pervade the Algerian society and the Muslim communities of the region have such a tangible religious element in their midst, but 'civil society' is part of every day discursive practices in Algeria, as elsewhere in the region, and religious associations are a part of this phenomenon.[3] This does not mean that civil society is 'really' there, especially in the form that many demanding Western definitions require, but one cannot simply dismiss this discourse and phenomenon as didactically pointless and politically irrelevant.) In political terms, the main threat that civil society posed to the institutional order in Algeria stemmed not from its increasing level of organisation but from its accumulation of symbolic capital. Because the Algerian regime had been especially effective in infusing its social and political institutions with ideological legitimacy, it was extremely sensitive to these symbolic challenges to its leadership. This fragility was heightened in the late 1980s by the increasing inability of the regime to accompany its propagandist discourse with an appropriate level of state subsidies designed to buy off social aggression.

THE 1988 OCTOBER RIOTS: THE SYMBOL OF A NEW ERA

In the late 1980s the worsening of the economic situation in Algeria provided propitious conditions for the development of movements of social protest. In a few years, since the end of the second oil boom in 1985, state export revenues had fallen by more than 40 per cent.[4] This shortfall in liquidities seriously undermined the heavily subsidised national economy and by 1988 the country's growth had reached a record low of –3.6 per cent. In the summer of 1988 the price of foodstuffs increased sharply on the black market, as state-subsidised goods became scarce. In the east of the country (Constantine) this situation became so extreme that food depots were ransacked by angry mobs. Social tensions were exacerbated by ad hoc 'liberal' reforms designed to improve the state management of the economy, which only succeeded in disturbing the 'socialist' routines of the administration. In this context the number of strike actions increased sharply and the year 1988 quickly established a new record for strikes.[5] In September a large strike action took place in the state-owned motor-industry complex of Roubia, just outside Algiers. As a large police force was mobilised, a tense stand-off interspersed with violent outbursts took place between striking workers and policemen. At the end of the month Chadli Benjedid, the Algerian President, denounced in a televised speech, 'the financial speculators' who were, in his view, the cause of all the economic ills of the country. In an attempt to limit the responsibility of the state in this economic crisis, he encouraged citizens to play a leading role in regulating the black market.[6] A few days later, in October, at the beginning of the school year, a sharp rise in the price of school materials placed an increased burden on impoverished Algerian families and provoked talk of strikes in schools and universities. At the same time, on 2 October the postal service went on strike in the Algiers region, thus worsening the pre-existing problem of circulation of information. From then on rumours of a general strike began to circulate in Algiers.

People in Algiers were expecting an outburst of violent protest and it was no great surprise to them when on 4 October trouble erupted. That evening 'striking' high-school students and unemployed youths went on the rampage in Algiers' lavish new commercial and cultural centre of Ryad-el-Feth. During the night clashes with the police caused the deaths of several children, and rumours of terrible police brutalities spread quickly all over town. The following morning schoolchildren, students and unemployed youths, who were friends and relatives of the persons killed overnight, organised a protest march in several suburbs of Algiers and directed themselves towards the town centre. This demonstration quickly turned into a riot. As people destroyed public amenities along their path, the police chose not to intervene in an effort to avoid a repeat of the events of the previous night.[7] In the centre of Algiers the rioting crowd ransacked several state-owned supermarkets, vandalised several offices of the state-party (the FLN), of the national airline (Air Algérie), and of the state-owned wine company, as well as the premises of a few luxury hotels and nightclubs. These young rioters did not have overtly political demands, but blamed the President, Chadli, for all their social and economic problems and for the police brutality. They claimed that they wanted to mobilise public opinion, and some even compared their revolt to the *Intifada* – an unlikely comparison in political terms but one that reflected the youthful character of the protest.[8] In the afternoon a long overdue police intervention caused more casualties among the rioters as the crowd was dispersed. However, far from discouraging the protesters, this repression and the non-recognition of their protest (which had received no coverage from the state-controlled television and radio) further exacerbated the anger of this youthful crowd and its determination to shake the regime. As night fell, rioting resumed in several of Algiers' poorer suburbs, and the local offices of the FLN and of the Local Councils were attacked and looted. Later that night the rioters moved back into the town centre where they ransacked and partially torched three ministerial buildings. Appropriately, these were the Ministry of Youth and Sports, the Ministry of Education and the Ministry of Commerce.

Up to that very moment this spate of rioting had not differed markedly from previous summers of unrest and it displayed all the characteristics of the 'food riots', which are well known in Algeria and in the region. (Two years earlier, in 1986, important riots had erupted in the east of the country (Constantine, Sétif), after a similarly tense summer of unrest, and had been brutally repressed.)[9] In October 1988, however, the combination of attacks on important symbols of state power (Ministries), the concentration of the troubles in the country's capital, and the coming of the Friday prayer – a traditionally propitious occasion for displays of popular anger – all encouraged the government to take strong preventive measures. On Thursday 6 October, two days after the beginning of the troubles, the Algerian President imposed a state of emergency in the Algiers region. For the first time since the end of the war of independence, all civilian authorities were placed under military control. The Algerian regime responded as if it was confronted by a military coup – which may credit the theses invoking a political manipulation of the rioters – and it sent armoured vehicles to protect the Defence Ministry, the FLN central committee and the radio and television buildings; as well as imposing a curfew. (In practice, however, these measures did little to halt the riots in Algiers' poorer suburbs during the night.) Early the following morning, army units were deployed alongside Algiers' main roads, tank brigades took up positions on the motorway and soldiers began to man strategic crossroads. In anticipation of further trouble, the government also announced that all schools in Algiers were to remain closed until further notice. All Air Algérie flights to and from Algiers were cancelled.

On Friday 7 October, the protest acquired a new dimension. The protest spread outside the Algiers area as Islamic fundamentalist leaders began to organise the crowd in post-prayer demonstrations. All of a sudden the regional capitals of the West (Oran), of Kabylia (Tizi-Ouzou) and of several other Algerian districts were shaken by an apparently well planned wave of demonstrations. The pattern of the demonstrations and the targets of the angry mobs were relatively consistent. Starting from the suburban mosques at the end of the Friday prayer, the protesters marched towards the main political and economic decision-making sites of each town centre. On their way they ransacked the FLN offices and the Local Councils, plundered the state-owned supermarkets, the luxury hotels, the offices of the national airline and, occasionally, attacked the Law Courts. Outside Algiers the security forces were generally unprepared to deal with such a powerful protest. Their lack of preparation ensured that they were often involved in bloody clashes with the demonstrators. (Clashes were particularly violent in Oran, where the army had been deployed hastily to protect the governor's office and the FLN regional office.) In Algiers the army's intervention was more carefully planned and altogether more successful at blocking the main protest marches without much bloodshed. In the suburb of Belcourt the soldiers negotiated with Ali Belhadj, the local preacher leading a 10,000-strong mob, in order to avoid clashes between the security forces and the demonstrators. Belhadj's intervention indicated that, at that stage, although Islamic leaders had used their organisational capacities and religious authority to transform an ill-focused food riot into a more explicitly political protest, they wanted only to attract the attention of the regime (to obtain political concessions), not to bring about its collapse. In fact, in his own Friday sermon, Belhadj had declared that he was ready 'to meet the authorities and to discuss the situation with them'. He even suggested that he could 'ask President Chadli to replace the state of emergency by the Islamic Law' (*Sharia*).[10] Although Islamic leaders appeared to orchestrate these demonstrations, they had only a tenuous control over the crowd. All over the country the most popular slogans in the demonstrations were always a mixture of Islamic, populist and democratic demands. Calls such as 'Allah Akbar' and 'Islamic republic' shared the crowds' favour with slogans such as 'the People make the laws' and 'reclaim your rights'. Increasingly, whilst Islamic leaders still recognised the legitimacy of the incumbent political authorities, the crowd adopted radical views in the face of an erratic police repression. As night fell and people continued to defy the curfew orders, rumours of mass shooting and torture by the army's Special Forces began to circulate in Algiers.[11] As rumours of atrocities by the armed forces spread, rallying calls like 'Chadli murderer' and 'down with the regime' became more common amongst demonstrators. 'Here it is worse than in Chile' the protesters claimed, when they heard that soldiers had received orders to shoot on sight in order to impose a curfew.[12] The lack of reliable information on the evolution of the protest – the state-controlled national media having decided on an information blackout – led people to take some preventive measures to protect themselves against the possible reprisals from the security forces. In several suburbs of Algiers, the protesters launched pre-emptive actions against police stations in order to confiscate their weaponry.

On 8 October, in the evening news, the Algerian Interior Minister mentioned 'the events' for the first time on national television. He recognised that a wave of disturbances had spread throughout the country and indicated that the 'security forces' had tried to stop the troubles but 'in vain'. In the government's name he regretted the 'considerable losses' that had occurred amongst the population and called for calm. His call was not heeded, and rioting continued throughout the night in the suburbs. The security forces asked hospitals not to hand back the bodies of the deceased to their relatives, in an attempt to avoid the organisation of new protest marches for the funerals. By 9 October the blatant lack of success of this heavy-handed military repression was becoming a serious worry for the Algerian regime. Its leadership decided to change tack and to adopt a more conciliatory approach towards the demonstrators. In an appeasing gesture the army began to organise food convoys to re-supply the recently looted state supermarkets with large quantities of foods that were previously in short supply. The state-controlled media announced that the government was taking the protesters' demands seriously and that the President would propose a solution in a televised speech the following day. On 10 October, a few hours before addressing the nation, the President invited to a crisis meeting several Islamic leaders who had been at the forefront of the protest movement: Sheikh Shanoun, Mahfoud Nannah, Abassi Madani, Ali Belhadj. After discussions with these leading figures of the Islamic movement, Chadli went on national television to address the nation. Opening his address with a mention of the economic crisis, the President gave assurances that the government would immediately guarantee lower retail prices and a greater availability of subsidised goods. Next, he swiftly moved on to concentrate on the political obstacles that were, in his view, at the root of all the current difficulties experienced in the country. He declared:

> My conviction is that it is time to introduce necessary reforms in the political field, and to revise some institutional structures and constitutional foundations in order to adapt them to the next stage ... On this matter, a project is being prepared which will be subject to the decision of the People ... We will eliminate the current monopoly of responsibility and will permit the official institutions of the State, the Parliament or others, to play their part in the control and monitoring of the State.[13]

Chadli concluded his declaration by mentioning the actions of the security forces and promised that he would take sanctions against 'those persons who have done wrong and have not fully assumed their responsibilities'. The main thrust of the President's message, as the Algerians understood it, was that it was time to democratise the political institutions of the country. That night the riots began to subside. The following morning, as abruptly as it started, the movement of protest ended. A day later, on 12 October, the President lifted the state of emergency. Tanks and soldiers were sent back to their barracks – though military tribunals were set up to try the people arrested during the riots. That Friday Islamic leaders called for appeasement in front of the large, expectant crowds that had been drawn to the urban mosques from all over the country to listen to their weekly sermon. On Saturday schools re-opened nationwide as pupils and students ended their 'strike'.

In October 1988, in Algeria, the President's 'democratisation speech', despite its rather vague and open-ended character, played a decisive role in the evolution of the polity at a violent conjuncture. Crucially, Chadli had emphasised the country's long-term political problems rather than the socio-economic factors and the repression that had triggered and fuelled the October riots. The unfavourable economic situation and the behaviour of the state apparatus, issues that were at the core of the popular protest, were in fact barely mentioned by the President (who knew how little he could do about them). By default, Chadli chose to give a prominent place to the reform of the political system, which he could initiate rapidly at a relatively low cost. (As Abdelhamid Brahimi, Chadli's Prime Minister until 1988, pointed out, before that time the President 'never did or said anything that indicated that he was interested in democratising the political system'.)[14] This unexpected political overture worked extremely well as a public-relations operation and brought about a very specific end to the riots, since it forced the rioters to reconsider their tactics in the face of these proposals. In practice, the proposal to eliminate the monopoly of state responsibility, and the odd-sounding proposition to let the official institutions monitor the activities of the state apparatus, signified the end of the one-party system and the beginning of a democratic transition. This unexpected outcome to the riots was certainly not the preferred solution for the Algerian military establishment or for the Islamic fundamentalists. (Perhaps it was not even the outcome that the protesters had hoped for, in so far as they had articulate demands.) From the army's perspective these political concessions seemed a dubious choice at a time when the riots were beginning to run out of steam (with food supplies running low in towns, the visible symbols of state power already either destroyed or under protection, and the soldiers improving the efficiency of the repression). At the other end of the political spectrum, the Islamic camp made very few direct gains in term of the 'Islamicisation' of the Algerian State.

In this context, as it happened earlier in Latin America, democratisation occurred principally by default.[15] Undoubtedly, the President's choices were instrumental in bringing this peaceful ending to the riots, but as subsequent events would prove, it was not simply a case of Chadli imposing his will upon the military or the Islamic fundamentalists. It was more a matter of creating a consensus and momentum on this issue among people in military and Islamic circles who had not been particularly interested in democratisation before. The President was prominent in the creation of this democratic transition, but the consensus that effectively put an end to the riots could not have been enforced by a single political actor or even by a few. Crucially, it was because many ordinary Algerian

citizens agreed that this democratic project was sufficiently representative of their aspirations and decided to back it up by their own
actions that Chadli's view were vindicated. What the 1988 October
riots actually achieved was an explicit deconstruction of the
post-independence political consensus based on the FLN–army–
administration system. More than simply showing the depth of
discontent or the strength of the Islamic opposition, the riots illustrated the failure of the Algerian regime to plan and manage
adequately the social and political practices of its citizens. For the
state, the resulting chaos highlighted serious structural and semantic
flaws in the organisation of the Algerian social and political system.
In this context, clearly, the prospect of a transition to democracy
opened up the possibility of injecting a new coherence into the
political system. What the events of October 1988 did not provide,
however, was a clear indication of how the socio-economic crisis that
crippled the country could be solved, or which political actors would
be best placed to take the country out of this difficult situation.

THE ALGERIAN DEMOCRATIC TRANSITION: SUCCESSES AND FAILURES

The first step taken in the reform of the state institutions and the
first effort to make the state apparatus more accountable was
Chadli's decision to put to the vote his own presidential mandate.
On 22 November 1988, just over a month after the riots, Chadli was
re-elected to the presidency by referendum – he was the sole
candidate – with over 80 per cent of yes votes and a turnout of nearly
90 per cent. Although the President had been blamed for the socio-
economic crisis before the riots, and even for the repression during
them, in the post-October political situation he had become by
default the best insurance that democratic transition had. Quite
simply, most Algerians had concluded that the President had to be
part of this democratic package; otherwise, they would have a new
'social contract', but no political leader willing and able to
implement it. In addition, as the few riotous days of October 1988
became fixated in the collective memory as a unitary event – the
'October Riots' – they introduced a symbolic breach in the historical
framework of the polity. This breach in the symbolic order that constituted the foundational event of Algerian democracy made it
possible to assign *a posteriori* new roles to each social and political

actor. By putting forward the image of a leader who had ended the state-party system and introduced political liberalisation, Chadli re-invented himself as the maker of democratic Algeria. (After the riots, the President also pardoned all those arrested during these events and condemned by military tribunals.) After his re-election Chadli endeavoured to re-orient the political debate towards the future in order to minimise an unavoidably acrimonious debate which would be centred on apportioning historical blame. In a very short time the redesigning of the constitutional framework to introduce political pluralism produced the new Algerian Constitution of 23 February 1989. This text, which authorised the creation of 'associ-ations of a political character' – i.e. political parties – was adopted by referendum with 73 per cent approval and a turnout of nearly 80 per cent.[16] Islamic leaders made a reality of this redefinition of the rules of the political game even before this official endorsement. Five days before the Constitution was approved, in a mosque of Bab-el-Oued, in Algiers, Abassi Madani and Ali Belhadj had announced the creation of one such political 'association', the Islamic Salvation Front (*Front Islamique du Salut*, FIS). (The party was then re-launched officially on 10 March.) This Islamic party was an outgrowth of The League of the Call (*Rabitat Dawa*), the national confederation Islamic fundamentalist associations that had come to the fore just after the October riots. Benefiting fully from the novelty effect, the lack of serious religious and political competition and the public impression that the Islamic movement had forced the regime into its conces-sions, this very first Algerian Islamic party immediately attracted a large following. In March 1989 the first issue of the FIS newspaper sold 100,000 copies.

Political pluralism was reinforced in Algeria by a reform of the FLN. Not only did the FLN lose its state-party status after the country's new constitution was adopted, but it also cut its ties with the military establishment in March 1989, when the military officers who had reserved seats on the executive committee withdrew from the party. The formal pluralist character of the country's new insti-tutional arrangements was officially approved by the FLN-controlled Parliament in September 1989, which recognised the legal existence of the Islamic and Berber parties. On a strict reading of the Consti-tution, Islamic and regionalist parties fell foul of a constitutional proviso that forbade the formation of political parties on an 'exclu-sively religious or regionalist basis'. In September 1989 these parties were, nonetheless, authorised according to a reading of the Constitution based on the argument that they were not *exclusively* religious or regionalist parties. This decision of Parliament, made under pressure from the President, constituted a significant political gesture by the Algerian regime. More than any formal constitutional basis, what the democratic process needed during these first few months of political transition was some *trust* to be injected into the social and political system. Unlike the devising of formal institutional reforms, the learning and diffusion of more tolerant, democratic and accountable political practices were, in Algeria as in any other new democracy, protracted endeavours. In 1989, the relaxation of censorship and the greater freedom given to the written press – the televised media remaining under state supervision – helped to sustain a better informed political debate. (In no time former employees of the official newspapers who had been adept at double-talk and propagandising state doctrine launched 'independent' newspapers extolling the values of democracy, pluralism, the freedom of the press and denouncing much of what they themselves previously stood for.)

However, the setting-up of political parties and the practical business of devising political manifestos and selecting party candidates remained a difficult undertaking, for both technical and psychological reasons. In addition to a lack of pre-existing institutional and financial structures for supporting a plural political system, the Algerian social and political actors themselves were not always fully convinced that it was worthwhile or even safe to engage in open political debates. From the moment the new Constitution was approved in February 1989 to the June 1990 elections, 14 new political parties were officially registered in Algeria. By contrast, over a similar period, between the June 1990 elections and the December 1991 elections, 36 new parties were created.[17] Even if we take into account the technical difficulties of creating political parties on a nationwide basis, it is clear that political engagements were held back by the fear of repression – at least until the first electoral contest. Tellingly, when asked why they did not register their party in time for the local elections of June 1990, the cadres of the moderate Islamic party *Ennahda* replied: 'we did not trust the government; we were afraid'.[18]

The FIS chose to trust the government and to be pioneers in representing political Islam. This risk-taking strategy, which consisted in participating fully in the process of democratic transition, was at first very well rewarded. In April 1990, just over a year after its creation, during the campaign for the local elections the Islamic party attracted between 600,000 and 800,000 people to a massive political rally in Algiers. At that time no other political party, not even the well-established FLN, could muster such a crowd for an electoral rally. More important, the FIS supporters did not only seek to mobilise the population of urban areas, which already knew well their Islamic fundamentalist views, but also made serious efforts to diffuse their political message among the more traditional sectors of the rural population. During the campaign for the local elections it was not unusual for the FIS supporters to go and meet villagers in relatively remote locations – where they were often the only political party to canvass. In the June 1990 local elections the victory of the FIS came, nonetheless, as a surprise to many domestic and foreign political observers. The FIS won over 55 per cent of the vote nationwide and, except for the Berber-dominated Kabylia and the Saharan regions, the Islamic party became near-hegemonic in the Local Councils in all the main urban centres of the country.[19] (In the three main towns of Algeria, Algiers, Oran and Constantine, it won respectively 33 Local Councils out of 33, 24 councils out of 26 and 12 councils out of 12.) For the population at large, however, the impact of institutional reforms and of political pluralism on the socio-economic crisis was less clear-cut than the electoral results that permitted the FIS to occupy the forefront of the Algerian political scene.

Despite economic concerns having been at the forefront of the revolt of 1988, the protest had been conspicuous for its lack of direct impact on the country's socio-economic situation. As government controls over the economy were relaxed and people felt freer to speak out, the number of protest movements and strike actions increased dramatically. The holding of democratic elections did nothing to prevent the number of strikes recorded in the country from reaching new highs in 1989 and 1990. (To the government's credit, however, the right to strike was officially recognised by Parliament in February 1990.) In this respect, the liberal economic policies devised by the new Prime Minister, Mouloud Hamrouche, failed to meet popular expectations. Despite the consensus reached by Hamrouche and the main Islamic, democrat and nationalist political leaders on the need to liberalise the economy, the population greeted with suspicion this rapid process of liberalisation that had dire practical consequences for the less well-off members of society. The lack of mutual under-standing between citizens and liberal reformers was duplicated on the international scene by the disagreements between the Algerian government and international lenders. Between 1989 and 1991 international financial institutions showed little interest in this new pro-democratic Algerian regime, and their engagement remained as limited as before the democratic transition. On the Algerian side, the remnants of a strong nationalist, Third Worldist and Arab Socialist ideology also ensured that the Algerian leadership often proved too intransigent for its own good (and that of the country).[20] Thus, the population remained highly suspicious of the intentions of the regime (and of the coherence of its policies) and doubtful that rich Western democracies and international institutions were doing all they could to help their country. Eventually, this seizing-up of the economic debate helped to focus people's attention on the political, cultural and religious issues that had remained marginal concerns before the democratic transition.

Emergent social and political actors like the FIS re-defined the important political issues of the day, and the boundaries of the political and religious fields. After the June 1990 local elections the growing attention given to these considerations overshadowed the relative managerial success of the Local Councils run by the FIS. Although the population did not experience a dramatic increase in living standards, the Islamic fundamentalists showed that they were able to provide relatively efficient social services by improving on the cost-effectiveness of the previous administration. (This had been no small achievement because, at that time, state funding of Local Councils had been drastically reduced – partly for budgetary reasons, partly for political purposes.) In this context, the first serious troubles encountered in the democratic transition were not brought about by another economically spurred social protest or by a reaction to an international event such as the Gulf War. (During the war, the FIS initially showed little interest in Iraq, as they were well aware of Saddam Hussain's lack of Islamic credentials and they were indebted to Saudi Arabia for its financial aid. They only began to support Iraq, under mounting popular pressure, when American troops landed in Saudi Arabia. As public interest in Saddam Hussain's adventures faded away, however, the FIS rallies rapidly failed to attract more than 50,000 persons at a time.)[21] The first serious crisis to test the willingness of the Algerian regime to democratise was a strictly political quandary that concerned the mechanisms of control of the electoral system. The near-fatal crisis of June 1991 began when the FLN-controlled Parliament attempted to redesign electoral boundaries prior to the parliamentary elections.

Having reflected on their poor results in the local elections, the FLN thought that it would be a good tactical move to redraw the constituencies' boundaries so as to favour their own candidates. To protest against this ad hoc redesigning of the electoral map by self-interested politicians, the democratic opposition parties called a general strike, and received the support of the Islamic parties. As the Parliament, backed by the President (who also felt that this manoeuvre was the only chance the FLN had left to avoid a complete rout), indicated clearly that it would not reconsider its decision. Desirous to avoid a confrontation with the regime at this stage, all political parties except the FIS withdrew their threat of a strike. The FIS leaders thought that their party was powerful enough not to have to submit to the FLN. Despite reservations of some senior party cadres concerning the capacity of the FIS to organise a strike, Madani's decision in favour of such protest action won the day. In the event, because of the Islamic party's lack of support within the trade unions, the FIS 'general strike' never took off and the party cadres had quickly to organise a series of demonstrations in Algiers to show their strength to the government. As life in the rest of the country continued normally, the FIS tried to show that its 'strike' could paralyse the capital by asking its supporters to continue occupying all the public places in central Algiers. These disturbances in the capital provided a convenient excuse for the military's tentative comeback onto the political stage. As the police declared that they was unable to cope with the disturbances, the Algerian President approved an intervention by the army to evacuate the 'striking' FIS protesters from the centre of Algiers. As the soldiers met resistance from the FIS, which also called for civil resistance in the municipalities under its jurisdiction, the military leadership decided to impose a state of emergency for three months. This period of emergency allowed the security forces to arrest the most vocal leaders of the FIS, who were charged with 'endangering national security'. Those arrests included the two main leaders of the Islamic party, Madani and Belhadj, who were imprisoned for their 'declarations of war'.[22]

In 1991, this wave of arrests of Islamic leaders and the temporary halt in the democratic transition still did not lead to a formal re-definition of the institutional framework. Although the military hierarchy asked the President to ban the FIS, Chadli chose not to do so and decided instead to postpone the elections by a few months to calm the situation. At that time, the President still hoped for a tight electoral contest between the FLN, the FIS and the secular/ democratic opposition parties that would produce no clear parliamentary majority. He envisioned the formation of a coalition government in which he could play a leading role. By authorising, or even requesting, a limited military operation, Chadli had hoped to reduce the appeal of the Islamic party and to boost the chances of the FLN. In practice, this bout of military repression set a dangerous precedent for all the parties involved in the democratic transition. (Anyway, it is doubtful how far this could help an FLN that was in a hopeless political situation – a fact that many inside the regime simply refused to recognise.) The repression unleashed in June 1991 undermined one main component of the democratic transition, the fragile trust between political actors, and between rulers and ruled. For the citizens as much as for the political players, this interruption in the democratic process indicated that the primacy of the political over the military, and of dialogue over coercion, was foundering. These strains were clearly visible within the regime itself, as Hamrouche, the liberal Prime Minister who had tried to negotiate an end to the 'strike' with the FIS, resigned in protest at the military intervention (or was dismissed for not agreeing to it).[23] From that moment onwards, many political actors implicitly turned their backs on the opportunities created by the democratic transition and began exploring alternative political options. At the FIS extraordinary congress of Batna, in August 1991, several members of the executive committee (*Madjliss Echoura* – literally, consultative council) were excluded for advocating an end to the party's participation in the electoral process and a more active preparation for extra-political actions. (Shortly before his arrest Belhadj himself had asked his supporters to stockpile weapons.) Abdelkader Hachani, provisionally the new leader of the FIS, succeeded in imposing his views on a strict electoral strategy and legalistic line, with the backing of the FIS mayors who were elected in 1990. Even though he understood that the democratic transition ought not to be taken at face value any longer, Hachani judged that 'the political legitimacy gained through the ballot box was the best insurance the FIS could get at the time'.[24]

In October 1991 the FIS machinery relaunched the campaign for the December parliamentary elections. Although the FIS had suffered from the repression during the three months of the state of emergency, the party recovered far more easily than its opponents had expected. In this respect it also benefited from the relative lack of enthusiasm on the part of the FLN and the other political parties for electoral campaigning. Repeating the mistakes of the 1990 campaign, the political opponents of the Islamic party rarely bothered to challenge the FIS supporters in relatively marginal constituencies.[25] In December Hachani's electoral strategy paid off and the electoral contest turned to the advantage of the FIS. On 26 December 1991 the FIS won nearly half of the parliamentary seats in the first round of the elections – taking 188 out of 430 seats by a straight majority vote.[26] The FLN gained a mere 15 seats and the FFS, the main democratic opposition party, took 25 seats (principally in Kabylia). This landslide FIS victory, only a few months after the military intervention, came as a surprise to many domestic and international actors. At first the reaction of the political community was muted. Soon, however, the disagreements about the process of democratic transition, which had remained unspoken before the elections, were voiced forcefully. Several Algerian political leaders demanded a formal redefinition of the institutional framework, with the help of the military if needed. Said Sadi, the leader of the smaller secular, democratic and Kabyle party, the Rally for Culture and Democracy (*Rassemblement pour la Culture et la Démocratie*, RCD) called for the cancellation of the elections. (Sadi declaring boldly, but unrealistically, that his party was 'ready to assume the entire responsibility for any eventual troubles'.)[27] A 'National Committee for the Safeguard of Algeria' was created under the impetus of Benhamouda, the leader of the official Algerian Workers' Union (*Union Générale des Travailleurs Algériens*, UGTA), and it called upon the military to stop the Islamic party, despite strong objections from the UGTA rank and file.

Many political leaders remained convinced of the importance of continuing the democratic experiment in spite of this unfavourable first round of voting. The Secretary General of the FLN, the reformer Abdelhamid Mehri, declared that his party could envision working with the FIS in a government of national coalition. (A suggestion that generated numerous protests by party cadres and members.) The FFS president, Hocine Ait Ahmed, warned, on 3 January 1992, at a rally organised by the FFS to 'save democracy', that 'to interrupt the electoral process would signify the endorsement of the ruling institution' – i.e. the FLN old guard and the military establishment. At this rally, which gathered a crowd of 300,000 demonstrators in Algiers, the malaise generated by this turn in the democratic transition was perceptible in the most popular slogan of the march: 'neither police state, nor Islamic state, but a democratic state'.[28]

Eventually even the Algerian Prime Minister, Sid Ahmed Ghozali, indicated the adherence of his government to the electoral process. On January 5, in a televised address, Ghozali encouraged Algerians to participate massively in the second round of elections, declaring that this was the sole guarantee of a free and fair democratic process. The following day, he even added on French radio that to present Algeria with a choice between an Islamic state and a military dictatorship was 'to invoke old *clichés*'. The position adopted by the Prime Minister and, implicitly, by the President was far from consensual and several ministers openly voiced their reservations. (A situation of open dissension that led Chadli to reply angrily that he 'needed the support of no one' to journalists who suggested at a press conference that he might not have the support of his government or of the military to pursue this democratic experiment.)[29] At the same time, the Supreme Court (*Conseil Constitutionel*), which was entrusted with the task of supervising the elections, declared that, despite a high number of formal complaints of electoral fraud, these appeals were unlikely to affect the electoral process as a whole or the outcome of the elections.

On the international scene, foreign governments began to indicate that they were quite ready to accept the outcome of these elections. The French Foreign Ministry declared that Franco-Algerian relations were unlikely to be modified by the results of this electoral process. The king of Morocco declared himself 'confident that whatever the results of the elections may be, the Algerian government would honour its engagements'.[30] The Algerian media too, generally believed that cancellation of the elections was unlikely. As the editorial of *Algérie-actualité* pointed out: 'there are observers and citizens, who hope, who think that the army might intervene to save a democracy that they, themselves have not been able to realise. It looks unlikely, not to say impossible, if the FIS does not make any serious mistake.'[31] On 9 January an Algerian newspaper asked Mohammed Boudiaf, a former leader of the war of liberation living in exile in Morocco, whether the military could and ought to stop the electoral process. Boudiaf, who was soon to play a major role in Algeria, replied that the military had no understanding of the situation and no serious alternative to offer. He declared:

> Now the FIS is here, they have the majority, they have to lead the country ... Either it is a democracy, or we turn against the FIS and jeopardise everything ... To argue that we can stop the FIS

experiment and still keep on being a democracy is to contradict oneself ... For what should we do next? Are we to dissolve the FLN? The other parties? Are we to leave them as they are? In 1988 it was time for change and we did not do it.[32]

Boudiaf accurately identified the dilemma that confronted the Algerian political elite and the military establishment at that crucial juncture. The formal political organisation and social consensus that had developed since the 1988 riots could not be modified by governmental decree without the entire democratic transition losing its meaning. If the political framework was to be modified, not only would the FIS electoral victory be negated, but all the political practices and understandings fostered in the country since the beginning of the democratic transition would be jeopardised. A surgical extraction of the elections of 26 November from the historical frame of the polity was simply impossible. Were such a political change to be made, the entire political transition would have to be rethought and restarted differently. As Boudiaf recognised, some occasions were more propitious than others for such momentous changes. Concerning the possibility of a successful political re-articulation at this very moment, he himself had serious doubts about the competency of its would-be military initiators.

4 The 1992 Coup d'État and Beyond: War as Politics Through Other Means (1992–94)

On 11 January 1992 the Algerian President, Chadli Benjedid, made the unexpected announcement on Algerian television that he had stepped down from office. He hesitantly read out a brief communiqué in which he indicated that the measures he had taken in favour of democratic and pluralistic political practices could no longer guarantee peace and order in the country. Chadli's conclusion was that his departure was inevitable because he could no longer continue to exercise his political functions without betraying the promises he had made to the Algerian citizens.[1] Shortly after the presidential intervention, a government official announced that the President had already dissolved the Parliament covertly, one week earlier. Finally, the Prime Minister made a declaration in which he indicated that, in the circumstances, he had asked the army to be deployed as a 'preventive measure'. As the Algerian population slowly began to realise that the democratic transition was seriously endangered, the deconstruction of the democratic institutional framework continued to unfold.[2] On 12 January the Supreme Court, which was in charge of the state institutions after the resignation of the President and the dissolution of Parliament, declared that this situation was not specified by the Constitution and decided to transfer (temporarily) all legislative and executive powers to the High Security Council (*Haut Conseil de Sécurité*, HCS), a pre-existing consultative body on security issues. The HCS was composed of the Prime Minister, A. Ghozali, the president of the Supreme Court (replacing the President), A. Benhabiles, the Justice Minister, H. Benkhelil, the Foreign Affairs Minister, L. Brahimi, the Interior Minister, L. Belkheir, the Defence Minister, K. Nezzar, and the Chief of Staff, A. Guenaizia – the last three members being senior military officers.[3] The HCS immediately declared that it had become impossible to pursue the electoral process in such circumstances and suspended the second round of parliamentary elections.

The decision of the HCS to halt the electoral process raised numerous objections among the political class. In particular, Hachani, the provisional leader of the FIS, denounced this decision as illegal. However, in a communiqué, he urged his supporters to show restraint. Hachani condemned this decision of the HCS that made it impossible for Algerians 'to choose their political project and their leadership via electoral contests', and that crushed 'the hope of re-establishing a relation of trust between the People and the government'. He castigated the members of the HCS as 'leaders of despotism' who acted 'in order to liquidate the Islamic project'. Hachani concluded that this new 'junta has betrayed God, the Prophet and the Faithful by usurping the People's choice, in order to satisfy the demands of despotism and the New World Order'. Yet, instead of ending his rhetorical flourish with a call to arms, Hachani argued that:

> confronted with this extremely difficult situation we must reinforce our bond with God, imploring him with prayers and days of fasting ... We call upon the people to arm themselves with vigilance and prudence, to be prepared to respond to any urgent matter dictated by the superior interest of God and Algeria.[4]

At this crucial moment, the originality of the FIS discourse resided in the moderation of its demands and in its strategy of resistance. The (unnamed) organisers of this putsch were excoriated for what they had done, but the message was clear: for the moment, one must bear stoically the grievous consequences of their actions. Under Hachani's banner the FIS endeavoured to build a large political consensus against the HCS. The Islamic party indicated that what was at stake was not simply an electoral result – indeed, Hachani barely mentioned the FIS victory – but a long-term democratic transformation of the country's institutions that concerned everyone. Conscious of its legitimacy deficit, the HCS apologised for the confusion that followed the departure of the President, and tried to present its intervention as a mere technicality in a constitutional imbroglio.

On 14 January the HCS officially handed over the presidential powers to a newly created institution, the State High Committee (*Haut Comité d'État*, HCE), which was to act as a provisional government until the organisation of new presidential and parliamentary elections at a later, unspecified date. The Head of the HCE was Mohammed Boudiaf, the former leader of the war of independence, who had been offered this presidency two days earlier in his Moroccan exile. The other four members of the committee were: A. Haroun, the Minister for Human Rights, A. Kafi, the president of the Association of Mujahidin (the war of independence veterans), T. Haddam, the Imam of the Paris mosque (who had just been flown in from France) and finally K. Nezzar, the Defence Minister. On the domestic and international scene the HCE tried to present itself as continuing the democratic transition by arguing that personalities close to the democratic, Islamic and nationalist currents were all involved with the committee. Domestically, however, this conciliatory tone and apologetic posturing encouraged the leaders of the three main political parties, the FIS, the FLN and the FFS, to denounce the rule of the HCE as unconstitutional and illegal. On 16 January these three parties met in order to establish a common response to this new political crisis. Soon afterwards the FIS announced that it was ready to set up a makeshift Parliament based on the results of the first round of the elections. Hachani declared that 'the 232 elected representatives can eventually assume their responsibilities, as they have a constitutional and a popular legitimacy'.[5] Abroad, this political agitation received a mixed response. The *de facto* new Algerian rulers (HCS and HCE) quickly received the support of neighbouring Arab countries like Tunisia, Libya and Egypt. These regimes were reluctant to see an elected, Islamic-dominated Parliament in Algeria because this victory of the Islamic fundamentalists would galvanise their own Islamic opposition and give them a potent political ally. As Ben Ali, the Tunisian President, declared himself 'confident of the prospects for Algeria', and Colonel Qaddafi, the Libyan leader, voiced his support for the new Algerian leadership, Mubarak, the Egyptian President, warned the international community 'not to interfere' with these new political developments in Algeria.[6] Whether they heeded Mubarak's advice or whether they reached this conclusion on their own, it remained the case that Western democracies generally remained extremely cautious and subdued. France and the United States declared themselves somewhat 'preoccupied' and 'worried' by the situation in Algeria but no official position and no action was taken in favour of, or against, the new Algerian regime.

A crucial test for the new Algerian regime was its handling of the Islamic opposition on the Friday that followed the interruption of the electoral process. On Friday 17 January the army was deployed in most Algerian towns to contain potentially virulent post-prayer demonstrations. No significant clashes between the crowds and the soldiers occurred, as the local imams generally followed the FIS advice and called for calm. The tension remained high, nonetheless, and two days later, on the evening of 19 January, small-scale disturbances erupted spontaneously in Algiers. A police station (*gendarmerie*) was partially torched in the town centre and two soldiers were killed in the suburbs. The following day, the police arrested several cadres of the FIS for their alleged involvement in these events. By far the most important event that week was the arrest, on 22 January, of the FIS leader, Hachani, for allegedly 'inciting soldiers to desertion'. The provisional government subsequently announced that it was taking new measures to prohibit all 'partisan activities' in the mosques. (Earlier on, the Information Minister had indicated that new reforms would be introduced to keep in check an 'uncontrolled' press, and several journalists had been arrested.) Completing this repressive built-up, on 23 January, the governor of Algiers issued a decree forbidding all gathering in the streets around the mosques at prayer time. On Friday 25 January the army was deployed once more on the streets of all the main Algerian towns, but no major incident occurred. Abroad, as the prospect for a rapid return to the electoral process appeared to be fast receding, Algeria's European neighbours increased their diplomatic activities. The European Union insisted that the Algerian authorities 'do all they can to restore a normal institutional life in Algeria by allowing all concerned parties to establish a peaceful dialogue and by permitting the democratic process to continue unhindered'. In addition, Mitterrand, the French President, warned that France was keen to 'maintain and develop her relation with Algeria but only if the principles that she judges essential – and progress towards democracy and respect of human rights are among them – are respected'.[7]

In Algeria, the political quagmire deepened in the face of increased police and army repression. An extraordinary FLN congress ended in disarray as the supporters of the Secretary General, advocates of an alliance with the FIS and the FFS, clashed with the conservative wing of the party, supporting the HCE and the military. On 29 January the tightening of the surveillance of the media led to the arrest of the editors of two FIS newspapers. A day later the Interior Minister forbade the Islamic party to collect funds in the mosques – the FIS had launched a charity appeal following a spate of flooding – declaring that he would not tolerate 'political associations that attempt to substitute themselves for the state'. The same day violent clashes erupted in one of Algiers' suburbs between 'Islamic youths' and policemen about to arrest an imam after his sermon. Two protesters were killed, eleven were injured and an FLN office was destroyed. On Friday 31 January numerous FIS cadres participating to the Friday prayer were arrested for 'vindictive preaching and slander against the country's institutions and the state leadership'. The clashes between the soldiers and the crowd that followed these arrests caused the death of one protester and left 20 others injured. On 3 February in a last-ditch attempt to convince a sceptical domestic and foreign public opinion that all was well in the country, Boudiaf, the president of the HCE, made a televised speech in which he signalled his intention to open a dialogue with the FIS leadership. He insisted at length that his government and the military supported the process of democratic transition and that their decisions and actions entirely respected the law. In the circumstances Boudiaf failed to convince a population and a political opposition that felt daily the arbitrary rule of the military on the streets. Two days later, on 5 February, serious clashes occurred in the provincial town of Batna between soldiers and demonstrators in front of the Law Courts where a local Islamic leader was put on trial for 'vindictive preaching'. The protest developed into a large riot that continued for two days and left an official (thus conservative) death toll of twelve. In response to these events the FIS called for a rally in Algiers the following week and asked Algeria's foreign partners to 'refrain from signing contracts and conventions'. At that moment, Haddam, the Imam of the Paris mosque, and the token Islamic presence on the HCE, decided to leave a committee that was heading for an all-out war with the Islamic opposition. His judgement and timing proved to be correct. On Friday 8 February, in a repeat of the 1988 October riots, violent clashes between the army and demonstrators erupted simultaneously in Algiers and more than 20 other towns throughout the country. As armoured vehicles and paratroopers were deployed on the streets, barricades were erected by the protesters and rioting spread like wildfire.

On 9 February 1992 a state of emergency was imposed in Algeria and the FIS was banned. That evening Boudiaf appeared on national television to announce these new political measures. In sharp contrast with Chadli's speech during the 1988 riots, the new

President's discourse contained neither a symbolic peace offering nor the promise of a political reform. Instead, Boudiaf focused on the socio-economic issues that were at the root of the Algerian crisis. 'Theft, illegal trafficking, nepotism', the President asserted, 'we are determined to bring them to justice'.[8] Boudiaf assured the people that he would resolve these problems without imposing new austerity measures or confiscating their newly gained political liberties. In the circumstances, however, the President's 'pragmatic' socio-economic programme was generally disliked by the public – especially, the part of his audience that had voted for the FIS a few weeks earlier. People realised that all political, judicial and economic powers were now officially in the hand of the HCE, the HCS and the military. In practice, the situation of a state of emergency gave the government the right to dismiss all the elected institutions that were deemed likely to hinder the actions of the state authorities. In addition, the Interior Minister was given the power to regulate the distribution of basic foodstuffs and services, to close all meeting places, and to place in administrative detention for an unspecified period of time any person that disrupted public order. Finally, military tribunals were given the authority to punish any infraction that threatened 'state security' (very loosely defined). The riots that had erupted in most Algerian towns on Friday continued until Sunday, involving mostly 'Islamic youths'. The very conservative official count for these three days of rioting indicated that 40 people died and 300 were injured, and that several thousands of arrests has taken place. The death toll established by the independent media was over 500. As the army units deployed on the streets showed their resilience and the state leadership its intransigence, street demonstrations subsided progressively in the face of repression. At the same time, however, an organised guerrilla movement began to emerge and on 10 February an Islamic guerrilla group killed ten policemen in a suburb of Algiers.

For nearly a month, from the moment Chadli resigned to the moment Boudiaf imposed a state of emergency, the new Algerian leadership (HCS, HCE and the military) had succeeded in repositioning itself at the head of a nominally democratic institutional framework. At the same time that the provisional government insisted that the democratic transition was still a reality – and demanded that people behave accordingly – the HCE, HCS and the military establishment discreetly reorganised the country's institutions to undermine their political challengers. In particular, the new leadership used the repressive capacities of the state apparatus to weaken the FIS infrastructure and, generally, the political opposition. The regime justified its change of policy by arguing that these political parties had themselves changed their stance, and that the state authorities were only responding to these developments. (Hence, the Imams' preaching became 'vindictive', necessitating prompt repression, the press became 'uncontrolled' and needed censorship, the Islamic associations were judged to be 'substituting themselves for the state' and needed to be chastised, etc.) At first the provisional government had only to deal with changes that were of its own making, in a context where the collective responses of the citizenry remained relatively predictable. Increasingly, however, the actions of the repressive apparatus created a situation in which many political activists and ordinary citizens had to reconsider their political views and practices. Young Islamic activists, in particular, found that it was increasingly justified to challenge violently a regime that had 'stolen' their democratic transition, abused people's trust and now mistreated them.[9] Furthermore, the *de facto* ending of the political debate and the imprisonment of crucial political players ensured that the political opposition lost much of its capacity to influence events directly. In the aftermath of the suspension of the elections, the patched-up policy of the FIS and of the main secular opposition parties (FLN and FFS) was simply one of non-cooperation with the provisional government. However, the slow evaporation of any prospect of a rapid return to the electoral process and the increased level of repression derailed this political strategy, as well as revealing the unpreparedness of the political opposition for a violent confrontation with professional armed forces. The FIS political strategy, in particular, was outpaced by popular protest simply because the party's cadres had been progressively removed by the regime and were not in a position to transmit instructions to their supporters. When the regime banned the FIS, the Islamic party had already melted into a mass of rank-and-file protesters. As Hachani subsequently admitted, the campaign of disobedience that launched the Islamic insurrection in 1992 had not been planned by the FIS leadership but was the unintended consequence of the breakdown in communication between the party cadres and the grassroots supporters.[10]

THE MILITARY IN CONTROL: THE REPRESSIVE OPTION

In January–February 1992 the Algerian military showed that intransigent repressive policies allied to an adroit manipulation of the institutional framework could crush a powerful popular protest and bring about a successful transition to authoritarianism. The coalition of military officers led by General Nezzar chose not to present themselves as the new leaders of the country but cleverly constructed a political façade that shielded them from popular discontent. Their political manoeuvres were facilitated by the fact that they succeeded in persuading the President to leave quietly and to take on most of the blame for the failure of the democratic transition. Furthermore, by inducing Chadli to dissolve a potentially unruly Parliament, the officers avoided facing an institutionalised political opposition to their rule. Subsequently, the empowerment of the State High Committee (HCE) permitted them to give the impression that the country was run by a civilian government. Only Nezzar was a member of this committee in his quality of Defence Minister but, crucially, he was not the head of the HCE. The careful selection of the committee's members allowed the military officers to give a semblance of legitimacy to the HCE. Boudiaf, the head of the HCE (and *de facto* Head of State) had an historical legitimacy, the imam of the Paris mosque had an Islamic legitimacy, the Minister for Human Rights a democratic one and the president of the war veterans association a nationalistic one. In the first few weeks of political agitation, this 'civilian-led' government helped to diffuse the risk of a massive popular upheaval in protest at the military intervention.

   Officially, this new civilian leadership decided to step up the repression against the opposition political parties – the FIS principally, but also the FFS, the reformers of the FLN and some smaller parties. The dissolution of the FIS in early February was followed by the systematic arrest of its cadres and the imprisonment of hundreds of sympathisers (and anti-government demonstrators). The supporters of the FIS were castigated for endangering 'the security of the state', and threatening 'civil peace' and 'national cohesion'. In less than two months over 10,000 alleged FIS activists were arrested and exiled to prison camps set up in the Sahara desert. These administrative detention measures – the persons arrested were generally not put on trial – were designed to prevent the Islamic party from organising large-scale protests in the urban centres and paralysing the country. In addition, in order to diffuse the threat posed by elected bodies such as the Local Councils, predominantly held by 'ex-FIS' members, the government dissolved them on the ground that they 'hindered the work of the state authorities', and replaced them with civil servants acting in executive committees (*Directions Exécutives Communales*, DEC). By March 1992 nearly half the Local Councils had been replaced. Realising that it did not have enough personnel to pursue this policy, the administration authorised the more cooperative councils to continue to exist, as a temporary measure. To draw attention away from the structural deficiencies of the administration and to create a semblance of popular support for its policies, the provisional government utilised its traditional clientele networks and 'mass organisations', like the UGTA syndicate or the war veterans association. Furthermore, in an attempt to reduce the disquiet created by the political repression, the regime offered financial incentives to the population. At the end of February Boudiaf announced the implementation of a $4 billion 'economic recovery package' (secured through foreign financial assistance).[11] This economic reprieve was short-lived, however, as the government quickly redistributed these funds profligately, either wasting them on ill-conceived social projects, or simply diverting them towards established clientelist networks. By April the regime was running short of cash and was forced to cut subsidies to most retail goods. To drum up popular support and to show its independence from the financial speculators, who were close to the military elite and who benefited from this situation of state of emergency, in May the provisional government launched several high-profile lawsuits against army officers accused of corruption. One senior officer, General Belloucif, was even imprisoned during this anti-corruption campaign. This initiative won Boudiaf some welcome popularity, but also a plentiful supply of powerful enemies. Although it might have looked as if the military establishment was willing to participate in the build-up of a credible civilian government by allowing some senior officers to be brought to justice, subsequent events would show that this situation was only an incidental consequence of the behind-the-scenes power struggle between top military officers.

In June 1992, soon after the start of the 'anti-corruption' campaign, Boudiaf was assassinated by one of his bodyguards, a member of the army's Special Forces. Although the exact circumstances of the assassination were never fully brought to light – an isolated act by a supporter of Islamic fundamentalists infiltrating the army, a military plot to eliminate someone with too great political ambitions, and so on – in the public eye Boudiaf appeared to be the victim of the military officers' behind-the-scenes struggles.[12] His assassination undermined the credibility of the government and cast doubt on the military's self-proclaimed non-involvement in politics. By this time, however, the risk of a general upheaval in protest against the military intervention had subsided and the military elite was not too shaken by the dramatic disappearance of the chief organiser of the political reconfiguration of the Algerian transition. The military elite assumed that if they were able to contain the growing military threat posed by the Islamic guerrillas – and defections within the army ranks made them take this risk seriously – the political turmoil would die out by itself.[13] In consequence, they paid less attention to finding a political solution to the growing problem of political violence and concentrated their efforts instead on stepping up their repressive tactics. This lack of political interest was illustrated by their choice of the lacklustre Minister for Human Rights, Kafi, for the HCE presidency, and by their decision to fill the post of Finance Minister with B. Abdessallam, a diehard socialist who had orchestrated the Algerian heavy industrialisation programme during the country's Arab Socialist period.) The prospect of a rapid return to democratic transition, already damaged by Boudiaf's disappearance, took another serious blow in July 1992 when a military tribunal sentenced the two FIS leaders, Madani and Belhadj, to twelve years in jail. Bent on a strategy of repression, the military stepped up its preparations against guerrilla movements by creating in August a special 'anti-terrorist' unit under the command of General Lamari. As the number of military operations against the Islamic guerrilla groups increased throughout the summer, the press began to be censored regularly. In October new 'anti-terrorist' laws were decreed to give more legal coverage to the actions of the 'security forces'. Completing this repressive build-up, in November the army redeployed itself in Algiers and its region. In response to the increased activities of the Islamic guerrillas in towns, the military imposed a curfew in this zone and became closely involved in the day-to-day running of public affairs.

In January 1993, a year after the end of the democratic transition, very few Algerians were surprised when the HCE, which was due to be dissolved at the end of that year, announced that it would remain in place for up to five years in order to create 'favourable conditions' for a new democratic transition. In February, a year after first being declared, the state of emergency was extended for one more year. At the same time, partly to make a gesture of appeasement toward the Islamic fundamentalists, and partly because its resources were stretched, the Interior Minister closed some Saharan prison camps and released over 8,000 FIS sympathisers who had been arrested a year earlier and detained without trial. (This did little to ease the tension and, soon afterwards, Nezzar, the unofficial Head of the regime, narrowly escaped an assassination attempt.) On the international scene, the new, uncompromising stance of the Algerian regime was also displayed in March 1993 when Algeria cut off diplomatic relations with Iran and the Sudan because of their alleged support for the Islamic insurrection. (A support which might have been diplomatically annoying for the Algerian regime but which was relatively inconsequential from the perspective of the Islamic guerrillas' logistics.) At home, in May, in response to another increase in guerrilla activities, the army had to step up its operations and to extend the area covered by the curfew outside the Algiers region to the Chlef, M'sila and Djefla districts. This increased military repression did little to halt the Islamic insurrection. Far from having a dissuasive effect it encouraged the unemployed youth and Islamic sympathisers, who bore the brunt of the police and army reprisals, to join the guerrillas. As an indiscriminate repression radicalised the pro-Islamic youth even more and as the inefficient economic policies devised by the socialist Finance Minister alienated even the non-'Islamic fundamentalist' segment of the population, the political solutions proposed by the military elite clearly showed their limitations. This uncomfortable political and economic climate hastened a reshuffle of the military leadership and of the government in the summer of 1993. In July, General Zeroual was nominated Defence Minister and General Lamari was promoted Chief of Staff. A month later, Redha Malek, the former Head of the political police, was nominated Prime Minister, while the Finance Minister was dismissed for opposing a debt-rescheduling deal with the International Monetary Fund (IMF). This 'new' leadership then set out to develop a more inclusive approach to solving the crisis by opening a dialogue with the political opposition and Algeria's international partners.

In October 1993 the HCE called up a 'National Commission for Dialogue' (*Commission Nationale de Dialogue*, CND) to set up the new political institutions of the country and to nominate a new Head of

State. Zeroual, the Defence Minister, indicated that the imprisoned FIS leaders would be associated with this process of reconstruction of the political institutions. Besides the FIS, the conference was designed to entice the secular political parties that were the most significant in terms of votes (FLN, FFS) that remained highly critical of the new Algerian regime. The CND raised some fresh hopes but, very quickly, the conditions imposed by the military during the pre-conference negotiations proved too constraining for many political parties and one by one they began to drop out of the conference list. By the end of 1993 it also became perfectly clear that no senior representatives of the FIS would be officially involved in the final decisions of the commission. By January, it was evident that the CND was a failure, and the HCE signalled that it was not ready to abide by the recommendations of the remaining participating parties. Most participants then withdrew from the commission. To deflect another blow to the credibility of its institutions, the HCE redefined the aim of the conference, which became consultative, and bestowed upon itself the prerogative to nominate the new Head of State. Eventually, the members of the HCE nominated to the presidential office one of their own, Liamin Zeroual, the Defence Minister. This nomination marked a low point for the credibility of the political front set up by the Algerian military elite, which had been unable to find a suitable and consensual political leader for the country. The military was obliged to produce a 'civilian' government from its own ranks – Zeroual having officially retired in 1990. Internally, this nomination did not signal a significant reorganisation of the military hierarchy. Zeroual was a candidate of compromise who had been chosen after much deliberation by the different clans that composed the Algerian military. Although Zeroual himself gained an increased leverage over his fellow officers because of his new functions (and his access to the international scene), his presidential role also meant that he could not be as involved in the minute details of the military affairs as he was before. (As Chadli's misadventure had illustrated a few years earlier, this meant that he was liable to be outflanked by his former 'allies' inside the military.) More than ever, Zeroual's authority over his fellow military officers was dependent upon the credibility and usefulness of political institutions that were in a shambles when he took office. For the Algerian polity as a whole, this tightening of the military hold over the institutional framework indicated that a prolonged period of authoritarian rule was to be expected. Accordingly, few were surprised in February 1994 when 'president' Zeroual extended the period of the state of emergency to yet another year.

THE ISLAMIC MOVEMENT: FROM POLITICAL OPPOSITION TO 'HOLY' WAR

In the early days of the conflict, the political opposition between 'radicals' and 'moderates' – or conservatives and reformers – inside the FIS was transfigured by the advent of the armed insurrection. These two political currents had different opinions on why it was most useful to have a stake in the state apparatus. 'Moderates' like Abbassi Madani and Abdelkader Hachani had argued that their political participation in the ruling institutions ought to be dictated by pragmatic considerations, such as its consequences for the Islamicisation of society. By contrast, the 'radical' current, represented by people like Ali Belhadj or Qamreddine Kerbane, had pointed out that this political involvement was a means of ensuring that the state repressive apparatus could not be utilised against the Islamic movement. After the June 1991 strike and the arrest of Madani and Belhadj, the 'radicals', led by Kerbane and Mohammed Said, had warned that the regime would increasingly use the security apparatus to suppress political dissent, and suggested that the FIS should take counter-measures by developing its military capabilities.[14] The 'moderates', led by Hachani, had retorted that these tactics were counterproductive and that, besides handing over the moral high ground to the regime, they would endanger the very institutions that the party wanted to utilise for the propagation of Islamic reform.[15] The electoral strategy adopted at the FIS congress of Batna in August 1991 collapsed six months later in January 1992, when the army abruptly took control of the state institutions and repressed the political opposition. Within a few weeks this repression effectively destroyed the organisational capabilities of the FIS by severing the links between the party leadership and the base. The 'moderates' suffered most from this repression, as the FIS members who were caught in this wave of arrests were the ones who confronted the soldiers with slogans and stones in street demonstrations. At about the same time, however, the more radical Islamic fundamentalists actors, inside and outside the party officialdom, began recruiting disgruntled FIS members and sympathisers stigmatised by police repression into underground networks, and prepared them for an armed uprising. Thus, civil disobedience turned into civil war.

After the military intervention of January–February 1992, the first important guerrilla organisation to challenge the new Algerian regime was the Armed Islamic Movement (*Mouvement Islamique Armé*, MIA) of Abdelkader Chebouti.[16] Other guerrilla groups particularly active during the early stages of the insurrection were organised by the veterans of the Afghan conflict. (Several hundred Algerians had received military training in Afghanistan or Pakistan before 1992.)[17] These groups staged small-scale but well-organised attacks on military installations and personnel. However, their leaders' previous military experiences and training led these organisations to adopt traditional guerrilla tactics and to set up bases in the hills surrounding the towns, particularly in the Algiers region. As Luis Martinez pointed out, this strategy proved to be a very ineffective mobilisation of the human resources of the Islamic fundamentalists and squandered the potential for a general upheaval that existed at that time in Algeria.[18] The strategy of making the rebellion progress from its mountain strongholds towards the urban centres left *de facto* the army in a position of strength in the towns. Because of this choice of tactics, the intensity of the guerrilla warfare remained relatively low throughout 1992 – the official death toll for army and police personnel remaining below 600 that year.[19] By the end of 1992 the guerrillas' initial hope of a rapid military campaign that would trigger the collapse of the military infrastructure and a massive popular insurrection began to fade away. In December, to boost the morale and legitimacy of the guerrillas, Belhadj smuggled letters out of jail to convey his support for the MIA. 'If I was outside the walls of this prison', Belhadj declared, 'I would be a fighter in the ranks of the army of my brother Abdelkader Chebouti.'[20] By that time, however, the Algerian army's superior firepower and organisation had already contained the first Islamic *maquis*. Confronted by this unexpected resilience from the military establishment, the Islamic guerrillas split over tactics. The core of the MIA withdrew from the Algiers region and moved into the rural areas of the East and West of the country where they hoped to establish more stable guerrilla bases. Simultaneously, splinter groups from the MIA and many 'Afghans' retreated in a more or less orderly fashion in the towns (especially Algiers), where they provided the impetus for an urban guerrilla movement.[21]

The urban guerrilla groups that emerged in 1993 in Algeria relied principally upon newly 'Islamicised' urban youths with little supervision from established Islamic fundamentalist leaders. After a fresh wave of governmental repression in late 1992 and early 1993, which had targeted rather indiscriminately disaffected youth and active supporters of the guerrillas, the young and poor became more radical in their choice of social action. In March 1993, a loose association of guerrilla groups was reorganised by the local commanders and ideologues of the Algiers area – Moh Levelley, Abdelhak Layada, Omar al-Eulmi, Djaffar al-Afghani.[22] The organisation became known as the GIA (*Groupements Islamiques Armés*, Armed Islamic Group) and gained its notoriety by organising a series of attacks against civil servants and members of the government. The political strategy of the GIA was to extend the range of legitimate guerrilla targets to politicians supporting the provisional government, high-ranking civil servants and people working in the security forces' administrative departments. By its actions the GIA sought to demonstrate the inability of the state to protect its own supporters and collaborators. Quickly the GIA raised the stakes by waging an assassination campaign that targeted potentially all the members of the state administration, as well as politicians, journalists and intellectuals who were perceived to be supportive of the regime or producing (alleged) 'anti-Islamic' propaganda. This radicalisation of its war tactics gave the GIA a tactical advantage in the psychological war against the regime, as well as justifying its claim to leadership inside the Islamic movement. At first this radicalisation of the insurrection found a degree of support among the poorer segments of the population who had suffered most from the military intervention – either directly because of the police repression or indirectly because of its disastrous economic consequences.[23]

The apparent success and sudden notoriety of the GIA induced a wave of defections from the FIS and the MIA, which provided staff for the new organisation. The most important FIS cadres to shift allegiances were Mohammed Said and Abderrazak Redjam, two members of the FIS executive committee (*madjlis*). These shifting allegiances underscored the divisions between the various Islamic tendencies that had rallied behind the FIS leadership during the democratic transition. Increasingly, the propaganda war between the different Islamic factions and ideological currents made it difficult to establish who was in control of what, especially when new splinter groups tentatively positioned themselves on the politico-military scene. In the second half of 1993 this reorganisation of the Islamic guerrilla movement and the expansion of the GIA into the areas controlled by the MIA led inevitably to violent clashes between these guerrilla groups. At the same time the GIA gained a dubious recognition on the international scene, when it organised the first series of attacks against foreign interests and foreign nationals. In September 1993 the GIA began by targeting foreigners who were perceived to be directly helping the Algerian government – the first foreigners assassinated were two French surveyors working in the oil sector. By the end of the year over 30 foreign nationals had been assassinated by the GIA, a situation that triggered a wave of departures of foreign residents. Early in 1994 this campaign of assassinations widened to include all foreigners, particularly Westerners and other non-Muslims, regardless of their activities or political views. The GIA had concluded that they were legitimate targets because their home governments indirectly supported the Algerian military. (None of the Western governments had taken sanctions against the Algerian military for its role in ending the democratic transition, and the continuing diplomatic, military and economic exchanges – with France most particularly – were branded by the guerrillas as blatant instances of active cooperation with the Algerian regime.) These tactics clearly succeeded in hindering the efforts of the Algerian government to attract vital economic investment into the country. In particular, they caused a slow-down in the activities of the oil companies, which had to repatriate many of their employees.[24] However, these actions also seriously tarnished the image of the Islamic insurrection on the international scene. The actions of the GIA undermined the efforts of the FIS cadres who had taken refuge in Europe and who were pushing for mediation by the Western democracies in Algeria to restart the process of democratisation.[25]

Domestically, the success of the GIA at targeting the political façade of the regime earned the movement the allegiance of the radical youngsters who had not belonged to the pre-1988 Islamic associations or to the FIS. Abroad and in the eyes of other Islamic and democratic actors, the radical guerrilla tactics employed by the GIA increased the difficulties of finding a political alternative to the existing military-backed Algerian regime. In addition, the inability of the guerrilla movement to present a unified politico-military front also ensured that the armed supporters of the GIA who dominated the urban scene could not gradually institutionalise their military control of the areas deserted by the state. Because of their political inexperience, the GIA leaders failed to combine effectively the activities of their armed groups with pre-existing political and associative networks to oppose the regime effectively. (The rise to supremacy of these Islamic warlords in 1992–94 took place in a context where the legitimacy of the Islamic fundamentalists was high, popular support for the insurrection was widespread and few political skills were needed to gain a prominent position in the Islamic hierarchy.) In fact, the GIA divergence of view with the FIS hierarchy even encouraged the Islamic party to support the formation of another armed movement. In July 1994 the Islamic Salvation Army (*Armée Islamique du Salut*, AIS) was created from the remnants of the MIA and with independent guerrilla groups. The AIS presented itself as the 'official' armed wing of the FIS and set out to counter the hegemony of the GIA on the guerrilla scene.[26] In the second half of 1994, despite some well-publicised successes – the attack on the French embassy, the hijacking of a French airliner – the GIA increasingly had to confront the problem of the stabilisation of the conflict and the difficulties created by their own tactics, which had isolated them domestically and internationally.[27] Unable to topple the military-backed regime on their own, and cut off from the political base of the FIS, the guerrillas of the GIA increasingly turned to a military strategy that was not subject to clear political objectives.

5 A New Authoritarianism: Guided Democracy Versus Radical Islam (1995–2000)

In February 1994, Zeroual, the newly appointed Algerian President, signalled his willingness to start a dialogue with the FIS by releasing from jail two influential members of their executive committee, Ali Djeddi and Abdelkader Boukhamkham. Two months later the President replaced his uncompromising Prime Minister – the former head of the political police – by a more malleable technocrat in order to create a political environment more favourable to a dialogue with the opposition. Throughout the summer of 1994, there were numerous unofficial contacts between the imprisoned FIS leaders and the President to try to find a negotiated solution to the crisis created by the 1992 military intervention. The rediscovery of the usefulness of an institutionalised Islamic opposition by Algeria's military elite had been an indirect consequence of the terror campaign orchestrated by the radical Islamic guerrillas of the GIA. The total lack of dialogue between the guerrillas and the regime facilitated the return of the politicised Islamic fundamentalists of the FIS on the politico-military scene. The new strongmen of the Algerian regime, principally Zeroual and Lamari, permitted the FIS cadres to reformulate a strategy that subordinated war objectives to political aims. In practice, the release of numerous party cadres in the first half of 1994 was instrumental to the formation of the AIS, the 'official' armed branch of the FIS, in July 1994. From the very beginning, the FIS–AIS association was meant to structure the guerrilla movement with a view to a negotiated solution to the Islamic insurrection. As Djeddi, one of the first cadre freed, indicated, these objectives were also those of the military leadership, which ask the security services of the army (*Sécurité Militaire*, SM) to facilitate the contacts between the FIS cadres and the guerrilla commanders.[1]

In September 1994, the President announced officially that there had been a correspondence between the FIS leadership and himself. The progress made in these talks encouraged Zeroual to transfer

Madani, Belhadj and Hachani from prison to house arrest. After another month of highly publicised negotiations, however, a final agreement proved impossible to reach and the talks broke down. Zeroual attributed this failure to the FIS leadership's lack of realism and particularly to Belhadj's political intransigence. In fact it was the lack of trust between the regime and the FIS leadership which was the main cause of failure of this first official attempt to negotiate an end to the insurrection. Since their arrest, Madani, Belhadj and Hachani had been in a situation where they judged that they could not call for an end to the fighting without the regime making a significant political gesture towards the Islamic movement – such as releasing them from prison. Were they to act otherwise, they thought, their followers would question their choices, perhaps think of capitulation, and their leadership would be in jeopardy, whilst their call for peace would remain a dead letter. Their negotiating position was complicated by the fact that the AIS only succeeded in re-organising militarily the Islamic opposition in the East and West (Ouarseni) of the country, whilst the GIA was firmly in control of the central Algiers area and the westernmost part of the country. Hachani indicated that, in these circumstances, Madani, Belhadj and himself agreed not to take any 'official' initiatives as long as they remained imprisoned.[2] As a result, talks with the regime broke down on the apparently trivial issue of whether the FIS leaders ought to be released before calling for an end to the insurrection, or whether their appeal for a truce should be a precondition for their release.

To maintain the political momentum and to avoid a possible backlash following the sudden rise in expectations among the population generated by these negotiations, Zeroual promptly declared that a solution to the crisis would come from the ballot box. He then officially announced the holding of a presidential election for 1995. Zeroual's attempt at circumventing the FIS by appealing directly to the people was implicitly aimed at drawing a line under the legitimacy crisis that had beset the regime since 1992. Predictably, given the circumstances, the main political parties of the democratic transition – the FIS, the FFS and the FLN – remained distrustful of this proposal. Alongside smaller political formations, they decided to convene their own 'peace conference' in December 1994, in Rome. Under the aegis of the San Egidio community, they tried to find a political compromise that could bring an end to the violence in Algeria. In January 1995 the parties to the Rome conference came up with a proposal based on holding new parlia-

mentary elections and the re-legalisation of the FIS.[3] Their propos-
itions, reported in most Algerian and foreign newspapers, caused
some interest, particularly among the governments of the European
Union. In France President Mitterand's interest in the initiative even
created a political crisis in his coalition government as his Prime
Minister, Chirac, and the French right more generally, did not
wanted to jeopardize France's economic and political relations with
the ruling Algerian elite. Ultimately, France's inertia prevented
definite political decisions to be taken by the members of the EU,
and the Rome proposal fell into oblivion. This absence of concrete
international action comforted Zeroual in his position of architect of
the Algerian institutional framework. He went ahead with his plan
for presidential elections and obtained the support of a handful of
political parties. The two principal parties which endorsed the
President's proposal and put forward candidates for the elections
were the moderate Islamic party led by Mahfoud Nannah, *Hamas*,
and the secular, democratic and Berberist party led by Said Sadi, the
RCD. Both parties had been firmly distanced by the FIS and the FFS
during the democratic transition, and they viewed this election as
an opportunity to claim the status of principal Islamic and secular-
democratic parties of the country. Zeroual also took steps to entice
the Islamic guerrillas into this process of 'national reconciliation' by
issuing, in March 1995, a decree of amnesty (*rahma*) aimed at those
members of armed Islamic groups who gave themselves up. (Until
then participation in the guerrilla movement had been punishable
by death in 'anti-terrorist' courts – a procedure that often amounted
to a summary execution ordered by local military commanders.)
Under the *rahma*, the guerrillas who were not accused of specific
blood crimes could be pardoned in exchange for their cooperation
– a method that had operated informally before.[4] Despite these conciliatory gestures, the regime kept up its repression and increased the
level of media censorship in early 1995 by promulgating new decrees
on the publication of so-called 'sensitive information'. As the FIS,
the FFS and the FLN decided to boycott this election and the GIA
promised to punish all those who cast their ballot, the meaningful-
ness of this political consultation became increasingly doubtful.

In December 1995 the presidential election took place without
any serious difficulties, in spite of the threats of the guerrillas. (The
army had mobilised tens of thousands of reservists a month before
the election to secure the areas where the polling was organised.) On
national television it was officially declared that Zeroual was

President-elect with more than 60 per cent of the votes and that the turnout for this election was nearly 75 per cent.[5] The moderate Islamic leader, Nannah, had obtained 25 per cent of the vote and the Kabyle 'democrat' Sadi nearly 10 per cent. With the national media firmly under state control and the foreign press *de facto* unable to cover the election because of the GIA assassination campaigns (and because of the government's reluctance to deliver visas to foreign journalists), the Algerian regime succeeded in conveying the impression that Zeroual was a consensual political figure who had received a clear popular mandate. In fact, the main success of the regime during these elections had been to tamper with the electoral results with enough discretion to be able to present this political contest as free and fair. Without doubt, as the opposition claimed and some press reports suggested, both the participation rate and Zeroual's share of votes had been artificially increased to show a massive popular involvement and to have the President endorsed by more than half of the electorate.[6] Even so, Zeroual was bound to win the contest, principally because many Algerians believed at the time that he was best placed to negotiate an end to the conflict, and because the other presidential candidates were even less appreciated and credible than the former General. (Sadi was a secularist Berber leader who had been among the first to call the army to intervene in 1992, whilst Nannah was the *bête noire* of the FIS.) As domestic public opinion appeared to condone the election, and as foreign governments congratulated the new President-elect, the political parties that had boycotted the election had to admit that their tactics had backfired, and grudgingly recognised the new political 'legitimacy' gained by Zeroual.

ELECTORAL MARKETING: FORMAL REPRESENTATION AND INFORMAL AUTHORITARIANISM

With this election Zeroual had scored an important political victory over the Islamic and democratic opposition parties and boosted the legitimacy of a regime that had come to power in dubious circumstances. A first consequence of this re-legitimisation of the regime was the downfall of the reformist leadership of the FLN and the return of the conservative elite of the party. In January 1996, as the FLN Secretary General, Abdelhamid Mehri, was forced to step down, the new executive changed the political line of the party and decided to participate to a coalition government. Zeroual's new ruling coalition also included representatives from the moderate Islamic party, *Hamas*. (After much deliberation the RCD decided not to join this ill-assorted coalition because of the strong reservations expressed by its base.) Although the President had been able to manoeuvre adroitly in the field of high politics to obtain the support of these political parties, this new coalition did not generate the expected level of grassroots support. In addition, Zeroual's new government quickly proved unable to deliver on the promises made during the election campaign – an abatement of the political violence and an economic recovery. Instead, the new political partners of the ruling coalition soon displayed the same authoritarian, nepotistic and kleptocratic tendencies as their predecessors. The lack of tangible progress towards a resolution of the conflict and the attitude of the government re-created a climate of low political confidence and, after a few months, whatever popular support Zeroual may have had at the time of his election had evaporated. In this context, as the President promised to complete his build-up of elected political institutions by holding new parliamentary and local elections in 1997, Zeroual also made sure that his interests would not be challenged by an unruly Parliament by rewriting the Constitution. In November 1996 the government adopted by decree a new Constitution granting large discretionary powers to the President.[7] In particular, the new Algerian Constitution gave the President the prerogative to nominate one-third of the Senate (second parliamentary chamber). It also made it necessary for any law voted by the Parliament to be ratified by a quorum of three-quarters of the senators to become law. (In practice, these dispositions ensured that the President's nominees *de facto* had a veto on any law voted by the Parliament.)

A few months later, in March 1997, Zeroual decided to respond to the wavering support of the established political parties (which had not been impressed by his constitutional rewriting), by launching his own party, the National Rally for Democracy (RND – *Rassemblement National pour la Démocratie*). Created three months only before the parliamentary elections, the RND was an unofficial state party whose purpose was to counter the influence of the FLN and the FFS, which had abandoned their boycott strategy and which sought to regain their past political importance. The RND was an ill-assorted assemblage of former civil servants and FLN cadres close to the President that was meant to provide Zeroual with reliable partners in the Parliament. For more than two months the RND conducted a lacklustre election campaign in a context of heightened military activities ahead of the elections. To ensure that the guerrillas would not disrupt the electoral process, the security forces mobilised over 300,000 soldiers and policemen to look after 37,000 polling stations. On this occasion, however, this show of strength angered the population, which felt that military might was only employed when it suited the regime's interests and not to protect ordinary citizens against rampant criminality and political violence. In the June 1997 parliamentary elections the Algerian regime chose once more to compensate for a lack of public confidence by tampering with the electoral results. The official results proclaimed that the RND had won over 40 per cent of the seats in the Parliament, the MSP (formerly *Hamas*) 18 per cent, the FLN 17 per cent, *Ennahda* (moderate Islamic fundamentalists) 9 per cent and the two Kabyle-democratic parties, FFS and RCD, 5 per cent each.[8] This time, however, the rigging operation was clearly observed – it was even captured on film by French TV crews – and the popular outrage that followed the announcement of these results produced the most important street demonstrations since the 1992 military putsch. The protest marches headed by the FFS, the RCD, the MSP and *Ennahda* were swiftly repressed by well-prepared security forces. Shortly afterwards the MSP dropped out of the protest after obtaining new governmental posts, alongside the FLN. Despite its success in containing these popular protests, this time the Algerian regime clearly failed to put its electoral marketing tactics to good use. The visibility of the electoral trafficking and the ensuing public display of anger undermined rather than consolidated the position of the regime. (Later on, a parliamentary inquiry set up by the opposition would even officially confirm that the parliamentary elections had been deeply flawed and ought to have been invalidated.) These rigging tactics showed crudely that electoral contests were primarily designed to provide the ruling elite with a façade of political legitimacy and not to elect representative political institutions.

After the June 1997 elections the Algerian regime tried to recapture domestic and international public opinion by announcing that it was close to reaching an agreement with the FIS–AIS organisation on the terms of a cease-fire. Quickly the negotiations between military officers close to Lamari and the AIS commanders Madani Mezrag and Ahmed Benaicha permitted the release from prison of Hachani in July 1997. A month later, it was the turn of Madani to be freed. The FIS leaders were meant to announce an 'official' cease-fire immediately after the release of Belhadj, as well as the formation of a new Islamic party. However, the internal rivalries between the President and the Chief of Staff delayed the announcement of the truce. Using the pretext of Madani's call to the United Nations Secretary-General to request a UN commission to investigate the role of the military in civilian massacres, Zeroual promptly placed the FIS leader under house arrest, barely one month after his release from prison. Eventually in October 1997 the truce was declared unilaterally by Mezrag, the chief military commander of the AIS, without mentioning a political settlement. Predictably in this uncertain political context the local elections of November 1997 failed to attract many voters, despite the official estimates putting the turnout level at 66 per cent. Once more the President's party, the RND, 'won' the election easily by taking just over 55 per cent of the Local Councils. The FLN gained over 20 per cent of the Councils, the MSP less than 7 per cent, the FFS, RCD and *Ennahda* less than 5 per cent each.[9] Again, all the political parties except the RND joined forces in street demonstrations in Algiers and other major towns in the days following the announcement of the elections results. The protest was as thoroughly repressed as the previous one, but it eventually led to the reallocation of several Councils. A few weeks later, as the mobilisation against this electoral fraud had barely dissipated, the elections for the Senate took place in an apathetic political atmosphere. The voters, who already knew that the second parliamentary chamber was controlled by the President's nominees, did not bother protesting against what were increasingly seen as vacuous electoral consultations and a ritualistic display of civic behaviour. As expected, the RND easily won the contest.[10] It was a non-event that did not even trigger protest demonstrations. Increasingly in 1997 the dilemma of Zeroual and of the ruling elite was that the more they were able to co-opt people and parties into a 'democratic' political process, the less they, themselves, appeared representative of the political aspirations of the electorate. As Zeroual became more and more successful in recreating some semblance of institutional order in the country, he could not help but become also the living example of all that was wrong with this new order and with the way the country was run. Zeroual's partial success not only encouraged his fellow military officers to keep on building this new institutional framework, but it also gave them an incentive to remove the increasingly discredited President-General from the picture. Pressed by his peers, Zeroual followed the example of Chadli and in September 1998 announced that he was stepping down from the Presidency and called for an early presidential election in 1999.

The military establishment tried to present the 1999 presidential election as a new departure for the country and indicated that it would not assign one of its members to the Presidency (as had been the case with Zeroual in 1994 and 1995). High-ranking officials and politicians close to the regime did their utmost to convince a sceptical public and political opposition (which had bitter memories of the previous elections), of the genuineness of this election. (Tellingly, Zeroual's sudden departure and the announcement of a new election had been noteworthy for the general lack of interest it generated among the population – a sign of the Algerian people's growing distrust of electoral contests.) A few weeks before the official start of the electoral campaign, the government's public relations efforts finally paid off. A number of leading opposition figures declared that they had received solid guarantees from the regime and had decided to run for President. In February, a record number of eleven candidates officially registered for the elections: Bouteflika, Taleb Ibrahimi, Ait Ahmed, Hamrouche, Djaballah, Sifi, Khatib, Ghozali, Boukrouh, Hanoune and Nannah. The Supreme Court (*Conseil Constitutionnel*) validated the candidatures of seven of the eleven candidates. Ghozali, Boukrouh and Hanoune were disqualified for failing to receive the endorsements of a sufficient number of elected representatives, while the runner-up in the 1995 presidential election, the moderate Islamic leader Nannah, was disqualified for failing to provide the certificate from the National Association of Mujahidin attesting his participation in the war of independence. (That Nannah could not meet the terms of this constitutional requirement for the Presidency raised numerous questions at the time. It would only become clear afterward that this affair had been engineered by the regime to prevent the moderate Islamic leader from joining forces with the rest of the opposition after the election.) The favourite among the presidential hopefuls was Abdelaziz Bouteflika, who was presented as the unofficial candidate of the regime. Bouteflika, a former high-ranking FLN cadre and Foreign Affairs Minister, had already been close to becoming the political façade of the Algerian regime in 1994–95, but the military eventually rallied behind Zeroual, who was deemed a more reliable choice in these troubled circumstances. Significantly, for the 1999 presidential election, several days before officially announcing his candidature, Bouteflika had 'spontaneously' received the support of the two pro-governmental parties, the FLN and the RND. (He had also received the support of half of *Ennahda*, the moderate Islamic party of Abdallah Djaballah, which fell prey to factional in-fighting under pressures from the political police.) The other main contender for the presidential election was Taleb Ibrahimi, a well-known pro-Islamic candidate from a renowned religious family – his father was the president of the Islamic Reform movement before the country's independence – who had been successively Education, Culture, and Foreign Affairs Minister. Taleb Ibrahimi's main campaigning theme was 'national reconciliation' and the inclusion of the 'ex'-FIS in the political process. On this occasion, and for the first time since it was banned, the FIS did not call for a boycott of the election but chose on the contrary to support Taleb Ibrahimi discreetly during the electoral campaign. (A few days before the end of the campaign, the executive committee of the FIS abroad even declared 'officially' that Ibrahimi was their preferred candidate.)

On 14 April 1999, the eve of the presidential election, the early polling organised for the security forces was marred by irregularities. (The independent media reported that in the barracks the voting slip of Bouteflika was the only one available, or that soldiers had to hand back the remaining slips to their officers after casting their ballot, whilst nationwide the representatives of the other candidates were forcibly prevented from supervising these polling booths.) Later that day, after convening a joint meeting, all the presidential candidates but Bouteflika decided to withdraw their candidatures.[11] In spite of this boycott, the government decided to go ahead with the election the following day. On election day the independent media reported a very low turnout of about 20 per cent nationwide, with lows of 5 per cent in the Kabyle region.[12] On state television, however, the official turnout was announced as over 60 per cent and Bouteflika was officially declared President-elect, winning more than 70 per cent of the vote. The following day in Kabylia tens of thousands of protesters invaded the streets of Tizi-Ouzou and Bejaia. Protests also began to be organised in Algiers and Oran, but the security forces rapidly repressed them. The former candidates declared that they did not recognise the validity of this election and called for protest rallies. In response, the government forbade all demonstrations and stepped up its 'security operations' in and around the capital to forestall any further protest action. On the international scene the immediate reactions to the election were muted. The French Foreign Minister declared that he was worried by this turn of events, whilst the US State Department said it was disappointed by the allegations of election rigging. In Algeria the newly 'elected' President, sure of the support of the military, chose to ignore the domestic protests and foreign censure that his shambolic election had triggered. In practice, Bouteflika discreetly contacted opposition leaders who had not been able or had chosen not to run for the election and behind the scenes set about rebuilding a political coalition of sorts based on the pro-governmental parties (RND and FLN), and the Islamic parties of Nannah and of *Ennahda*'s runaway faction. This political base, similar to that of former President Zeroual, allowed Bouteflika to contain the challenge mounted by the other presidential candidates, whose united protest had begun to falter. (Besides their opposition to Bouteflika, these politicians had little in common, and they proved unable to transform their initial protest action into a unified political front.)

To buttress the legitimacy of Bouteflika's presidency, the regime's military backers chose to revive the prospects of an agreement between the FIS–AIS and the government, as they did after the 1997 parliamentary elections. On 1 June 1999 the military commander of the AIS, Mezrag, wrote a communiqué indicating that he was ready to formalise the truce declared unilaterally by the AIS in October 1997. Two days later the very official *Algérie Presse Service* publicised the contents of the letter, which were then aired on state television during the evening news. On 4 June a communiqué from the presidential office indicated that Bouteflika would respond to this demand 'by giving a legal framework to this initiative'.[13] Two days later, in a well-executed *pas de deux*, Mezrag answered favourably the President's proposal in a second communiqué where he signalled the intention of the AIS to renounce definitively all military activities and his willingness to place the organisation 'under the authority of the state'.[14] (The AIS commander indicated that these conditions corresponded to 'a plan drawn up with the leadership of the National Popular Army' – i.e. the Algerian military.) The presidential office immediately issued a communiqué stating that 'the President will invite the government to adopt a new project of law to be submitted to the Parliament'. (The RND-dominated Parliament would duly rubber-stamp this project of law a few weeks later.) On 11 June Madani, the jailed FIS leader sent a message to Bouteflika to add his personal support to Mezrag's initiative. Soon all the influential FIS cadres, at home and abroad, voiced their support for Mezrag's initiative. Noticeable by their absence, however, were the endorsements of Hachani and Belhadj. Importantly, too, Taleb Ibrahimi and Ait Ahmed voiced doubts on the potential of this accord between the regime and the AIS to solve the crisis. They were particularly concerned by the fact that this agreement did not address the issue of the re-legalisation of the Islamic party, the problem of the 'disappeared' and the ending of the state of emergency (in place since 1992).[15] Their doubts concerning the political usefulness of this agreement were reinforced by Bouteflika's subsequent declarations concerning the release of Madani and Belhadj (which the President made conditional on their complete retirement from political life) and regarding the prospects for political pluralism, which Bouteflika viewed as a catalyst for the problems of the country.[16] The President proposed nonetheless to hold a referendum on his agreement with the guerrillas and on the associated general amnesty – dubbed the 'law on civil concord' – within three months.

On 16 September 1999 the 'law on civil concord' was approved with a massive 98.6 per cent approval and an 85 per cent turnout.[17] At last the domestic and international politicians and the media that had been so critical of his election hailed the new Algerian President as a credible political leader who had become the peace broker of the Algerian civil war. This normalisation of the relations between the regime and the Islamic fundamentalists of the AIS successfully diverted domestic and international attention from the dubious means by which the new Algerian President had come to power. Just as Zeroual's legitimacy had been boosted in 1994–95 by the popular belief that he was best placed to offer a rapid negotiated end to the conflict, at the end of 1999 Bouteflika's legitimacy was propped up by the signing of the 'law on civil concord'. In both cases, however, these short-term solutions to the problem of political violence strengthened the hold of the military establishment on the political system and marginalised the role of the electoral process in selecting the country's leadership. At the start of 2000, with the disbanding of the AIS, the reduced level of violence present in the country comforted Bouteflika in his position of peacemaker. However, any expectation that a normal political life would soon restart was dashed in February 2000 when the state of emergency was prolonged for yet another year. Unsure of the support of the population and unable openly to oppose the military establishment, Bouteflika decided not to modify the delicate balance of power that had been created in Algeria after several years of civil conflict. This lack of political dynamism, which was presented at first as political prudence, became a serious problem as soon as people realised that the decrease in guerrilla activities did not lead to an era of socio-economic revival and to a greater opening out of political activity. As politicians and ordinary citizens began to question the ability and the willingness of the President to go beyond the status quo, the promise of a new dawn for the Algerian polity which had briefly shone at the start of the new millennium was quickly eclipsed by a return to the climate of mutual defiance that had characterised the relationship between the citizenry and the ruling elite since 1992.

ON THE MARGINS OF POLITICS: THE MILITARY AND THE ISLAMIC GUERRILLAS

The military

From the very beginning the political transformations that took place in the political sphere in Algeria favoured a concentration of military authority. Since the 1992 coup, most particularly, the jockeying for the dominant positions inside the military establishment has directly underwritten the reconstruction of political order in the country. Before the democratic transition all the important decisions directly or indirectly concerning the military were taken in a collegial fashion by senior officers under the nominal leadership of Chadli. The country's military forces were divided between different factions (clans) that had gained their political 'legitimacy', military power and economic autonomy during the war of independence (1954–62) and under the Boumediene presidency (1965–78).[18] Although Chadli had tried to reinforce his authority by creating new military ranks – the rank of General was created in 1984 to be awarded to the President's allies – this had little effect on the overall military structure, since opportunities for real advancement – i.e. increased military and economic capacities – were pre-empted. In 1988, the army's awkward intervention during the October riots had given Chadli the opportunity to reorganise the military hierarchy. Several commanders of military regions and heads of the army High Command were pushed aside and younger officers – nonetheless veterans of the war of independence – were promoted. General Nezzar became the Head of the military High Command, General Zeroual the Head of the Land Forces, Colonel Lamari the

Head of the Fifth Military Region. The situation of the newly appointed officers remained precarious, though, as they tried simultaneously to assert their authority over their fellow officers and to remain in tune with the new political developments generated by the democratic transition. By September 1989 General Zeroual had already been dismissed for criticising Chadli's reform of the army and Lamari had been promoted to his post.

In June 1990 the first political defeat of the FLN at the hands of the Islamic opposition and the continuing democratisation of the political institutions had encouraged Chadli to demarcate clearly the function of President from that of Commander in Chief. (Since the 1965 coup by Colonel Boumediene (then Defence Minister) the functions of President and Defence Minister had been combined. Furthermore, since the 1967 attempted coup by Colonel Zbiri (then Chief of Staff), the President had also been the Chief of Staff.) In July, Chadli re-created the post of Defence Minister and appointed his ally, General Nezzar, to the post. Within a year the military establishment had found a new stability. In June 1991, during the FIS 'strike', this newly found equilibrium gave the military High Command the confidence to challenge the decisions of the executive and to win over the President to their cause. The repression of the FIS by the army and the three-month period of state emergency that ensued did not trigger any reshuffling of the military leadership but led instead to the downfall of Hamrouche, the liberal Prime Minister who had chosen to negotiate with the Islamic party. The new stability and confidence of the military hierarchy gave them an important tactical advantage six months later when the authority of the President and of the official political apparatus was challenged through the ballot box. Although the victory of the FIS in the parliamentary elections did not directly challenge the position of the President, the military establishment and the ruling elite feared the increased organisational capabilities that the FIS could develop once in power, and they lacked confidence in their capacity to turn the tables on the Islamic fundamentalists in open political contests.[19] This pervasive fear of an uncontrollable rise of Islamic fundamentalism encouraged a coalition of officers led by the Defence Minister, Khaled Nezzar, to dismiss the President in January 1992 and to dismantle the political institutions that he had put in place.

Following the putsch changes in the military hierarchy reflected the varying fortunes in the Islamic insurrection and the successes and failures of the strategies devised by the top-ranking officers to solve the crisis. In August 1992 the increase in guerrilla activity led to the creation of a special 'anti-terrorist unit', commanded by Lamari, which rapidly grew in strength over the following months. To counter the activities of the radical Islamic guerrillas, Nezzar also sought to open a dialogue with the FIS and to this effect recalled his former ally, Zeroual. (Zeroual had officially retired from the army in 1990, shortly after his dismissal from the High Command, and had therefore not been involved in the repression against the FIS.) In July 1993 Zeroual was nominated to the 'civilian' post of Defence Minister. At the same time the hardliners within the military – the so-called 'eradicators' – proponents of a straightforward eradication of the guerrilla groups, were given more room for manoeuvre when Lamari, their chief advocate, was promoted to the post of Chief of Staff. By the end of 1993 the rivalries between Nezzar, Zeroual and Lamari led to a showdown and to the departure of Nezzar. In January 1994 Zeroual was nominated Head of State and combined the functions of President and Defence Minister. A few months later, however, the failure of Zeroual's negotiations with the FIS gave a boost to the uncompromisingly military strategy devised by Lamari, who was promoted to Major-General (the highest rank in the Algerian military). As these two strongmen asserted their authority and undermined one another, changes were recurrent inside the military hierarchy, especially at the level of middle-ranking officers. Between 1995 and 1997 most regional commanders who were veterans of the war of independence were replaced by younger officers who had only been in charge of operational army units since the beginning of the civil war. These newcomers had fewer connections with the clans of the war of independence and owed much of their authority to the senior officers nominating them.

The political, economic and military autonomy of the clans in each military region was also diminished as the regional command centres that had been at the core of the pre-1988 power structure were left unstrengthened compared with units like the anti-terrorist force or the *gendarmerie*. Not only were these specialised units made up of well-trained and well-paid professionals while the regular army had to rely on conscripts (whose numbers and morale had been in free fall), but they were also equipped with modern military hardware, technically superior to that of the regular army. In addition, the military importance of the regional commands was indirectly undermined by the creation of rural militias. Created in 1995 from a pre-existing 10,000-strong rural police force, these paramilitary forces had grown by 1997 to an estimated 200,000 fully armed men.[20] In this context, the strategic military capabilities were increasingly concentrated in the hands of the officers in the High Command heading the specialised units – most of whom were close allies of Lamari, the Chief of Staff. This concentration of military power into fewer hands and the strategic reorganisation of the armed forces did not always correspond to a desire to improve the efficacy of the war against the Islamic guerrillas. As the Chief of Staff himself pointed out in 1998 (upon signing a defence treaty with South Africa and buying her sophisticated weaponry), the Algerian army needed no such sophisticated armour to crush to Islamic guerrillas. 'We are not going to fight a flea with a hammer', Lamari pointed out.[21] His comments may have been bravado but they also underscored an important organisational trend in the Algerian military. In practice, the distribution of modern military hardware was used to strengthen selected units and officers who were part of specific patronage networks.[22] In Algeria, as elsewhere in the region, the chain of command was organised more to prevent military coups by fellow military officers than to wage war effectively. (As the 1997–98 civilian massacres made clear, despite their superior firepower the army was in fact often unable to repel guerrilla attacks and to protect the population because the chain of command was organised in such a way that local commanders needed a direct authorisation from the regional commander or the High Command before ordering any movement of troops.)

In 1998 the behind-the-scenes power struggle between Lamari and Zeroual overflowed onto the political stage. Confidential army reports were leaked to the press and revealed the gross misdemeanours during the October riots committed by one of the main presidential allies and the strongman of the political police, Col. Betchine. This political and media campaign, orchestrated by Lamari's supporters, led to the resignation of Betchine and the ousting of an already weakened Zeroual. Following Zeroual's announcement, in September 1998, of an early presidential election, Lamari vaunted the merits of the new 'Algerian democracy' in a speech intended for the armed forces. After applauding the choices of the President, which, in his view, placed Algeria 'at the level of nations with strong democratic traditions', the Chief of Staff expressed his appreciation for the efforts of the armed forces which had made it possible 'to work at the edification of a lawful state which can survive persons and conjunctures'.[23] He concluded with a warning that 'accession to power and alternation of power by means of elections must be, from now on, irreversible practices and the foundations on which rest democracy, the state of law and social justice'. Lamari's discourse was noteworthy for the lip service paid to democracy and it underscored the military leadership's lack of an alternative ideological framework to justify its control of the state institutions – a *de facto* consequence of the state of emergency in place since 1992. (This lack of justification was even more apparent in Zeroual's resignation speech, when he proudly claimed that, while in 1992 Algeria was about to be 'sacrificed on the altar of a supposed democracy', in 1998 this danger had subsided and had been replaced by 'a return to the kind of democracy to which Algerians could legitimately aspire'.)[24] Although Lamari dropped the pretence of having a legitimate political role in Algeria, he had already determined the roles that political and military actors should play in the forthcoming presidential election. When he indicated that the military would certainly not contest the winner of an electoral process, he implied that the successful candidate would have to reach an agreement with the military before the elections. Furthermore, when he pointed out that this 'electoral' system would be the only mode of accession to power, he also warned the population and the political opposition that any popular protest, boycott or political agreement against this 'official' process of legitimisation would not be tolerated by the military. In 1998 the rise to prominence of Lamari signalled a diminution in the prospects for a genuine democratic transition and the continuing impotence of the existing political institutions. However, Lamari's indirect rule did also strengthen the possibility of a long-term agreement between the military elite and the political parties. The period of 'enlightened dictatorship' that opened in 1998 with Lamari's accession to a quasi-hegemonic position inside the military ensured that limited political changes could take place without risk of the armed forces intervening to stop them halfway. Today it remains to be seen whether Lamari and his allies will choose to pursue the kind of 'pacted' transition that constituted the hallmark of the Latin American wave of democratisation in the 1980s. All that can be said with certainty at the beginning of the new century is that the choices of the military and the pace of change will be dictated by the international political and financial pressures that are applied to Algeria, as well as by the behaviour of the remaining Islamic guerrillas.

The Islamic guerrillas

From 1992 onwards, the 'revolutionary' war tactics of the Islamic guerrillas were the main catalyst for the Algerian civil conflict. Despite their relatively weak military capabilities – no armour, no artillery, no air power – these groups created a major social upheaval by taking advantage of the crisis created by the collapse of the democratic transition. By targeting the representatives of the state and all those deemed to support the regime or to benefit from it, the armed Islamic groups exacerbated the state elite's distrust of the citizenry and encouraged it to use harsh repressive policies. In turn, the citizens' distrust of the state authorities was encouraged by the regime's own counter-insurgency policies (policies which created, among other things, a problem of the 'disappeared' similar to that of the Latin American military regimes of the 1980s).[25] In 1993–94, as the army decided to dig in and to weather the storm, the guerrillas undertook increasingly spectacular terrorist actions to create a semblance of political and military momentum. However, dramatic operations like the GIA attack on the French embassy and the hijacking of a French airliner in 1994, or the GIA-sponsored bombing campaign in France in 1995, were smokescreens which hid the fact that the army was winning the war of attrition in the Algerian urban areas.[26] At that moment, the main failure of the Islamic guerrillas was not to adjust quickly enough to the new politico-military and socio-economic situation that they themselves had helped to create. In 1994–95, after several years of conflict, the GIA groups were still targeting the visible symbols of the state, they were still parasitic upon the local economy – financing their cause locally by raising so-called Islamic taxes – and they had not created any credible political institutions to replace those of the military-backed Algerian regime. (The only significant attempt to institutionalise the structures of the Islamic insurrection was a rapprochement in May 1994 between the FIS and GIA factions led respectively by Said and Gousmi – an accord described in the 'Communiqué of Unity' – but the implementation of this agreement proved elusive and this alliance was quickly disavowed by the executive committee of the FIS in exile.)[27] Inexorably, a better-equipped and better-financed Algerian army pushed back the major part of the GIA from the suburban areas, and transformed the conflict into an essentially rural one.

In the countryside the GIA had difficulty finding targets that were appropriate for the kind of terror campaign that had become its trademark. The core GIA groups – first under Djamel Zitouni, then under Antar Zouabri – proposed increasingly radical interpretations of the Koran and made grander political claims to sustain their status of '*mujahidin*'. As the GIA became more embroiled in the war and was confronted simultaneously by the domination of the Algerian military in the towns, the formation of rural militias in the countryside and to the politico-military opposition of the FIS–AIS, its leadership decided to compensate for the reduction of its territory by multiplying the number of potentially legitimate targets. They branded FIS and AIS members as traitors and apostates and vowed to eliminate them. (In November 1995 two former members of the FIS executive committee, Said and Redjam, who had rallied the GIA but had become increasingly critical of its tactics, were executed by their brothers-in-arms.) More important, after the November 1995 presidential elections the GIA leadership declared apostate those Algerians who had voted in the elections, making them legitimate targets for the guerrillas. From 1995 onward the GIA also began to eliminate the members of the rural militias that had been created by the Interior Ministry that year.[28] The creation of these pro-governmental militias hindered the activities of the armed groups but at the cost of dragging more civilians into the conflict. In time the villages of the Algerian countryside became small fortresses, complete with watchtowers and armed guards, and an unofficial curfew was rigorously imposed from dusk to dawn. In 1996, as the GIA began targeting the civilians who supported the rural militias, the violence became endemic and more intimate, and the death toll for civilians of all ages and of either sex began to increase sharply. (Up to 1995 the official death toll for women and children killed was below 300, from a total number of fatal casualties over 10,000.)[29] At the same time the increasing intricacy of the violence involving the killings of civilians by militiamen, the occasional clashes between militias, or between the police and the militias, became an embarrassment for the Algerian state itself.

The GIA targeting of civilians linked to state-sponsored militias led them to commit large-scale massacres in February 1997, during the holy month of Ramadan. This Ramadan witnessed the highest number of casualties in such a small space of time since the beginning of the insurrection: over 400 civilians were killed in the first two weeks of that month during raids on villages of the Mitidja plain, around Algiers. The GIA had declared these persons apostates and had punished them accordingly, rendering 'justice' by ritually

beheading the guilty party, as in 'proper' Islamic trials.[30] Without
doubt, some of the operations allegedly conducted by the GIA were
the work of *agents provocateurs* from the military intelligence and the
political police.[31] (Areas like the towns of the Mitidja plain or the
poor suburbs of Bab-el-Oued and Belcourt in Algiers, known to be
'hotbeds' of Islamic fundamentalism, were also the scene of bombing
campaigns and punitive raids.) However, after several years of
escalating conflict, the uncompromising ideological stance of the
members of the GIA as well as their more mundane war experiences
could easily justify, in their eyes, these deadly tactics.[32] Increasingly,
the GIA was bent on pursuing a military strategy based on escalating
human costs and reduced popular support. Their questionable
politico-military choices were clearly on display in 1997–98 during
the campaign for the local elections and during the holy month of
Ramadan. In November 1997, as political parties were campaigning
throughout the country, the GIA managed to assassinate ten out of
8,500 candidates. A few weeks later, in January 1998, in what proved
to be the bloodiest month of Ramadan since the beginning of the
civil war, 1,000 persons were assassinated by the GIA in the first
twelve days of the holy month. Even the Interior Minister had to
recognise that the security forces were unable to protect the rural
population against this violence, and the regional military
commanders had to tell people in rural areas to form their own
militias and to defend themselves.[33] This capacity of the GIA to
catch the attention of both the government and the population illustrated the continuing relevance of its challenge to the state
institutions. Despite their lack of extensive popular support, the
radical Islamic guerrillas had thus far been able to sustain their
activities and to recruit a sufficient number of replacements to
compensate for their own losses. In 1997–98, the number of guerrilla
actions and the geographical range of the groups remained relatively
stable, as did the level of casualties outside the period of Ramadan.
(Between October 1997, the date of the unilateral AIS cease-fire, and
October 1998 the guerrillas managed to kill between 23 and 41
soldiers, policemen or militiamen each month, without any trend
indicating a reduction in the killings.)[34] Although the political
challenge of the GIA had peaked in 1994 and its insurrectional
potential was seriously dented by 1998, the situation that prevailed
in Algeria at the time still made it worthwhile for a segment of the
population – the impoverished, the thoroughly indoctrinated, those

with the 'right' familial connections, etc. – to persist in violent opposition to the state and the rest of society.[35]

In 1999 several GIA factions began to realise the shortcomings of their strategy and to distance themselves from earlier policies and leaderships. In a context where the military-backed regime was clearly not going to be toppled by the armed Islamic groups, the guerrillas adopted a more pragmatic stance and tried to force the regime to grant them political privileges in exchange for their military submission. The main window of opportunity for this type of arrangement was provided by the law on 'civil concord' devised jointly by the AIS and the Algerian military. The prospect of a general amnesty and the opportunity for guerrilla fighters to invest their war booty in the legal economic sector persuaded several independent and GIA-affiliated guerrilla groups to rally behind the AIS. Others, like Hassan Hattab's Group for Preaching and Combat (*Dawa wa Jihad*), which had began to challenge the supremacy of the mainstream GIA in the Algiers/Kabylia sector, saw this as an opportunity to form an alliance with all those either not tempted by the truce or disenchanted with the current actual GIA leadership.[36] The guerrilla factions led by the AIS began to disband in September 1999 after signing the amnesty deal and financial package proposed by the military. As a result, the intensity of the guerrilla activities diminished significantly in Algeria: 1999 was one of the least violent years the country had seen since the beginning of the conflict. (That year, a little under 1,500 persons were killed in the Islamic insurrection. This situation marked an improvement on 1998, when just over 3,000 people were killed).[37] In the first half of 2000, however, instead of continuing to decline, the level of violence remained roughly the same. A reorganised GIA and, particularly, Hattab's group, which had decided to continue the struggle until the regime itself became more 'Islamicised', ensured the continuity of guerrilla warfare. In the second half of 2000, and particularly at the time of the Ramadan (November/December), there was a noticeable revival of guerrilla activity and a substantial number of civilians were killed.[38] This coincided with the stalemate reached on the political front on the issue of the re-legalisation of an Islamic party. (Taleb Ibrahimi, the unsuccessful candidate in the 1999 presidential election, was refused permission by the Interior Minister to legally register his pro-Islamic party, the *Wafa*, in November 2000.) The disappointing level of political benefits resulting from the law on civil concord galvanised the Islamic groups that had remained outside this peace process and convinced former guerrillas or aspiring *mujahidin* that it was not the time to abandon the armed struggle. In 2001, after the terrorist attacks in the United States, the GIA and Hattab's group were placed on the US Department of State's list of the terrorist organisations linked to bin Laden's network. These international connections enjoyed by Algerian guerrilla groups, despite having little direct military influence on the civil war, contribute indirectly to inhibiting the dialogue between the Algerian regime and the 'politicised' Islamic fundamentalists. Finally, the lack of political dialogue can only encourage the remaining guerrilla groups to continue to use terrorism as their main strategy, and it can only entrench the authoritarian practices of the military strongmen of the Algerian regime.

6 A Civil Society in Transition: Survivalist Strategies and Social Protest

COPING WITH VIOLENCE AND DEPRIVATION: SURVIVALIST STRATEGIES

The new situation that all Algerians had to face after the 1992 putsch was the sudden irruption of political violence into their lives. The outbreak of guerrilla activities coupled with the arbitrariness of state policies weakened and destroyed long-standing formal and informal social and political arrangements. People came to believe that political violence was the main engine of change and that they had no choice but to take part in this necessary evil if they wanted to remedy the social, economic and political inequalities that affected them. This 'democratisation' of violence also reinforced the perception of the state as a 'predatory' one and of the guerrillas as organised criminality. Inevitably the disintegration of the pre-existing social and political order forced a reconfiguration and redistribution of the forms of authority that could be deemed 'legitimate'. Without employing well-defined standards of political legitimacy, non-government actors like the political parties, the associative networks, the guerrilla groups and the militias imposed their views and practices in those areas of society partially deserted by the state. Depending on the needs of the moment (and their own capabilities), these actors themselves attempted to meet some of the main tasks of the state – defence of the population, regulation of economic activities, legitimisation of violence, etc. As the army succeeded in preventing the Islamic guerrillas from establishing stable bases and from controlling well-defined territories, the dispersion of the armed Islamic groups created a situation of diffuse insecurity. The guerrillas moved continuously from district to district, going to areas previously unused to fighting whenever the army concentrated its efforts on a region that had been up to that point one of its strongholds; and the army simply reciprocated. In this context, in the countryside social relationships became more firmly grounded in a traditional, kinship-based system of allegiance. In urban areas, by contrast, social life and social protest were principally reconstructed from the remnants of the democratic and Islamic associative movements. Everywhere trust and betrayal were part of a highly complex game in which individuals solved apparently intractable dilemmas by changing their political views and their practices opportunistically.

In the rural areas the months and years of ebb and flow of each group of combatants' zone of control taught the population to choose carefully strategies that minimised risk and collateral damage. The unexpected but always possible irruption of war into everyone's life favoured self-reliance and a minimal political cooperation with the powers-that-be. Eventually such non-cooperative practices also became instrumental in producing new security dilemmas and in fuelling the country's socio-economic crisis. The political conflicts of the 1990s grafted themselves onto pre-existing antagonisms between social groups (families and clans) and fuelled sectarian violence. In rural areas the dilemmas of the civil war were built upon the earlier 'socialist' mismanagement of the agricultural sector. As Martinez remarks, many of the contemporary blood feuds are long-running disputes involving lands that were redistributed by successive French and Algerian administrations to reward their allies during various conflicts.[1] In the 1990s the government's half-baked reform of the agricultural sector and its practical inability (or unwillingness) to clarify the system of land ownership directly aggravated these local antagonisms.[2] The decades of 'socialist' management of the agricultural sector had also created a rural economy less dependent on agricultural production than on the redistribution of state subsidies. As the level of state subsidies steadily declined in the 1990s because of the liberalisation of the economy, the level of unemployment and under-employment rose. In this near-subsistence rural economy the option to join a guerrilla group suddenly became an opportunity for the unemployed.[3] The activities of the guerrilla groups (rackets, contraband and theft) represented attractive (if risky) business ventures for those in need. The Algerian regime was quick to grasp this economic argument and it proposed new subsidies for those rural communities which agreed to form pro-government militias. In addition, the militias and rural police forces themselves became an important source of income for the local population – either because their employees were on the payroll of the state or because they permitted people to become involved in the informal economy, just like the Islamic guerrillas. (Famously, in

June 1997, the mayor of the town of Relizane and his militiamen were arrested for leading organised crime in their district.)[4] Overall, however, these new government incentives did little to raise the living standards in the countryside or to persuade the peasants to cooperate in earnest with the security forces. More often they merely permitted local people to build up a small capital that was utilised to migrate to the towns when the funds dried up, or when the security situation seriously deteriorated.

In rural locations these social choices were determined more by local conditions than by ideological preferences. (In this respect, despite the propagandist efforts of the FIS in the countryside during the democratic transition, the commitment of the rural population to political Islam remained a very pragmatic affair.) In these rural communities even the local *nomenklatura*, an alliance of civil servants and local notables, interpreted the directives of the administration and of the government according to the local balance of power. This was often needed because the central administration in Algiers had difficulties in assessing correctly the political and socio-economic situation in the remote parts of the country. (In rural districts it was not unusual for the central administration to send financial assistance to people who had already emigrated or joined the guerrillas. In such cases, the local administrative personnel would accept these funds in the absentee's name and channel them into their own clientele networks.)[5] The series of cuts in state subventions to local institutions made throughout the 1990s, particularly after the 1994 IMF debt-rescheduling deal, had seriously weakened the traditional patronage networks of the local elites and increased the intensity of the competition for financial resources. Faced with this situation, for many individuals and clans joining the guerrillas or their support network was often a calculated risk to enhance one's bargaining position; or it was a consequence of losing out in the local power struggle. In practice, the local economy continued to function in the rural communities even under conditions of intense guerrilla activity because the low political content of the struggle permitted the different parties to reach informal working agreements. Frequently there was unofficial recognition of each group's zone of influence and activities. The local administration and the militias often knew the guerrillas personally and they lived alongside the people who organised their logistical support.[6] In this precarious environment the armed Islamic groups could use the economic facilities of the provincial towns for their logistical needs and, in exchange, the local militias and population obtained guarantees that the guerrillas would not raid their town or village. Inevitably, these tacit understandings stabilised the relations between warring factions locally, but at the cost of promoting insta- bility on a larger scale.[7] Furthermore, through provocation, greed or misfortune, local struggles for influence could easily turn into savage blood feuds in which the atrocities committed by the guerrillas matched those of the militias. (The incidents of August 1997 in the village of Ain Hamra were a typical instance of these clashes – albeit with an unusually high media coverage. When a section of the militia of a neighbouring village was decimated by a bomb placed near this locality, the rest of the militia launched a punitive campaign against the families of the village that were relatives of the guerrillas. Their houses were burnt down and all the men who happened to be at home were executed.)[8] Although the massacres of civilians by the GIA hit the headlines in the late 1990s, most commonly the guerrillas satisfied their religious ardour by collecting 'Islamic taxes' and by controlling black market activities.[9] In the east of the country, the situation had even taken a quasi-official turn after the 'unofficial' cease-fire agreed between the AIS and the army in 1997 gave the AIS fighters a *de facto* judicial immunity in the areas in which they were stationed. At the other end of the country, near the Moroccan border, the war economy had also become extremely complex after the 1994 border closure with Morocco, and widespread smuggling activities blurred the lines between the guerrillas, the militias and organised criminals.[10]

If the violence generated by the Islamic insurrection was the most noticeable feature of the Algerian countryside in the second half of the 1990s, in the urban areas by contrast, the socio-economic crisis was the main cause of the transformation of the social and political situation. Because the towns had been among the main strategic assets of the Algerian regime from very early on, by 1995 the reduced necessity of responding to physical threats simply meant that the majority of urban dwellers resented even more the incompetence and perceived iniquity of the regime. The persisting tension between the ruling elite and the citizenry centred on the management of (relatively) abundant but ill-utilised economic resources, such as the oil revenues.[11] As before the beginning of the civil conflict, social exclusion and social discontent were underpinned by a rise in urban population and a concomitant decrease in state economic and administrative capacities.[12] The civil war in the countryside worsened the phenomenon of rural emigration and exacerbated the social tensions in the main Algerian urban areas (Algiers, Oran, Constantine, Annaba).[13] A housing shortage and tighter governmental control in the town centres helped divert the waves of rural migrants towards the suburban housing estates and the shantytowns. This unprecedented arrival of refugees stretched the capacities of the urban local councils to breaking point. (In Oran, between the beginning of the conflict in 1992 and 1996, the main shantytown received nearly 70 per cent of its inhabitants.)[14] Such a trend is unlikely to be reversed in the near future given the exactions of the radical guerrillas in the countryside and the continuing economic crisis. For these rural migrants the relative lack of violence and the proximity of economic resources ensure that the shantytowns remain attractive locations. (Furthermore, wherever newcomers already have familial connections in a shantytown, a communal organisation is quickly re-created and the shantytown becomes a replica of the village, 'in town'.) In parallel with this phenomenon of rural migration, the population of the towns' newly urbanised periphery also increased dramatically.[15] There, because the population was already made up of urban dwellers, the resentment against the government was fuelled by the perception of having being pushed by an incompetent administration into a suburban fringe where the risk of violence is greater and the infrastructures almost non-existent. Because state planning was often incoherent, this rapid phenomenon of urbanisation led to a ghettoisation of the suburban districts. In practice, public transport, as well as functional (and secure) roads and railway lines were only available between economically successful and privileged sites. (A situation made worse by the 1994 IMF deal, which led the state to run public services on the cheap or to hand them over to private enterprises which promptly dropped all unprofitable activities.) This state of affairs resulted in the cutting-off of the suburban belts (and the shanty-towns) from the towns' main amenities. In these underprivileged areas spatial segregation reinforced economic divisions and the process of social exclusion accelerated.

The lack of social integration became even starker after the intro-duction of economic reforms devised by the IMF. The Algerian government's privatisation of state enterprises led to multiple closures and left hundreds of thousands of workers without wages. In 1998 the Algerian Prime Minister indicated that the privatisation of state enterprises had directly or indirectly led to the loss of

380,000 jobs in just over three years.[16] As the system of compensa-
tion for redundancy due to privatisation or closure of state
enterprises never functioned properly (and as the state pension
system became increasingly dysfunctional), hundreds of thousands
of Algerians were forced to reorganise their lives outside the 'legal'
economic system. In 1996 nearly 1 million Algerians – about 20 per
cent of the country's workforce – worked in the 'informal' sector.[17]
For the state the rise of the black market economy meant that, from
the mid-1990s onward, nearly half of the country's currency
circulated outside the state-controlled banking sector. (Despite the
efforts of the IMF, the opportunities for Algerians to invest their
savings in private businesses has not improved significantly, thanks
to the reluctance of the Algerian authorities to suspend their political
supervision of investors.)[18] This informal reorganisation of the socio-
economic arrangements in the polity undermined the capacity of
the state apparatus to supervise economic growth and to police social
change. As the Algerian regime became even more dependent on the
oil revenues to finance its rule, Algerian society reorganised itself
even more on the basis of the solidarity networks of civil society that
continued to function even under those adverse conditions.

In the late 1990s, as the state-funded welfare system was rapidly
disintegrating, survival depended increasingly on familial solidarity
and charity networks. In Algeria this associative system is structured
principally by Islamic organisations (charities) and, to a lesser degree,
by Berber cultural and pro-democratic associations.[19] The social work
of both Islamic and Berber associations is generally associated with
a cultural or religious propaganda that implicitly supports an alternative, democratic or Islamic, political order. The Islamic
associations claim to embody a better form of social order because of
their religious faith, whilst the Berber associations have an efficient
community network (particularly in the large urban areas and in
Kabylia) based on local democracy and cultural ties. In these circumstances, it is extremely difficult to separate the causal
mechanisms that make these associations such effective models for
collective action, from the religious or identity-based beliefs that
underpin their social work. (Reciprocally, it is difficult to separate
the practical causes of the chronic inefficiency of the state administration from the ideological commitment shown by the civil servants
– or their lack thereof.) Regardless, however, of their specific social,
political or religious programmes, because these associative networks
are grounded in a repressed counter-culture which aspires to changes

that go well beyond the implementation of an effective system of governance, their discourses invariably contribute to the popular resentment against the ruling elite. In Algeria this implicit antagonism between civil society and the state has been aggravated since 1992 by the state of emergency. Over the past decade all the components of civil society have had to confront the coercive side of a state system that is not particularly eager to listen to the complaints or demands of the population. Hence, whether they contribute to a patient work of social reconstruction or whether they chose to challenge the regime directly, these associative networks reinforce the mutual defiance that exists between civil society and the state apparatus. Unwittingly, and despite their effective social work, they frequently constitute an additional hindrance to the success of the socio-economic and political reforms tentatively proposed by the state.

THE ARTICULATION OF SOCIAL PROTEST: DEFYING THE REGIME

In Algeria, as in most of the Muslim world, the Islamic associative networks are one of the main social structures permitting popular mobilisation and the articulation of social demands. However, since the 1988 October riots, the attention of the Algerian regime (and of foreign players) has been focused not on the Islamic associative system but on the political and armed products of Islamic fundamentalism. The exceptional political situation that developed in Algeria after 1992 helped to conceal the fact that the articulation of political Islam cannot be fully appreciated without an understanding of the activities of these associative networks that pervade society. The FIS had emerged from the associative movement in 1989 and, although it is unlikely that after several years of political violence an Islamic party will today grow organically out of the associative movement, the 'subversive' ideological and organisational potential of these 'apolitical' Islamic associations remains as strong as ever, particularly among the youth.[20] (Significantly, at the end of 1993 a survey conducted among adolescents at the end of their secondary education in Oran, showed that the 'values' that they most recognised and respected were those of religion and family, while everything connected to the nation and nationalism trailed far behind.)[21] Indeed, from the perspective of the Algerian regime, the fact that the Islamic associative movement is not composed of social activists advocating direct political action is a mixed blessing. Precisely because they do not link their social work explicitly to political reform, many Islamic associations can evade the mechanisms of political repression devised by the state security apparatus. Unlike what happened during the first few years of the civil war, when their open support for the FIS had led to their *de facto* politicisation and had made them the targets of police repression, in the second half of the 1990s the Islamic charities only advocated an Islamicisation of the social sphere. (Nowadays, just as they did before the democratic transition, Islamic charities spend most of their time and energy redistributing wealth, integrating the unemployed and the young, helping the settlement of impoverished migrants, etc.)

The Islamic charities

Islamic charities have been able to quickly regain their position in the social structure because the worsening socio-economic crisis has forced the government to seek the support of civil society and to become more discriminating in its use of repression. In this political context the Islamic associations have had to make plain their non-political character.

Sheikh Shamseddine, the leader of one of the main Islamic charities in the Algiers' suburb of Belcourt, explicitly rejects any form of political involvement. More than apolitical, Shamseddine argued, his association was 'anti-politics'.[22] Shamseddine considered that the popular success encountered by his association, like that of any other good Islamic charity, was simply the consequence of their effective management of scarce human and financial resources. This rigorous management permitted them to be more efficient than the social services of the state and continuously to attract new members and new donations from wealthy benefactors.[23] This tangible effort, he said, contrasted with the vacuous propaganda of the various political parties (including Islamic ones), which were only interested in gaining votes. The Sheikh and the cadres of the association judged that because they helped the poor, the state ought to welcome their support, just as in 'the West'; it was natural for 'civil society to take part in the everyday running of society'. In the Algerian context Shamseddine recognised that he had trouble eliciting the support and the goodwill of the state administration, and attributed this uncooperativeness to the absence of a strong 'democratic tradition' in the country. He also recognised that, although his association did not intend to produce a politicised discourse, it could not help but articulate the social demands of a population frustrated by an unresponsive state administration. Shamseddine considered that his organisation embodied the aspirations of 'ordinary Muslims', as distinct from the 'Islamists wanting to create an Islamic state' – i.e. the FIS – and from the 'false Muslims', who were so-called 'Islamic terrorists' – i.e. the GIA.

The distinction operated by Sheikh Shamseddine is typical of the Islamic associative movement in Algeria. It combines a condemnation of the actions of the guerrillas with an approval of the Islamicisation of society, but remains silent about the role of those activists wishing to Islamise the state itself. (Evidently this silence often encourages the Algerian regime to hinder the work of associations, which, through their social achievements, give people incentives to support nominally Islamic policies and politicians.) This ambiguous doctrinal positioning of the Islamic associations is complicated by the fact that the cadres of these charities use a propagandist discourse that blends strands of 'popular' Islam in the case of local matters, and strands of 'fundamentalism' regarding international issues. Most frequently, however, these views are not expressing a precise political argument but are only a reflection of the fact that the Islamic charities cater for many urban and rural poor with varied and unorthodox religious beliefs. These associations cannot afford to demand rigid discursive practices or to enforce strict religious rules, but must compromise with their members and emphasise working agreements at the expense of formal professions of faith. In practice the discourse of these social activists is frequently a non-structured one that only makes sense locally (or temporarily), and only serves to justify their own localised efforts and to elicit the sympathy of the people concerned. (In which case, it would be misleading to present their discourse as one of James Scott's 'hidden transcripts', which the dominated groups display when dealing with the dominant one.)[24] Aside from their practical achievements, the success of these Islamic charities arises from the fact that their loosely rational discourse reflects the heterogeneous beliefs of the poorer segments of the Algerian population and the unsophisticated understanding of progress favoured by the poor. Accordingly, if this discourse constitutes a subversive ideology, it is only in the sense that it symbolises the (widening) divide between amateur/popular and professional/official understanding of social change. Without doubt the various religious and political beliefs implicitly advocated by these Islamic associations converge towards some general notion of 'good' Islamic order and governance. Yet, because the cadres of these charities are very careful not to address strictly political issues, the questions that would arise from a political analysis of their situation remain unasked. Certainly, the members of these associations can offer complex answers to these questions if pressed, and certainly, too, they can be willing to mislead people. Mostly, however, they are far too involved in their day-to-day struggle with local poverty and Islamicisation to spend much time and effort trying to devise the means to reform the state institutions. (In this case it is not Scott's hidden transcripts but Pierre Bourdieu's *doxa* – the ideas and practices that 'go without saying' – that best captures the rationale of this Islamic discourse.)[25]

In Belcourt Sheikh Shamseddine regretted the lack of democratic attitudes within the Algerian administration and its ineffective social policies, but only suggested to the authorities that they should listen more carefully to the recommendations of social scientists (and pointing out that 'good governance' was based on the work of 'scientists', he did not fail to remark that Islam was 'on the side of science' and that his own social and educational efforts were devoted to the promotion of such 'science').[26] However, the Sheikh and the cadres of the Islamic associations had no clear idea of how these 'scientists' would become the mentors of the government, nor did they knew very precisely how they would resolve the country's socio-economic crisis. Like most Algerians they were convinced that 'science', Islam and democracy could happily be merged together. Because their own social experience and local solutions permitted them to deal expeditiously with the religious, political and economic problems of their members, they were persuaded that these local solutions could also be employed as expeditiously and felicitously at the state level. This idea was stated by the FIS during the democratic transition. However, its leadership soon realised that if the party could capitalise on the popular belief that, as Ali Djeddi puts it, 'they were better managers than the state', they had to seriously rethink the practical reform that they could introduce without undermining the organisation of the country's entire administrative and economic system.[27] In an effort to define this 'Islamic democracy', Belhadj had even proposed that a body of Islamic scholars having both practical experience and theological expertise should provide the moral supervision needed to keep in check the choices made by the people and their representatives. These 'experts' would not be simple FIS activists, but would need to be scholars knowing the *ijtihad*; nor would they be the *ulama*, who did not participate enough in the everyday running of the community – and who were in any case far too close to the authorities. Specifically, Belhadj suggested a separation of powers in a mixed democratic system that combined non-elected but popular religious and social experts with an elected body of political representatives.[28]

Today, without the support of a (genuine) institutionalised Islamic opposition, the crude and often unrealistic aspect of the solutions proposed by the Islamic associative movement reduces the chances of these activists contributing meaningfully to a resolution of the country's problems, especially in national politics. However, this practical-minded social approach guarantees an enduring popular support for the Islamic charities and for the political actors who might emerge from the associative movement. In the suburbs of Algiers, as elsewhere in the country, very few non-Islamic organisations have developed an approach to social and political reform that is tailored to the capabilities and understanding of the average Algerian citizen. Frequently the non-Islamic organisations present in civil society, just like the legal political parties, lack the capacity and/or willingness to reach down towards the poorer social groups that constitute the bulk of Algerian society. Consequently, the criticisms made by the ruling elite and liberal circles of the Islamic associations' lack of understanding of socio-economic and political issues are perceived by the population as mere ritual criticism tainted by cultural prejudice. Such criticisms only reinforce the popular belief that non-Islamic activists and political parties (as well as foreign players) are not interested in helping ordinary people but only in bickering over state ownership and the control of the country's natural resources. Indirectly, therefore, they reinforce the standing of the Islamic associations and their image as social actors who distance themselves from high politics in order to focus on local accountability. Certainly, as the presence of a powerful Berber pro-democracy movement in Algeria indicates, there is no principled opposition between effective associative networks and non-Islamic social institutions, even in a Muslim polity, but there are nonetheless strong socio-historical contingencies.

The Berber associations

Unlike the Islamic charities, the Berber associations do not constitute a pervasive social network that slowly wins the hearts and minds of the population. They are a nucleus of modernist and democratic forces whose turbulent behaviour can be a focal point and a trigger for anti-government opposition. Although traditionally critical of the central government in Algiers and well capable of unruly behaviour (1963 Kabyle insurrection, 1980 Berber Spring), the Berber community and most particularly its large Kabyle component became allies by default of the Algerian regime after 1992. The more liberal, secular and culturally distinct Kabyle community had been staunchly opposed to the Islamic fundamentalists during the democratic transition. Although the FFS decided to support the FIS against the autocratic leadership of the new Algerian regime, the Kabyles remained strong opponents of the Islamic guerrillas (particularly so after the assassination of secular intellectuals by the GIA had polarised public opinion.)[29] Over the years, however, as the political threat posed by political Islam was contained by the Algerian regime, the Kabyle community increasingly resented the political, cultural and economic tutelage imposed by the state elite in Algiers. The regime's neutralisation of the legal political opposition ensured that the Kabyles could not satisfactorily express their discontent in official electoral contests, despite the participation of parties like the FFS or the RCD that were well attuned to their demands. It was against this background that Kabyle civil society forced the regime to take seriously the issues of minority rights and of the democratic control of the state institutions by launching two series of violent protests in 1998 and 2001. In June 1998 the riots that erupted in Kabylia constituted the first popular uprising since the end of the democratic transition in 1992. This wave of rioting was triggered by the assassination of the popular Kabyle singer and Berber activist, Matoub Lounes, supposedly by Islamic guerrillas. The protest started in Tizi-Ouzou, the regional capital of Kabylia, on 26 June 1998, when townspeople turned in anger against the state and its representatives upon learning that Lounes had been killed on the outskirts of the town. The rioters ransacked the tribunal and the regional offices of the Ministries, and attacked the state-owned banks and airline offices. The following day the protest spread to most Kabylian towns, where the protesters ransacked the state buildings and the offices of the pro-governmental parties (the FLN and the

RND). Even though Lounes' assassination was attributed to the Islamic guerrillas, all over Kabylia the rioters specifically targeted the symbols of the state. The spokesperson of the Berber Cultural Movement (*Mouvement Culturel Berbère*, MCB) branded the President and the Prime Minister as 'accomplices of the murderers' and 'allies of the fundamentalists'.[30] Protesters regarded the regime as responsible for the climate of insecurity that existed in the country *and* for specific acts of violence against Berber activists. (This state of affairs was partly attributable to the fact that Lounes had already been shot and wounded by the police a few years earlier, when he was campaigning for the Berber cause.)[31] In addition, Lounes' death occurred just a few days after the government had decreed that only Arabic could be used in the administrative and educational systems. Tamazigh-speaking (and French-speaking) Berbers resented this new law as yet another attempt to marginalise their culture. Hence, during the riots, all the most popular slogans, beside 'state murderer' ('*pouvoir assassin*'), had a distinctive cultural twist: 'we are not Arabs', 'no to Arabicisation'.[32] (All signposts, posters, adverts, plates written in Arabic were also destroyed or erased during these demonstrations.)

The spontaneity of the protest and its distinctively anti-government and culturally based character were espoused by Berber associations like the MCB under popular pressure. Such a synergy was more difficult to create (and probably less desirable to maintain) for parties like the FFS and the RCD, which had to deal with the situation politically, at the national level. These parties quickly realised that the cultural flavour of the revolt prevented the protest from spreading outside Kabylia – except among the substantial Kabyle communities of Algiers and Oran, where it was rapidly suppressed by the security forces – and, therefore, would prevent the Kabyles from obtaining significant political concessions from the regime. The explicitly Berber symbolism used during the protest alienated the other sections of Algerian society, and despite the relevance of the issues raised by the Kabyle community – such as the role of the security apparatus, the arbitrary character of many state policies, the lack of accountability of state institutions – their movement appeared as a secessionist tendency in Algerian society. This perception was reinforced by the fact that the protest targeted a wide range of symbols that were important for non-Berber Algerians, such as their Arab heritage. (Nannah, the leader of the main pro-governmental Islamic party, condemned the Kabyles for their reckless opposition to the dominant Arab-Islamic culture of

Algeria.) Finally, a more practical reason for the lack of enthusiasm on the part of the non-Kabyle populations was their own lack of appropriate alternatives. The Kabyles had the opportunity to condemn both the actions of the state and of the Islamic fundamentalists because they possessed alternative social and political structures that avoided this polarisation. Such an opportunity did not occur elsewhere in Algeria, where a powerful non-Islamic associative movement simply did not exist, and where society was divided into mutually antagonistic pro-Islamic and pro-governmental institutions. (Indeed, the Islamic guerrillas who later claimed responsibility for Lounes' murder declared that they considered that Lounes was 'one of the fiercest opponent of religion' who 'supported those who fought against Islam'.)[33]

The protest movement slowly subsided, as the government promised to reconsider some of the more contentious aspects of the law on Arabicisation and as the army stepped up its operations against the Islamic guerrillas in the region. The failure the Kabyle riots to spark a nationwide protest movement and to provoke significant political reform signalled the increased isolation of the Kabyle community in the country. This sense of isolation, as well as a concomitant ostracism, increased over the following months and set the scene for another, longer and stronger, outburst of violence in the spring of 2001. The Kabyle revolt that ran from April to July 2001 illustrated the radicalisation both of the opposition between this community and of the Algerian regime, and of the opposition between the Berber and Arab components of Algerian society. The event that triggered this new outburst of violence was the accidental killing of a schoolboy by a *gendarme* (a member of the *gendarmerie*, the police force attached to the military) on 18 April 2001. This killing, which nearly coincided with the anniversary of the 1980 Berber Spring, was the starting point for a series of violent demonstrations in Kabylia against the *gendarmerie* and for the recognition of the cultural specificity (and local autonomy) of the Berber community. On 19 April over 10,000 people participated in a protest march organised by the MCB in Tizi-Ouzou. On 22 April riots erupted in the neighbouring district of Bejaia and, as the week progressed, the number of towns touched by this wave of rioting increased. As this wave of violent anti-government demonstration finally spread to all districts of Kabylia, the Algerian President was forced to launch an official inquiry into the behaviour of the security forces, in order to appease the Kabyles. This inquiry was welcome because the confrontation between the security forces (especially the *gendarmerie*) and the demonstrators had been particularly bloody – the *gendarmes* killing 50 protesters in just one week.[34] In 2001 as much as in 1998, the Kabyle-dominated political parties, FFS and RCD, had been unable to control this sudden movement of popular discontent. (The RCD, which had joined forces with the FLN and the MSP in Bouteflika's ruling coalition a few months earlier, was even forced to quit the government under pressure from the streets.) After a few weeks of tentative mediation by political parties, the Kabyle revolt began again on 21 May in Tizi-Ouzou with a massive demonstration organised by the council of village assemblies, which gathered over 500,000 Kabyles. On 25 May new riots erupted in the region; lasting several days, they caused the death of many more protesters. Increasingly at that time, the opposition was organised by the traditional Kabyle village assemblies (*aarch*). A few weeks after having organised their massive demonstration in Tizi-Ouzou, the council of village assemblies succeeded in moving the protest to the capital, Algiers, where a huge demonstration took place on 14 June. This protest march, in which there were frequent and violent confrontations between the hundreds of thousands of demonstrators and the security forces, did nothing to improve relations between the Kabyles and the regime, or to foster friendship between Arabs and Berbers. On the contrary, this show of strength by the Kabyle community antagonised the inhabitants of Algiers and encouraged Bouteflika to forbid all demonstrations in the country (a political decision that did not prevent recurrent outbursts of violence continuing to occur in Kabylia over several weeks.)

The break between the Kabyle community and the state authorities, symbolised by the havoc created in Algiers by the Kabyle demonstrators, was the result of years of latent political opposition and months of violent confrontations with the security forces in this region. The climate of latent insurrection that prevailed in Kabylia progressively loosened the hold of the government over this community. Over the many weeks of recurrent rioting, the administrative and institutional structure of the state – regional assemblies, regional offices of the Ministries, local councils, etc. – had been physically dismantled by the protesters, and informally replaced by a system of local administration. After a while, even the *gendarmes* were forced to live retrenched in their barracks, letting the Kabyle police forces and militias provide a semblance of law and order. The political parties closest to the Kabyle community were taken aback by the scale of civic disobedience and by demands that frequently went beyond the reforms that they were proposing. Even the associative structures of the MCB were swept away by a popular protest movement that reached down to the village level. In fact, before being undermined by their own anarchic tendencies, the village assemblies were the chief organisers of the protest in Kabylia in 2001. That this traditional representative structure of Kabyle local democracy should have taken over from the political parties and from the MCB indicated how effective the Algerian regime's neutralisation of political society had been. Inevitably, this neutralisation of the Kabyle-dominated parties tended to reinforce anarchy within civil society as well as to radicalise the protest movement. This radicalisation of Kabyle civil society was well illustrated by the fact that in 2001 the slogans of the demonstrators were not only anti-government but also supported the Islamic guerrillas. Slogans such as, 'Hattab, the People are with you', were used by protesters in spite of the fact that Hattab's group was believed to have been behind the assassination of Lounes, three years earlier.[35] This tentative (symbolic) reconciliation of the Kabyles with the armed opposition, at a time when the Islamic guerrillas no longer represented a powerful political force in the country, did nothing to redefine the relationship between secularist and Islamic current in Algerian society. However, the actual behaviour of the Kabyles and their endorsement of pro-Islamic political violence did undermine the political pretensions of the pro-democracy parties close to this community. Whatever hopes the FFS may have had of becoming the leading liberal-democratic party in the country were dashed by these two successive revolts by its Kabyle supporters. In national politics, unlike the Islamic associative movement (which is simply denied an official legal political voice by the regime), Kabyle civil society is rendered powerless by the connection that is made in the popular psyche between the pro-democratic parties that have emerged from this community and the specific culture (and demands) of this community. Today the Algerian regime may well be satisfied by these divisions in civil society and by the inability of any one social movement to formulate coherent political demands with a nationwide appeal. Yet, there is an obvious drawback to this. Historically, one of the main challenges for the Algerian leadership has always been to create a sense of national identity and to forge a modern notion of citizenship. The situation that now prevails in the country undermines the very notion of Algerian citizenship that had emerged from the state-building endeavours of the French and the nation-building efforts of the FLN. The longer this situation lasts, the more difficult it will be to reconstruct viable national social and political institutions, particularly if they are to be properly grounded in elective democracy.

7   The International Arena: Strengths and Weaknesses of the New World Order

THE POLITICAL ECONOMY OF THE CONFLICT: THE ROLE OF INTERNATIONAL ACTORS

In Algeria, after the 1992 coup, to secure the cash incomes of the state (and of the army) became a top priority for the new military rulers of the country. The financial situation of the Algerian state had never been very bright from the mid-1980s onwards, but the sharp rise in oil prices that resulted from the Gulf War at the beginning of the 1990s had given the regime some breathing space. This had been highly beneficial to the country, as the sale of oil and gas represented 95 per cent of Algeria's export revenues and 45 per cent of its GNP.[1] When the military took control of the state institutions in January 1992, however, the Gulf War had just ended – and with it the fear of oil shortages. The sharp decrease in oil prices that followed was highly detrimental to the Algerian polity, especially as the previous government had bargained on a protracted conflict (and high oil prices), and had contracted new loans accordingly. At the start of 1992 the new Algerian regime faced the prospect of a large current account deficit and a cash shortage. It had to ask its creditors – mostly Western governments and European and Japanese banks – to reschedule its loan repayments in order to avoid bankruptcy. The French authorities proved extremely receptive to this argument, and in February 1992 the Algerian government secured a $1.5 billion refinancing deal from a group of private creditors led by the Crédit Lyonnais, a bank owned by the French State. The French government also made it clear that it would not change the terms of its annual $1 billion export credit loan to Algeria, despite the military intervention and the ending of the democratic transition. Because France was one of Algeria's main creditors and trading partners, and because of domestic political issues linked to the presence of a large Algerian community in France, the French government was eager to see the situation stabilised in its southern neighbour.

Thus comforted by this external support, the Algerian provisional government immediately announced the implementation of a $4 billion economic programme designed to relaunch the domestic economy. This recovery programme was deliberately over-ambitious and worked principally as public relations exercise. Two months later, however, the government ran short of cash and had to suspend the financing of social programmes and to stop subsidising the price of most retail goods. Needing to generate new income quickly, Boudiaf, the civilian Head of State, decided to open the Algerian gas sector to foreign investment and facilitated joint ventures with the state-owned oil and gas company, SONATRACH.[2] Soon several major Western companies (Total, BP, Mobil, Agip, Arco, Repsol) began to negotiate oil and gas contracts. In June 1992, barely two months after announcing the partial liberalisation of the oil and gas sector, Boudiaf was assassinated. The military 'minders' of the regime then entrusted the urgent task of solving the country's financial difficulties to a diehard socialist, Belaid Abdessallam, who had been the architect of Algeria's industrialisation programme in the 1970s. The newly promoted Finance Minister quickly implemented policies that undermined the confidence of foreign investors. As Abdessallam suspended some of the decrees that allowed unlimited access to foreign investments, re-imposed government controls on imports, and refused any devaluation of the Algerian dinar, the oil companies decided to withhold most of their contracts and investments in Algeria.[3] Fortunately for the Algerian regime the southern European countries, who were extremely worried by the risk of massive emigration linked to the potential collapse of the Algerian state, provided financial compensation for this reduced involvement by the oil companies. In October 1992 the Spanish government granted a $1 billion export credit to Algeria. (The Spanish Foreign Minister, Javier Solana, was also the first foreign minister from the European Union to travel to Algiers and to display his support for the Algerian regime publicly.) In November, in a more convoluted fashion, the Italian government also ensured that the state-owned electricity company, ENI, signed an important gas contract with the Algerian state-owned oil and gas company.[4] Like France, Italy and Spain hoped that their timely interventions would allow the Algerian economy and the Algerian state to cope until the political crisis that shook the country was resolved – democratically if possible, undemocratically if that was the best way to ensure stability in the polity.

In spite of these timely interventions by Algeria's European neighbours, by the end of 1992 the Algerian economy was beginning to feel the strain of the idiosyncratic 'socialist' policies devised by Abdessallam, as well as the economic costs of the civil conflict. The state's budget already had a deficit of 7.4 per cent of GNP (which contrasted sharply with the positive balance of the previous year (+2.4 per cent)), and the forecasts for 1993 were that the budget deficit would double while the debt–service ratio would reach 80 per cent.[5] To cope with this situation, the Algerian government printed more money, thus fuelling inflation, and contracted more loans, thus increasing the debt burden. In the spring of 1993 growing inflation and the need for more cash facilities led many inside the Algerian ruling circles to consider asking the International Monetary Fund (IMF) and institutional creditors (the Paris Club) for a rescheduling of the country's debt – an idea strongly opposed by the Finance Minister. Eventually the country's growing socio-economic difficulties triggered a mini-crisis inside the military establishment, and as a new team of military strongmen took charge of the political affairs of the country in August 1993, the socialist-minded Finance Minister was finally evicted and the IMF's help sought. The French government then offered its services as a go-between in the negotiations between the IMF and the Algerian regime. Many French politicians favoured the theory that economic development in Algeria would weaken the virulence of the Islamic fundamentalist protest. (As the French Prime Minister, Alain Juppé, explained to Parliament at the start of 1994, 'under-development provides a fertile terrain for the growth of pernicious ideologies'.)[6] In addition, the efforts of the French and of other European governments to pass on the responsibility for the financial survival of the Algerian regime and for the economic recovery of the country to the IMF were dictated by their fear of becoming the prime targets of popular discontent and of political violence. (Significantly, at the end of 1993 and at the start of 1994 the campaign of assassination of Westerners by the GIA had become particularly virulent in Algeria.) In May 1994, after several months of intense negotiations, the Algerian government finally reached an agreement with the IMF on a programme of structural economic reforms. This accord paved the way for a debt rescheduling of $5 billion by the Paris Club that nearly halved the debt–service ratio of the country, bringing it down to 46 per cent.[7] In addition, the Algerian regime obtained a $1 billion stand-by loan from the IMF.

The funds diverted from the repayment of the debt permitted the Algerian regime to finance some of its most vital administrative functions in the face of a growing level of depredation by the Islamic guerrillas as well as modernising its repressive apparatus. (This financial support was particularly needed at the time, as the strength of the guerrilla movement had increased, and it was no longer possible for the state apparatus and the military to withstand this challenge by drawing on their reserves, as they had done in the early stages of the conflict.) Predictably, in 1994 military expenditure increased dramatically (by 140 per cent) and the combined budgets of the Ministry of Defence and of the Interior Ministry accounted for approximately 15 per cent of the state budget.[8]

The financial survival of the Algerian regime was secured in 1995 when it renegotiated with the IMF an 'extended-facilities' loan guaranteeing $1.8 billion a year over a three-year period. Following the IMF agreements, the Paris Club authorised another $5 billion rescheduling of the Algerian public debt and the London Club (private creditors) authorised a $3 billion rescheduling of the country's private debt.[9] Thus, in just over a year, the Algerian regime gained access to over $15 billion through a series of debt reschedulings and loans from foreign governments, banks and international financial organisations. In return, the IMF package forced upon the Algerian regime a series of measures intended to liberalise the economy. In particular, it required that the Algerian authorities reduce their budget deficit, reduce inflation, cease subsidising retail goods, open the interior market to foreign investments and privatise state-owned enterprises. By contrast, few of the requirements concerning democratic accountability that the IMF tentatively introduced in all its programmes at that time were included in the Algerian package. In practice, even the requirements for financial accountability and transparency were quite lax during the first few years of the Algerian programme. In 1995, the newly appointed Algerian Minister of Privatisation even complained publicly that 'the rescheduling money was being used for personal enrichment by public servants'.[10] Besides the chronic corruption, the main difficulty of the Algerian restructuration programme was the bailing-out of public enterprises. When the IMF programme began, state enterprises still employed nearly one-third of the country's workforce (1.7 million workers) and were responsible for 70 per cent of the national industrial production.[11] In 1995, the Algerian government spent DA148 billion to pay the debts of the state-owned enterprises before privatising them (at a bargain price and to businessmen close to the ruling elite). These expenditures prevented the regime from balancing its books and resulted in a budget deficit of DA168 billions.[12]

In practice, the main success of the IMF programme was the deregulation of the energy sector, which was instrumental in attracting foreign investors. (Earlier on, those projects had also been jeopardised by the assassination of foreign nationals by the GIA – an assassination campaign that had obliged the oil companies to repatriate most of their foreign staff based in Algeria.)[13] The deregulation of the energy sector, coupled with the curtailing of the activities of the Islamic guerrillas near the oilfields – where the Algerian military had created a special 'exclusion zone' for Algerians in April 1995 – and the election of Zeroual to the Presidency in November 1995, persuaded the foreign companies to go ahead with their projects. As a result, in December 1995 BP signed a $3.5 billion oil-exploration contract; in January 1996, Total signed a $1.5 billion deal and, a month later, Arco signed another $1.5 billion contract.[14] These three major deals represented a total investment in the country greater than all the foreign investments in the oil and gas sector in the preceding five years. By 1996, too, the new political arrangements devised by the Algerian regime to enhance its credibility on the international scene increasingly won over international public opinion, and foreign governments thus felt freer to reschedule bilaterally their share of the Algerian public debt with less fear of public disapprobation. Between March and June 1996 Algeria's three main trading partners, the United States, France and Italy, rescheduled $4 billion of the country's debt in a series of bilateral agreements. This rescheduling of the Algerian public debt and the contracts signed with foreign oil companies finally enabled the Algerian government to balance its books and by the start of 1997 the country was even cited as an example of successful structural adjustment by the IMF.

Despite the increased access to international finance, the Algerian domestic economy and the Algerian population benefited little from this external support. In 1997 industrial production declined by 7.2 per cent and the domestic economy contracted by 1.2 per cent.[15] These poor performances were principally a consequence of the fact, that while the programme of privatisation and closure of the (labour-intensive) state industries kept the level of unemployment at a high 30 per cent nationwide, the foreign investments were concentrated in the capital-intensive oil and gas sector. At the start of 1998 the

IMF offered to prolong its programme of structural reforms (and its loans) for another year, but this proposal was rejected by an increasingly confident Algerian regime, which boasted $6 billion in foreign currency reserves. Soon, however, these reserves shrank as the government had to begin repaying its loans and as the price of oil plummeted on the international market. As the period of grace in the debt rescheduling agreement ended, the servicing ratio of the debt rose from 30 per cent at the end of 1997, to 47 per cent at the end of 1998.[16] At the same time, the fall in oil prices caused a 25 per cent shortfall in export revenues. Thus, at the end of 1998 and throughout 1999 the Algerian government had to diffuse a growing popular discontent by reviving the prospect of political changes at the top and by promising an end to political violence. This strategy was temporarily successful, but by the end of 1999 and, increasingly, in 2000, discontent grew ever stronger as the new President, Bouteflika, advanced at a snail's pace on the road to national reconciliation and to political and economic reform. By that time, however, a sharp rise in the world price of oil and the growing willingness of Algeria's Western partners to recognise the legitimacy of the regime and to support it financially permitted the Algerian government to finance new social and economic distributive programmes that eased social tensions. (Increasingly in 2001, particularly after 11 September, the willingness of the United States and the European Union to overlook the authoritarian character of the Algerian regime in order to enlist it in a global coalition against Islamic terrorism resulted in the setting-up of generous economic agreements – especially in the case of the signing of the Mediterranean partnership with the EU.)

The changing economic and political fortunes of Algeria in the recent past typify the pattern of development of a country and a regime dependent on the international community and market for its survival. Today more than ever, the fluctuations in the price of oil and gas commodities on the world market and the changing priorities of the international community constitute an endemic cause of instability for the country. Today, not only does Algeria lack the financial reserves that could cushion the more serious drops in the price of oil but also, following the restructuring programme of the IMF, the country has abandoned all ambition to develop a strong, production-oriented domestic economy. At the start of the twenty-first century, because of the continuing inability of the ruling Algerian elite to generate structural legitimacy, the country must rely on the good will and timely interventions of Western governments and international financial organisations to diffuse the recurrent risk of social upheaval linked to a reduction in its oil and gas revenues. For political and geostrategic reasons the United States and the European Union prefer to keep afloat the dubious system of governance devised by Algeria's military rulers through a system of direct and indirect (IMF and Paris Club) aid rather that pressing for genuine and thorough political and economic reforms. The endemic but moderate instability of the Algerian state, though relatively benign for the international community thus far, constitutes nonetheless a highly distressing situation for the Algerian population. This popular discontent fuels the ambition of the Islamic fundamentalists to reform (or topple) the secularist ruling elite and indirectly contributes to the overall instability of the country. Increasingly today, this domestic struggle has indirect international repercussions, as the radical transnational Islamic fundamentalist movements that have clearly designated Western finance and Western political elites as the main culprits for all the ills of the Muslim world are physically and ideologically strengthened by this state of affairs.

ALGERIA AS THE FUTURE OF DEMOCRATISATION IN THE MUSLIM WORLD

In the 1990s the Algerian regime vividly illustrated how access to the financial resources of the international system could prop up a state apparatus which had little popular support. 'New World Order' or not, the messy scramble for power that characterised the arrival of a new, self-proclaimed state leadership in Algeria by means of violence did not jeopardise the political privileges associated with the ownership of the state institutions. This ownership of the state institutions, painstakingly validated on the international scene by Algeria's ruling elite via an energetic diplomatic campaign allied to a pragmatic utilisation of the country's position as oil and gas supplier for Europe and the United States, guaranteed to the new masters of the country access to the financial, political and military facilities offered by supranational organisations. More than 30 years after the decolonisation period, an old question came once more to the fore: whether the 'international community' – read: the dominant Western powers – and an organisation like the United Nations did not promote stability at the international level at the

cost of the internal viability of some states.[17] The very similar accu-
sations aimed more recently at a financial organisation like the
International Monetary Fund – of favouring an integrated global
economy at the expense of a viable domestic economy for some
countries – are just one more addition to this debate. Clearly, in the
1990s the inability of the international community to influence
political developments in Algeria in a positive manner indicates that
there are still serious and damaging shortcomings in its present
policies and attitudes towards political and socio-economic development in the Third World, as well as a palpably poor understanding
of all the implications of its foreign policy choices.[18] Despite being
Algeria's main creditors and trading partners, Western democracies
failed to created a genuine 'New World Order' in North Africa exactly
as they failed to do so in the Gulf. In practice, they only succeeded
in encouraging the re-creation of the kind of authoritarian order that
characterised most of the Third World from the end of the colonial
era to the end of the Cold War.

This 'failure' to promote democracy (and peace and economic
stability) is attributable to three main factors that can be presented
in chronological order. First, during the democratic transition proper
(1988–91) Western democracies and international financial organisations were concentrating their political efforts and financial
resources on the democratic transitions taking place in Eastern
Europe and the Soviet Union. Furthermore, many international
players came to believe at the time that an unstoppable worldwide
movement toward democratisation had been generated by the end
of the Cold War and the collapse of the Soviet bloc. (A current of
thought most vividly illustrated in writings such as Samuel
Huntington's *The Third Wave* and Francis Fukuyama's *The End of
History*.)[19] Secondly, at the time of the putsch by the Algerian
military, there was an ideologically based resistance to action
amongst Western democracies. They viewed the Algerian democratic
transition as particularly problematical because of the involvement
of an Islamic fundamentalist movement unsympathetic to Western
ideals and Western-style liberal democracy. The Islamic fundamentalists' efforts at redefining the democratic agenda were judged
particularly pernicious by Western political elites, which came to
view Algeria as the likely starting point for the kind of 'domino
theory' scenarios imagined by Cold War theorists. This fear of an
Islamic domino effect grew during the Gulf War, when a majority
of Islamic fundamentalist movements in the region decided to

support Saddam Hussein (despite the latter's more than dubious Islamic credentials).[20] In addition, the reports of various security services made public in Europe and in the United States at the time, suggesting that the Algerian regime was trying to develop a military nuclear capability, also led Western governments (and public opinion) to consider very carefully who was to be in power in the country.[21] In these circumstances Algeria became the first casualty of a geostrategic order in which political changes were not constrained by Cold War strategic calculations to halt the spread of communism but by the constraints of a New World Order, which had as one of its main component the fear of Islamic fundamentalism.[22] Thirdly, and finally, the principal element that prevented prompt action by the international community once the Algerian civil war had begun was the technical difficulty of a direct intervention. The United Nations, and the United States in particular, had just experienced a serious setback in their humanitarian-inspired intervention in Somalia. Furthermore, for the European countries as much as for the United States, this emerging civil conflict shared too many common factors with the Lebanese civil war for Western democracies to consider seriously taking up again the role of mediator in another potentially disastrous endeavour.

In the end Western democracies chose not to intervene directly, either to 'save democracy' in Algeria or to stop this new Islamic fundamentalist 'wave'. Instead, they put the polity affected by this phenomenon in an unofficial 'quarantine'. Algeria was in effect subjected to a policy of confinement designed to minimise the security risks for Western countries and the dangers of Islamic contamination in North Africa. As the intensity of the Algerian civil conflict increased, embassies were partially shut down, visas were delivered with extreme parsimony, land borders were closed off, international flights were not longer operated by companies other than the Algerian national carrier and, for the foreign oil companies established in the Sahara, special 'exclusion zones' for Algerians were created by the army and private security companies. Only once, and very briefly, did the UN Secretary-General try to generate a momentum for a greater international involvement in the Algerian conflict. In 1997 the newly appointed Kofi Annan remarked about the Algerian civil war that, 'as the killings go on and the numbers rise, it is extremely difficult for all of us to pretend it is not happening'.[23] However, the Secretary-General soon realised that, despite the many calls by leading Algerian opposition leaders and by Western pro-democracy groups for a greater UN involvement, the members of the Security Council, and particularly France, were not particularly keen to see this conflict treated as something other than an internal Algerian affair. For their part, regional organisations like the Arab League, the Organisation of African Unity or the European Union did not have any significant leverage on the Algerian regime or did not wish to use it for fear of negative domestic or international repercussions. (The European Union eventually sent a low-key mission of inquiry in 1998, at the height of the massacres of civilians in Algeria, in order to satisfy its domestic public opinion, but this was in no way sufficient to have any effect on the authoritarian tendencies of the regime or the terrorist options of the guerrillas.)[24]

In the Muslim world the Algerian crisis constituted a real-life experiment for all those autocratic regimes confronted by public opinion and a political opposition demanding simultaneously a greater democratisation and Islamicisation of the state institutions. For these autocratic elites the Algerian experiment provided important lessons for the re-formation of authoritarian institutions supported by radical components of civil society. It also showed them how growing internal disorder and the manipulation of the democratic process could reinforce the position of the state apparatus as the sole intermediary between the citizenry and the international community. In Algeria the regime was propped up by the *de facto* embargo that was a consequence of the foreign powers' reluctance to operate inside Algeria and of their demand for greater control over the movement of the Algerian nationals, especially outside the country. The Algerian regime benefited fully from the willingness of Western democracies to provide economic and military aid to the state apparatus to prevent the spread of this internal disorder onto the international scene – in much the same way as during the Cold War Western democracies had supported those regimes which they judged were best able to deal expediently with the subversive activities of their designated enemies.[25] The financial efforts undertaken by Western creditors to ensure the financial survival of the regime was only one aspect of these foreign policy choices. The adjustment programme agreed with the IMF in 1994 permitted principally the financing of political repression and the modernisation of the security apparatus, as well as ensuring that the administration could function at the height of the Islamic insurrection. Furthermore, if the improvement in state finances had little effect on the country's domestic economy, it did permit the financial reorganisation of the state apparatus on the basis of oil revenues, thereby further insulating the regime against domestic social upheavals. Indirectly, the liberalisation of the economy repeated what older 'socialist' policies had done, namely, making the population more dependent on the state by limiting the opportunities for an independent bourgeoisie/civil society.[26] In Algeria, this (very) incomplete economic restructuring and liberalisation was able to address what had become since the mid-1980s one of the main challenges for non-democratic countries with a pseudo-socialist economic system, namely, the task of rescuing the state finances by slowing down the growth of the state apparatus, while still retaining political control.[27]

For all those regimes faced with drastic IMF-led restructuring plans, the most difficult task is to ensure that a greater degree of popular sovereignty and state accountability will make the population accept these austerity measures and the socio-economic inequalities inherent in a deregulated capitalist economy.[28] In Algeria, the very real withdrawing and reduction of the state's activities in the early stages of the Islamic insurrection facilitated the uncontrolled emergence of private entrepreneurs. As the risk of state collapse diminished, the regime encouraged the private sector to continue to assume this new economic role (together with social responsibilities) to compensate for the reduction in the state distributive networks. However, the state elite also aimed at controlling (or regaining control over) the activities of these economic actors unconnected to their redistribution networks through administrative and legalistic procedures.[29] This was clearly not done purely to facilitate an economic recovery, but in order to keep a watchful eye on the financial resources of those social groups that might mount a political challenge to the ruling elite. In addition, by selectively implementing the IMF recommendations and by regulating access to foreign capital and markets, the state elite also became a main beneficiary of the process of liberalisation.[30] These policies facilitated the emergence of a two-speed economy where the more profitable enterprises and sectors of activities were acquired by the members of the state elite (or their friends) in their capacity as private citizens, and the loss-making companies and activities were run on the cheap by the administration, or dismantled and sold to less well-connected private entrepreneurs. If this very one-sided process of liberalisation did compensate for the overall reduction in the state distributive capabilities, it predictably failed to generate growth. Because this process of economic liberalisation obeyed a political logic – i.e. to permit the state elite to transform some of its most conspicuous political privileges into less controversial economic assets – it is principally in those terms that its outcomes have to be evaluated. Thus, the partial opening of the state apparatus to elected politicians, particularly in the social and (domestic) economic fields, permitted the old ruling elite to spread the blame for the failures of liberalisation on to the opposition parties. The military elite could therefore let popular discontent focus on this political 'front', whose incapacity to cope with the socio-economic crisis added to the conviction of many Algerians that electing a government accountable to the people might in their case be irrelevant.

For regimes like Algeria's, the principal challenge in a partial re-legitimisation of the state's institutions and in the formation of a new bourgeoisie is to ensure that the state apparatus does not break down despite the reduction of its economic and repressive capabilities. The ruling elites must devise a system of legitimisation of political authority which is distinct from and less dependent on the distributive functions of the state apparatus. Thus, in the North African and Middle Eastern context, the nation-states that possess a modern state apparatus and an established ruling dynasty (Morocco, Jordan, etc.), are better placed to deal with such a reform of the state than nationalistic regimes (Algeria, Egypt, Syria, etc.), which must appeal to an increasingly challenged sense of national pride and historical legitimacy. In these neo-traditionalist monarchies the boundaries between the prerogatives of the monarch and those of the state may not be fully demarcated, but people are aware of the distinct character of each and of their areas of friction, which does provide some guarantee against over-extreme social and political reforms. (Obviously the main drawback of this situation is that acute political skills are demanded of rulers who may have little political experience and who are not, as hereditary monarchs, easily replaceable on grounds of political incompetence.) For countries like Algeria, which are directly under the control of autocrats of the military kind, the reform of the ruling elite and the re-legitimisation of the state apparatus on a non-distributive basis is necessarily more ambitious and difficult to control. In its more elaborate configuration, the (partial) reform of an authoritarian regime can produce a form of pseudo-democracy – of which the Turkish Republic is today the most successful current example. The same idea of 'democracy as façade' was also that tentatively promoted domestically and internationally by the Algerian regime in the second half of the 1990s, and quite successfully from 1999 onward. The main benefits of this system of governance are that it allows the regime to hand over apparent control of the state apparatus to an elected civilian government and to foster a relatively functional, multi-party, political environment. From the perspective of the ruling elite this façade of democracy serves to shield the military establishment from popular resentment and to limit the activities of the political opposition – particularly the Islamic fundamentalists – in a strictly regulated political arena. The main drawback of these political arrangements is that they cannot cope with even a mild political crisis. (Significantly, from the 1960s to the 1980s Turkey was the scene of a military coup every ten years or so.)

Despite the hopes raised by the Turkish regime in the early 1990s, when it was presented as a model for the democratic integration of Islamic movements into a secular republic, the limitations of this model of government quickly became apparent at the end of the decade, especially when the military evicted from power the ruling Islamic party *Refah* (judged to be implementing anti-constitutional, non-secularist policies).[31] Although this 'eviction' went smoothly in Turkey, it nonetheless illustrates the drawbacks of the system. In Turkey as elsewhere, the main problem for such a two-tiered system of political rule functioning under military supervision is not the occasional waywardness of an Islamic party, but simply the evolution of the citizenry's political opinions and voting behaviour. With these arrangements, the country's main power brokers, the military officers, must act intermittently and informally to control and redirect the changes brought forward via the multi-party system that the official institutions cannot validate on their own (because they do not possess enough political power *sui generis*).[32] Conspicuously, in Algeria, in 1999 and 2000, not only did the military have to intervene to rig the elections but it also had to intervene recurrently in the political debate to ensure that Islamic politicians with a potentially wide electoral appeal could not join forces with the legal political parties and that the authorised parties did not overstep the limits that it had imposed. In this situation, the formal institutional arrangements conceal the real informal channels of power that prevent the institutionalised political leadership from devising a programme of genuine political and constitutional reform. (They cannot do so principally because they are totally without popular legitimacy and have no authority over the security apparatus.) This state of affairs is largely responsible for the fact that many political activists cannot be enticed into participating in the official electoral process, whilst the electorate loses interest in the empty rituals of politics. Most worryingly for Algeria's Western partners, this situation convinces the electorate that it is international finance and military power that are the supporting pillars of this 'democratic' system, and it encourages the most determined amongst them to formulate their political demands directly in those terms.

EXPORTING THE *JIHAD*: THE INTERNATIONALISATION OF RADICAL ISLAMIC ACTORS

In the Algerian conflict the threat posed by radical Islamic groups on the international scene has been relatively disconnected from the ability of the Islamic guerrillas to overthrow their domestic opponents. In Europe, in the early years of the Algerian civil war, there was a *de facto* separation inside the Muslim community between those Islamic networks working for the political return of the FIS in Algeria – and, more discreetly, for the military victory of the guerrillas – and those Islamic associations wanting to Islamicise Western society and to re-Islamicise the Muslims living in the West. In France, typically, the government let the FIS sympathisers express their political demands freely and organise solidarity networks for their allies in Algeria, but they made it clear that the FIS should not fire up the religious demands of the Muslim community in France itself. This tacit agreement was endorsed by senior Islamic leaders and FIS cadres abroad; particularly Sheikh Sahraoui, who became the guarantor of this social peace and a valuable mediator for the French authorities.[33] This understanding between the various European governments and the Islamic community did not change significantly even when some FIS sympathisers tentatively turned to provisioning with weapons the guerrilla groups operating in Algeria. Between the end of 1993 and the start of 1994 several support networks operating in the European Union bought some light weaponry in the former communist countries of Eastern Europe (Croatia, Slovakia, Slovenia and the Czech Republic) and organised their shipments from French and Italian ports.[34] Almost immediately, however, their transit routes via France, Italy and Germany were dismantled by these countries' police forces and the smugglers were caught. Although several important FIS cadres were arrested and investigated in connection with this affair, most were quickly released when they agreed to work with the authorities to help to restrain the belligerent tendencies of the Muslim/Algerian community. In the summer of 1994, however, this tacit division of labour between groups working on the domestic front and those operating on the foreign scene was jeopardised when French citizens of Moroccan and Algerian origin organised a terrorist operation against European tourists in Morocco. The French police then uncovered a network of radical Islamic fundamentalists made up of French nationals of North African origin, who had been recruited among the youth of Paris' poorer suburbs and, in some cases, had received military training abroad (in Afghanistan). This discovery was extremely worrying for the French at the time, especially because the Algerian GIA had clearly signalled its intention to bring its political struggle to France.

The final blow to the tacit agreement that had prevailed between the French authorities and the Muslim community in France was the assassination of Sheikh Sahraoui on 11 July 1995. This event marked the end of the previous consensus on the desirability of keeping apart those Algerian groups trying to topple the Algerian regime from those Islamic networks trying to reform (or destroy) Western society from the inside. Then, on 25 July 1995, a bomb exploded in the Parisian underground, leaving 10 people dead and 57 wounded. It was the start of a bombing campaign that lasted nearly three months (until 7 October). Despite the small number of casualties – no one was killed in subsequent explosions – these random attacks in the underground and the railway network created havoc in France and radically transformed the attitude of the French authorities (and of the population) toward the Muslim community in general, and the Algerian and Islamic fundamentalists movements in particular. The declared aim of these GIA-sponsored bombers was to force the French government to change its foreign policy towards Algeria and to end its financial and military support for the Algerian regime.[35] The bombers failed to reach their objective as the French police dismantled what proved to be a poorly organised network of apprentice terrorists. (The police nonetheless found evidence that the operation had been financed by Rachid Ramda, an Algerian living in London who himself had a financial connection with bin Laden's al-Qaida organisation.) In France the bombing campaign had been organised by a small group of GIA sympathisers operating in three cells located in areas of Paris, Lyon and Lille. The leaders of these cells were two Algerian students, Boualem Bensaid and Ali Touchent, and a French citizen of Algerian origin, Khaled Kelkal. Apart from Kelkal's group, which was partly composed of petty criminals, the members of these cells were not listed by the police and had no previous record of this type of violent terrorist activity. Bensaid's group was composed of three French nationals recently converted to Islam and one Algerian who owned a butcher shop, whilst Touchent's group was made up of French youths of North African descent, who were part of the local Islamic associative scene.[36] These examples of 're-Islamisation' and of the radicalisation of the French youth of North African origin vividly illustrated the mechanics of the internationalisation of the Algerian conflict. In this respect, the route followed by Kelkal is very typical of this type of politico-religious metamorphosis.[37] Born in Algeria but raised in France, Kelkal suffered from a lack of social and economic integration, common in many poor suburbs of large French cities. Having turned to petty crime for a living, he was briefly sent to jail where he was 're-Islamicised' by his fundamentalist cell companion, a Muslim Brotherhood sympathiser. After his time in prison, Kelkal tried to make sense of his conversion by taking a full role in a grand Islamic project and, because of his origins, chose the struggle of the Islamic fundamentalists in Algeria. He went back to Algeria in 1993, where he contacted members of the GIA and received some military training. Back in France a year later, Kelkal promoted the GIA doctrine and organised an operative cell composed of young Muslims like himself, the sons of North African immigrants, who found in this radical Islamic vision the means to transcend the lowly social position that was theirs in French society.

The risk of political radicalisation of those members of the Muslim community living in Western democracies who feel excluded from the dominant liberal, secular and individualist system of social integration, though it is unlikely to be the spark for a mass movement that can shake a country, must nevertheless be taken very seriously in view of the recent increase in the capacity for destruction of transnational terrorism. From the 1995 bombing campaign in France to the far more dramatic events of September 2001 in the United States, the dangers of revived religious and political confrontations as well as the more straightforward domestic security risks for Western democracies that result from this identification of a part of the citizenry with supranational Islamic ideologies and causes are directly linked to the conditions of political opposition in the

Muslim world. This does not mean, however, that the links between armed Islamic movements fighting for state power in a specific country and in radical transnational Islamic groups are at the root of the problem (or even a good indicator of what the problem is). Indeed, the kind of informal separation of nationalistic and transnational Islamic causes that prevailed in France before and, more ambiguously, after 1995 is often evident today in the Muslim communities of Western democracies. Revealingly, none of the ten country-specific terrorist organisations linked to al-Qaida – including the Algerian GIA and GSPC – which the Bush administration quickly blacklisted after 11 September, played any significant part in the hijacking operation. In fact, most of the hijackers were Saudi nationals who did not belong to any such national-based armed Islamic movement. Furthermore, if subsequent investigations did reveal that several Algerians, Franco-Algerians and French citizens of North African origin were indeed likely to have been involved in the al-Qaida operation, these persons were not members of the GIA or the GSPC. In particular, Zacarias Moussaoui, a French citizen of Moroccan origin whom the US investigators presented as one of the hijackers who was unable to get on the plane, appeared to have been recruited by al-Qaida members without the mediation of any North African militant Islamic group.[38] (A week after the attacks in New York and Washington, the French justice department also revealed that a French customs officer had taken flying lessons in the United States in one of the flying schools in Florida that had been utilised by several of the hijackers, and that these lessons had been paid for by one of bin Laden's brothers, Yeslam. A few days later, Lofti Raissi, an Algerian pilot living in the UK, was also accused by the British police of having been one of the instructors of several of the members of the commando that hijacked the planes. But again, none of them were members of the Algerian armed Islamic groups.)[39]

In the end, the efforts of the EU countries to dismantle the Algerian Islamic networks in Europe, which were most successful in Italy and in Spain, only revealed that these groups were principally engaged in organising logistical support for the Islamic guerrillas in Algeria, especially the fabrication of false documents. Although the Italian and Spanish cells of the GSPC had clear financial connections with the al-Qaida organisation and they served as contacts for those Muslims wanting to receive military training in Afghanistan, their participation in the grand scheme of al-Qaida to destabilise the United States was at best incidental.[40]

What emerges from the series of events of the last few years is that conflicts in the Muslim world in which Western democracies are directly or indirectly involved can easily focus the hatred of a part of the Muslim community living in the West, and particularly the youth. However, there are strong indications that those persons recruited to undertake violent actions against Western democracies are not the same as those recruited in nationalistic Islamic movements. While the latter are generally personally touched by an existing conflict and have clear and practical objectives in sight, the former only associate themselves to these causes via an ideology and they have rather vague (if ambitious) expectations of change. For Western democracies it would be counterproductive to link their own fight against international terrorism – especially when this only includes violence against Western democracies – with the numerous country-specific struggles involving armed Islamic movements throughout the world. In practice, if the boundaries of the communities that have a stake in a specific national struggle – Algeria, Palestine, Kashmir, etc. – can be easily defined and potential troublemakers blocked by preventive coercive action, the identity of the terrorists who have been implicated in the attacks in France and the United States shows that the main security threat for the Western democracies comes from a much wider pool of people. Not only is this pool of potential terrorists not easily identifiable (and eliminable), but the wide-ranging and often indiscriminate security measures designed to repress the activities of country-specific Islamic movements can themselves lead to the radicalisation of a greater number of Islamic sympathisers. In this context – paradoxical as it may sound – the more the security drive orchestrated by the United States and the European countries is successful in eliminating those easily identifiable targets that are the Western-based Islamic networks supporting armed insurrections in the Muslim world, the more those transnational Islamic networks who do not recruit on the basis of country-specific struggles will become the main outlet for radical political Islam.

8 Conclusion: Learning and Unlearning to be Democratic

The Algerian democratic transition and civil conflict vividly illustrates several of the most intractable dilemmas of political transitions involving autocratic regimes, Islamic fundamentalist movements and fragmented civil societies. When in 1988, under the pressure of the street, the Algerian regime attempted to solve the country's socio-economic crisis by proposing a programme of political liberalisation, it started up one of the very first genuine democratic transitions of the contemporary Middle East and North Africa. Unfortunately, this original effort at creating a new consensus on governance and at redefining the relationship between state and society quickly ran into trouble. If this political liberalisation permitted the Algerian citizens to rediscover their own decision-making powers, it did not contribute to resolving the very practical socio-economic and political problems that the departing elite had been unable to solve. On the contrary, democratisation aggravated the social tensions and the opposition between rulers and ruled. When the citizens were forced to make precise political choices on their own and to define explicitly social and religious boundaries, the existing consensus on what being Algerian or Muslim meant – or what a legitimate state was – foundered. This lethal side effect of the process of democratisation that plagues all political transitions is best summarised by Alexis de Tocqueville's well-known remark that 'the most dangerous moment for a bad government, is usually when it begins to reform itself'.[1] In this respect, the most damaging aspect of the open-ended process of democratic reform launched by the Algerian President in 1988 was that this redistribution of political authority, which did indeed favour the swift empowerment of many individuals and social groups that were previously excluded from the political debate, was not accompanied by an improved understanding of the mechanisms permitting political pluralism to function effectively.[2]

In the aftermath of the national riots of October 1988, the new political assertiveness of the Algerian populace produced a highly voluntarist and minimally self-reflective process of institutional reform. After two decades of political and socio-economic inertia, the sudden rise in conflicting demands for rapid and thorough institutional changes helped to create a climate of social and political instability. Many political actors, inside the regime or from the opposition, and the citizens themselves did try hard (at times) to make the democratic transition succeed. Unfortunately, their poor understanding of exactly what this process was meant to achieve, as well as their very limited knowledge of the political mechanisms at work, meant that they repeatedly did more harm than good. Without seeking to diminish the responsibilities of each group of actors for this failure of the democratic transition, one must realise how much these outcomes were the unintended consequences of each sides strategies. Much more than the disreputableness of some of the political players involved, the quarrelsomeness of many ordinary Algerians, or the misfortunes and external contingencies that befell the country at that time, it was this lack of clear understanding of what could be achieved and of the means to do so that were crucial in this dramatic failure of democracy.

With the benefit of hindsight we can see that the Algerian political class, the Algerian people and even the international community, all played a part in creating and maintaining the current Algerian imbroglio; each more or less consciously, each more or less willingly. At a more general level, the principal problem for the international community – in its ambitious sense of a community of nations – is that it must endeavour to build a free and fair system of international relationships with member-states that do not consistently share these normative precepts. If political theorists and international-relations specialists are more or less in agreement that there are, in theory, no insurmountable obstacles to the transformation of an 'anarchic' international order into a civilised international community, they also point out that there are serious *practical* obstacles to achieving this.[3] The practical problems that impeded the efforts of the international community – read: the group of rich Western democracies which are Algeria's main creditors and trading partners – in this North African context stemmed principally from the fact that the process of democratisation was accompanied by a process of 'Islamicisation'. Western democracies had to make a difficult compromise between their short-term economic and domestic political objectives and the long-term developmental needs of liberal democracy in a Muslim polity. In this case their foreign policy choices were far more influenced by the demand for easy access to oil and gas resources, the ambition to regulate north–south migratory movements and the prospects of having a Western-friendly regime on Europe's southern flank than by the moral and political imperative to let people decide for themselves how they should be governed. This strategic positioning by Western countries sharpened the dilemmas over the practical requirements of democracy in Algeria, particularly the means through which the Algerian electorate was supposed to acquire its new democratic skills. During both the democratic transition and the civil war the behaviour of the Algerian population repeatedly reminded home-grown and foreign liberals and democrats that to strive for political tolerance, prudence and moderation is not necessarily the main pre-occupations of citizens confronted by harsh socio-economic conditions and political repression.[4] The social and political choices of the Algerian citizens showed that, without the proper set of formal and informal socio-political institutions, civil society was unlikely to devise on its own a working political order that resembles the one currently prevailing in Western democracies. However, these failings in collective action remain the responsibility of the Algerian domestic political class far more than that of the international community or of Algerian citizens. Ultimately, it is domestic politicians who bear the crucial responsibility for building the kind of effective institutional system that permits the electorate to produce informed and meaningful political choices.

Causally and historically, one of the main obstacles to the formation of a functional democratic political order in Algeria has been, is and will remain for some time to come, the lack of organic connection between the citizenry and the institutions of the state. The best opportunity for establishing such a connection on a democratic basis, as well as the most conspicuous failure of political dialogue, was the 1989–91 democratic transition. At that time, plainly, the technical skills of the political elite were more at fault than the substance of the reforms proposed. Because the political reforms which were implemented leaned excessively towards one political movement – that of Islamic fundamentalism – they polarised civil society and reawakened the fears and personal ambitions of the military-conservative elite. Having failed to create a consensus on democratic governance, the political transition unwittingly facilitated the (re-)establishment of dysfunctional and unrepresentative political institutions under military supervision. For the state elite, whether under the reformers (1988–91) or under the conservatives (1992–), the deeper cause of this inability to produce effective reforms is simply its failure to appear as a credible embodiment of the aspirations of the citizenry. After several decades of one-party rule and, today, after ten years of a state of emergency, the ruling elite is simply too used to a system that buys social peace with political repression and economic redistribution to perform well in a competitive electoral system. This lack of political credibility and electoral competitiveness is at the heart of the failure to democratise and liberalise the Algerian polity. Furthermore, in Algeria, as in most countries of the Middle East and North Africa, the Islamic fundamentalists relied on the pervasive Islamic self-help networks to make sure that they were better attuned to popular demands than the state elite and the democrats. Unfortunately, the Islamic fundamentalists' very limited political experience at state level led them to underestimate the political and military dangers that threatened the democratic transition. In Algeria the FIS did not take the necessary action to assuage the fears or moderate the ambitions of those actors who had the capacity to halt this political process. Thus, in as much as the state elite failed to acquire a sufficient amount of popular recognition and acceptance for the governance skills it had already acquired in running the country, the Islamic fundamentalists failed to transform their formidable popular support into an institutionalised political force. (As for the liberal-democratic parties, they remain numerically and politically far behind these two contenders for state power, principally because of their historically shallow political roots in the region. Furthermore, they have made very few gains over the years because they are repeatedly caught up between a state elite that utilises political patronage to obtain the compliance of the more traditional segments of the Algerian population, and Islamic movements that take advantage of the effective social work of the ('apolitical') Islamic self-help network to win the favour of the urban poor and the lower middle-classes.)

Between 1992 and 2002 these failings on the part of the Algerian political class have not only been instrumental in transforming the Algerian democratic transition into a vicious civil conflict, but they are also responsible for maintaining the country in its current situation. The Islamic fundamentalists have repeatedly failed to negotiate an entry with the Algerian state elite and the international community into the legitimate political system. Furthermore, they have seen their public image seriously tarnished by the actions of the Islamic guerrillas and are no nearer to being accepted as credible and experienced political representatives nationally or internationally than they were ten years ago. For the Algerian Islamic fundamentalists, as for any Sunni Islamic fundamentalist movement, the most important cause of failure is their endemic organisational frailty. Unlike Shi'ite Islam, which is organised by a well-defined clergy, Sunni Islam does not possess any clear religious hierarchy. What the FIS did quite successfully in Algeria between 1989 and 1991 was to federate the country's various Islamic tendencies around an Islamic leadership validated by a political system of representation. Inside the Islamic movement, particularly for the more radical players, the FIS leadership was able to impose its arguments concerning the Islamicisation of society using a pragmatic rhetoric: democratisation favours Islamicisation, thus political democracy is desirable. From a theological point of view, however, they did not, and could not, either fully endorse liberal democracy or completely disavow (armed) *jihad* as an inappropriate form of religious expression. The FIS leaders did not impose a theologically based code of political conduct because they lacked the religious authority to create a consensus on 'proper' Islamic practices. At best they subjected the need for political democracy and the pertinence of *jihad* to the practical requirements of government. (Thus, Ali Belhadj, the main ideologue of the FIS, could profess simultaneously that any Muslim had 'the right' to refuse the positive laws of the state and 'to launch on any occasion a war against them because they represent the official facade of the *Jahiliyya*', and indicate by his own political conduct that for their own good, and for the greater glory of God, people were best advised not to exercise their right to rebel but to exercise their right to vote instead.)[5] The main drawback of the FIS's pragmatic approach was that, once its leaders were confronted with a closing down of political activity, they lost their leverage over other Islamic activists. When the political organisation of the FIS collapsed in 1992 in the face of military repression, the means to obtain a consensus on non-violent, Islamic political movements were destroyed. This political closure remains, ten years later, the main obstacle to the formation of a cohesive Islamic current that could ensure the return to a more moderate form of political Islam based on electoral consultation. Today, in Algeria, as in the rest of the Middle East and North Africa, the lack of access to government power for opposition parties ensures that no Islamic actor can build a strong political movement that places the requirements of political democracy above the possibility of (armed) *jihad*.

In Algeria the implosion of the Islamic movement was undoubtedly welcomed by the state elite and secular politicians, but this episode did little to rehabilitate their own political organisations in the eyes of the citizenry. After the 1992 coup conservatives proved themselves no better than reformers at producing an organisation that could engage with the electorate and convince people to support their policies or vote for them in free and fair electoral contests. The FLN and its pro-governmental successors have been unable and/or unwilling to abandon the old socialist organisational model of political and economic patronage that views politics as a zero-sum game. Unlike the Islamic fundamentalists, they have not considered very seriously the role that the citizens must play in actively creating and sustaining a (democratic) political order and, therefore, they have not produced any convincing effort at civic education. Today, as before the democratic transition, the Algerian regime rejects from the start the possibility that the population may rightly and properly disagree with its policies. Consequently, the possibility of transforming popular opposition into constructive criticisms and activities is pre-empted. This autocratic political style undermines the state elite's own attempts to utilise the institutional resources of the state to 'reform' the citizenry and to teach people the secular and republican values that might constitute an alternative to Islamic fundamentalism. As the Prime Minister in power at the time of the coup d'état, Sid Ahmed Ghozali, remarked on the occasion of the tenth anniversary of the coup:

> Until now, we have not proposed to the Algerians any alternative to the FIS and the regime. The rift between the state and the citizens has grown ever larger. The citizens do not make any distinction between the state, the regime and the parties. In their eyes, they are all worthless. As long as we ask people to choose between the plague and the cholera, 75% of Algerians will not vote. And the remaining 25% will vote for the FIS or its look-alikes, as with these people there is no abstention and mobilisation is always maximal. We are therefore in an extremely unfair situation where an Algerian society not in tune with the Islamic fundamentalists theses, would bring to power, if it had the opportunity, an Islamic fundamentalist government.[6]

Ghozali concluded that, in these circumstances, it would be better not to have any elections at all rather than to keep rigging them until the electorate makes the 'right' choice on its own. The members of the Algerian state elite currently in power may have a better appreciation of the domestic and international rewards to be gained by this cosmetic exercise but, by their tactical choices, they clearly indicate that they share Ghozali's mistrust of the Algerian electorate. As time passes, this mutual distrust between the regime and the population can only become more entrenched and can only increasingly impede the initiation of a more heuristic approach to political education and compromise. Hence, in as much as the challenge for the Islamic fundamentalists is to find the political means to overcome the absence of a religious hierarchy, the challenge for the ruling elite is to find the means to remain a recognised political force without direct access to, and support from, the state institutions.

Today, very few rays of hope enliven the situation of the Algerian polity. The prospects for genuine political reforms in Algeria are far less promising than they were at the end of the 1980s. In the absence of a heaven-sent leader who would have the strength and genius to reform the regime single-handedly from within, the best chance of restoring social and political peace in the country must come from a patient recolonisation of the state apparatus by democrats and moderate Islamic actors. The most likely group of democratic activists to form the basis for such a transformation comes from the Kabyle community. In the Kabyle region pro-democracy parties like the FFS (and more dubiously the RCD) and social movements like the association of tribal/village councils (*aarch*) have managed to create and sustain a meaningful political debate and a strong civic spirit within the community. Despite the civil war and the political intrigues of the regime, these social and political actors have maintained, regionally, the kind of organic connection between rulers and ruled that the state and the legal opposition parties have failed to create or sustain at the national level. However, the social and political achievements of the Kabyle community must be disseminated throughout the political system and among the non-Kabyle populations in order to become truly significant. Only such an expansion can transform this liberal-democratic current into a serious complement and counterweight to the ideas and practices of both the state elite and political Islam. To succeed, this endeavour will require first that the reformers inside the regime and the pro-democracy parties overcome their petty squabbles and form productive alliances with the predominantly Kabyle parties. In addition, such a democratic alliance, if it becomes reality, cannot succeed without at the very least the indirect support of the main political force in the polity: the Islamic fundamentalists. These Islamic activists remain necessary political players because they are extremely apt at engaging people in a political debate at the micro-social level.

It may be true that for the Islamic fundamentalists, whatever the wishes of the masses might be, the citizens' best interest is to be found in a fuller implementation of the religious order set forth in the Holy Scriptures. However, the patient social dialogue that the grassroots Islamic associations have generated to convince the citizens that this is indeed the case has done much more to develop among them the skills of participative democracy than any governmental policy. This capacity for promoting political deliberation has not been dented by the failure of the Islamic guerrillas to score a decisive military victory – quite the contrary. The failure of the militaristic option has strengthened the case for a strictly electoralist political strategy among the cadres and leaders of the movement. Because of their political weight, however, these moderate Islamic actors are given very little room for manoeuvre by a regime that has become extremely risk-adverse. Consequently, the process of normalisation of relations between the Islamic fundamentalists and the state elite is fraught with dangers. Well-established Islamic leaders and movements can easily squander their legitimacy capital in pursuing sterile compromises with reluctant and self-interested governmental intermediaries – as has been the case with the party led by Nannah. Furthermore, a purely formal political rapprochement between the Islamic fundamentalists and the state elite is unlikely to permit any reduction in the violent opposition between state and society if it is not quickly followed by concrete changes. (The evolution of the security situation after the 1999 general amnesty illustrates this point perfectly.) Only if moderate Islamic leaders can maintain a trajectory in high politics that avoids violence and the treacheries of the regimes with sufficient consistency – and if they receive some domestic and international encouragement for doing so – will the Islamic movement succeed in introducing into national politics the kind of popular social dialogue that it established in a local context. In a best-case scenario such a dialogue will take several years to take root.

The role of, and role for, the demos remain at the core of the Algerian state's current predicament. In this polity, as in most non-democratic countries, the difficulty in building a working consensus on legitimate government stems from the fact that the institutions of the state participates only minimally in the formation of the political consciousness of its citizenry. If democratic practices are principally conceived in terms of the didactic relationship established between the citizens (with their more-or-less coherent demands) and the political elite (with its more or less appropriate governance skills), then the political usefulness of Algeria's tentative democratic transition will have largely been squandered.[7] Today the Algerian regime has no way of knowing at all precisely what the population can devise by itself and for itself as an appropriate form of social and political order, and how to deal meaningfully with it. On the other hand, the citizens can only learn to formulate coherent political views with extreme difficulty, because of the lack of political structures honestly designed to this end. In Algeria, as in most countries of the Middle East and North Africa, this dual inability to understand and regulate political change is principally attributable to the fact that the institutional system is not designed to provide accurate information about, and to, the population. This lack of genuine institutionalised political representation ensures that the population is unlikely to learn any more about liberal-democratic practices than it already knows, and it may even forget this. (Indeed, an average Algerian knows much more today about guerrilla warfare, counter-insurgency methods, electoral manipulation, state corruption, and political and religious intolerance than they know about the means, ends and rationale of liberal democracy.) In this context, the repeated failure and the continuing inadequacy of domestic and international efforts at producing a genuine, institutionalised political dialogue between rulers and ruled ensure the continuing relevance in this country (as in the rest of the region) of autocratic methods of governance and violent forms of civil disobedience.

The tragic evolution of Algerian democratic transition and civil conflict vividly showed that the demos is a political entity indissociable from the social and political practices deployed to act upon it. Politicians worldwide can be expert users of the maxim 'do as I say, not as I do', but without a clear correspondence between their own actions and the response they expect from the population at large, it is unlikely that the current illiberal and violent tendencies that permeate any society – be it Algerian or European, Muslim or Christian – will ever crystallise into something akin to a functional liberal democratic system.[8] In particular, any liberal notion about 'good governance' developed by Western democracies has very little chance of permeating into the Algerian demos if no one is there to make a case for it at the ground level.[9] In the present circumstances the reckless misuse of democratic rituals by the Algerian regime is extremely detrimental, since it not only frustrates civil society's ability to reform the state but also increasingly prevents people from developing fair, tolerant and democratic political practices. (In this respect Western democracies' repeated endorsements of rigged electoral processes do very little to convince any intelligent citizen of the true 'virtues' of democracy and of democratic parties.) In such a context, it will be extremely difficult to restore confidence and effectiveness in the Algerian political system and to permit the active participation of the demos, not in undermining the state system as happens today, but in cooperating with it. The political choices that the polity will make in the future will reflect what people have learnt, individually and collectively, during a decade of civil conflict and years of autocratic rule in democratic disguise. As things now stand, it seems to me that the process of unlearning the unpalatable social and political skills that the Algerian citizens have recently acquired will demand intervention by thoughtful and dedicated social educators that only a new generation of (domestic and foreign) political activists will be able to foster. In the meantime, democratic regression and the entrenchment of authoritarianism are bound to be the lot of Algeria and the shape of things to come in this region of the world.

Notes

1 UNDERSTANDING POLITICAL DEMOCRATISATION AT THE BEGINNING OF
   THE TWENTY-FIRST CENTURY

1. John Dunn, 'Responsibility without power: states and the incoherence of the modern conception of the political good', in *Interpreting Political Responsibility* (Cambridge: Polity Press, 1990).
2. See Dale F. Eickelman and James Piscatori, *Muslim Politics* (Princeton: Princeton University Press, 1996).
3. Samuel P. Huntington, *The Clash of Civilisations and the Remaking of the World Order* (New York: Simon and Schuster, 1996).
4. See Bernard Yack, *The Longing for Total Revolution: Philosophical Sources of Social Discontent from Rousseau to Marx* (Princeton: Princeton University Press, 1985); John Dunn, 'Revolution', in T. Ball, J. Farr and R. Hanson (eds), *Political Innovation and Conceptual Change* (Cambridge: Cambridge University Press, 1989).
5. See Forrest D. Colburn, *The Vogue of Revolutions in Poor Countries* (Princeton: Princeton University Press, 1994); John Dunn, *Modern Revolutions* (Cambridge: Cambridge University Press, 1989).
6. Guillermo O'Donnell, Phillipe Schmitter and Lawrence Whitehead, *Transitions from Authoritarian Rule: Prospects for Democracy*, 3 vols (Baltimore: Johns Hopkins University Press, 1986). A noteworthy early work is Dankwart Rustow's 'Transitions to democracy: toward a dynamic model', *Comparative Politics*, 2 (3), 1970.
7. John Esposito and John Voll, *Islam and Democracy* (Oxford: Oxford University Press, 1996).
8. Francis Fukuyama, *The End of History and the Last Man* (New York: Free Press, 1992).
9. On polite civil societies see particularly Edward Shils, 'The virtue of civil society', *Government and Opposition*, 26 (1), 1991; Jean L. Cohen and Andrew Arato, *Civil Society and Political Theory* (Cambridge MA: MIT Press, 1992).
10. Guillermo O'Donnell, 'Illusions about consolidation', in L. Diamond, M. Plattner, Y. Chu and H. Tien (eds), *Consolidating the Third Wave Democracies* (Baltimore: Johns Hopkins University Press, 1997), p. 45.
11. Adam Przeworski, *Democracy and the Market: Political and Economic Reforms in Eastern Europe and Latin America* (Cambridge: Cambridge University Press, 1991); 'Minimalist conception of democracy: a defence', in I. Shapiro and C. Hacker-Cordon (eds), *Democracy's Value* (Cambridge: Cambridge University Press, 1999).
12. See Michael Taylor, 'When rationality fails', in J. Friedman (ed.), *The Rational Choice Controversy: Economic Models of Politics Reconsidered* (New Haven: Yale University Press, 1996); 'Structure, culture and action in the explanation of social change', *Politics and Society*, 17, 1989; 'Rationality and revolutionary collective action', in M. Taylor (ed.), *Rationality and Revolution* (Cambridge: Cambridge University Press, 1988).
13. Phillipe Schmitter, 'Interest systems and the consolidation of democracies', in L. Diamond and G. Marks (eds), *Reexamining Democracy: Essays in Honour of Seymour Martin Lipset* (London: Sage, 1992), p. 158.
14. Samuel P. Huntington, *Political Order in Changing Societies* (New Haven: Yale University Press, 1968); Theda Skocpol, *States and Social Revolutions* (Cambridge: Cambridge University Press, 1979). More recently, see Jack A. Goldstone, *Revolution and Rebellion in the Early Modern World* (Berkeley: University of California Press, 1991); Timothy P. Wickham-Crowley, *Guerrillas and Revolution in Latin America: A Comparative Study of Insurgents and Regimes since 1956* (Princeton: Princeton

University Press, 1992); Philip G. Roeder, *Red Sunset: The Failure of the Soviet Union* (Princeton: Princeton University Press, 1993); Michael Bratton and Nicholas van de Walle, *Democratic Experiments in Africa: Regime Transitions in Comparative Perspective* (Cambridge: Cambridge University Press, 1997).

15. See John Dunn, 'Practising history and social science on "realist" assumptions', in *Political Obligation in its Historical Context* (Cambridge: Cambridge University Press, 1980).

16. Colburn, *The Vogue of Revolutions in Poor Countries.*

17. The best overall picture of Algeria is given in John Ruedy, *Modern Algeria: The Origins and Development of a Nation* (Bloomington: Indiana University Press, 1992). Concerning the Islamic movement, see particularly François Burgat, *L'Islamisme au Maghreb* (Paris: Karthala, 1988). About the military see William Zartman, 'The military in the politics of succession: Algeria', in J.W. Harbeson (ed.), *The Military in African Politics* (New York: Praeger, 1987). Finally, for an appraisal of 'Algerian socialism', see Mahfoud Bennoune, *The Making of Contemporary Algeria, 1830–1987: Colonial Upheavals and Post-Independence Development* (Cambridge: Cambridge University Press, 1988).

18. See Theda Skocpol, 'Rentier state and Shi'a Islam in the Iranian revolution', *Theory and Society*, 11 (3), 1982; Jack A. Goldstone, 'Predicting revolutions: why we could (and should) have foreseen the revolutions of 1989–1991 in the USSR and Eastern Europe', *Contention*, 2 (2), 1993.

19. Antonio Gramsci, *Selections from the Prison Notebooks*, ed. and tr. Q. Hoare and G.N. Smith (London: Lawrence and Wishart, 1971); Louis Althusser, 'Ideology and ideological states apparatuses', in *Lenin and Philosophy, and other essays*, tr. B. Brewster (London: New Left Books, 1971).

20. Ernest Gellner, *Conditions of Liberty: Civil Society and its Rivals* (London: Hamish Hamilton, 1994); Huntington, *The Clash of Civilisations.*

21. See the contributors to Augustus Richard Norton's *Civil Society in the Middle East*, 2 vols (Leiden: E.J. Brill, 1995), and compare Frédéric Volpi, 'Language, practices and the formation of a transnational liberal-democratic ethos', *Global Society*, 16 (1), 2002.

22. Guillermo O'Donnell and Phillipe Schmitter, 'Tentative conclusions about uncertain democracies', in O'Donnell, Schmitter and Whitehead, *Transitions from Authoritarian Rule.*

23. See Frédéric Volpi, 'Democratisation and its enemies: The Algerian transition to authoritarianism 1988–2001', in Robin Luckham and Gavin Cawthra (eds), *Governing Security: Democratic Control of Military and Security Establishments in Transitional Democracies* (London: Zed Books, 2003).

24. Carl Schmitt, *The Concept of the Political*, tr. G. Schwab (Chicago: University of Chicago Press, 1996).

25. Gilles Kepel, *Jihad: Expansion et Déclin de l'Islamisme* (Paris: Gallimard, 2000).

26. See Fawaz A. Gerges, *America and Political Islam: Clash of Cultures or Clash of Interests?* (Cambridge: Cambridge University Press, 1999); Vladimir Tismaneanu, *Fantasies of Salvation: Democracy, Nationalism, and Myth in Post-Communist Europe* (Princeton: Princeton University Press, 1998); John Esposito, *The Islamic Threat: Myth or Reality* (Oxford: Oxford University Press, 1992).

27. See Raymond Geuss, *The Idea of a Critical Theory* (Cambridge: Cambridge University Press, 1981).

28. See Pierre Bourdieu, *Outline of a Theory of Practice*, tr. R. Nice (Cambridge: Cambridge University Press, 1977).

29. Pierre Bourdieu, 'Political representation: elements for a theory of the political field', tr. G. Raymond and M. Adamson, in J.B Thompson (ed.), *Pierre Bourdieu: Language and Symbolic Power* (Oxford: Polity Press, 1991); Max Weber, *Economy and Society*, ed. G. Roth and C. Wittich (New York: Bedminter Press, 1968), especially chapters 11 and 14.

30. O'Donnell and Schmitter, 'Tentative conclusions', p. 5.
31. About the strategic utilisation of the Shi'ite symbolic imagery by Khomeini and the clergy see, Yan Richard, *Shi'ite Islam: Polity, Ideology and Creed*, tr. A. Nevill (Oxford: Blackwell, 1995); Mansoor Moaddel, 'Ideology as episodic discourse: the case of the Iranian revolution', *American Sociology Review* 57, 1992; Gene Burns, 'Ideology, Culture, and Ambiguity: The Revolutionary Process in Iran', *Theory and Society*, 25 (3), 1996; Charles Kurzman, 'Structural opportunity and perceived opportunity in social movement theory: the Iranian Revolution of 1979', *American Sociological Review*, 61 (1), 1996.
32. See Esposito and Voll, *Islam and Democracy*.
33. See Emmanuel Sivan, 'Arabs and democracy: Illusions of change', *Journal of Democracy* 11, July 2000; Nazih N. Ayubi, *Over-Stating the Arab State: Politics and Society in the Middle East* (London: I.B. Tauris, 1995); Sami Zubaida, *Islam, the People and the State: Essays on Political Ideas and Movements in the Middle East* (London: Routledge, 1989).
34. Robert D. Putnam, *Making Democracy Works: Civic Traditions in Modern Italy* (Princeton: Princeton University Press, 1993).
35. See Eickelman and Piscatori, *Muslim Politics*.
36. Samuel P. Huntington, *The Third Wave: Democratization in the Late Twentieth Century* (Norman: University of Oklahoma Press, 1991); David Armstrong, *Revolution and World Order: The Revolutionary State in International Society* (Oxford: Clarendon Press, 1993); and compare Huntington, *The Clash of Civilisations*.
37. On the Gulf War see James Piscatori, 'Religion and realpolitik: Islamic responses to the Gulf War', in J. Piscatori (ed.), *Islamic Fundamentalisms and the Gulf Crisis* (Chicago: The American Academy of Arts and Sciences, 1991).
38. See United States Department of State, '2001 report on foreign terrorist organisations' (Washington, October 2001).
39. Kepel, *Jihad*.
40. For critical responses to Kepel's suggestions, see Francois Burgat, 'De l'islamisme au postislamisme, vie et mort d'un concept' and Olivier Roy, 'Les islamologues ont-ils inventés l'islamisme', both in *Esprit*, No. 277, August–September 2001.
41. See Andrew Linklater, *The Transformation of Political Community: Ethical Foundations of the post-Westphalian Era* (Cambridge: Polity Press, 1998).
42. Concerning the negative consequences of 'anti-terrorist' policies for human rights, see Amnesty International, 'United Nations General Assembly, 56th session 2001, draft comprehensive convention on international terrorism: a threat to human rights standards' (London, October 2001).
43. See *Le Monde*, 26 September 2001; *Le Monde*, 10 October 2001.
44. See Claire Spencer, 'Algeria: France's Disarray and Europe's Conundrum', in B.A. Roberson (ed.), *The Middle East and Europe: The Power Deficit* (London: Routledge, 1998).
45. See Sivan, 'Arabs and democracy'.
46. Larry Diamond, 'Is Pakistan the (reverse) wave of the future?' *Journal of Democracy*, 11, July 2000.
47. Alexis de Tocqueville, *Democracy in America*, part II, tr. G. Lawrence (Chicago: Encyclopaedia Britannica, 1990), p. 281.

2   POLITICAL IDEAS AND PRACTICES IN HISTORICAL PERSPECTIVE

1. See Nazih N. Ayubi, *Over-Stating the Arab State: Politics and Society in the Middle East* (London: I.B. Tauris, 1995); Joel S. Migdal, *Strong Societies and Weak States: State–Society Relations and State Capabilities in the Third World* (Princeton: Princeton University Press, 1988).

2. See John P. Entelis, 'State–society relations: Algeria as a case study', in M. Tessler, J. Nachtwey and A. Banda (eds), *Area Studies and Social Sciences: Strategies for Understanding Middle East Politics* (Bloomington: Indiana University Press, 1999).

3. See John Ruedy, *Modern Algeria: The Origins and Development of a Nation* (Bloomington: Indiana University Press, 1992); David Prochaska, *Making Algeria French: Colonialism in Bône 1870–1920* (Cambridge: Cambridge University Press, 1990).

4. As Bernard Lewis pointed out, these two types of allegiance were only locked together in the nineteenth century, as part of a strategic manoeuvre by the Ottoman Sultan to counter the expansion of Western powers. Bernard Lewis, *The Political Language of Islam* (Chicago: University of Chicago Press, 1988).

5. See Jacques Berque, *French North Africa: The Maghrib Between Two World Wars*, tr. J. Stewart (London: Faber and Faber, 1967); Philip Khoury, *Syria and the French Mandate: The Politics of Arab Nationalism 1920–1945* (London: I.B. Tauris, 1987); Elie Kedourie, *England and the Middle East: The Destruction of the Ottoman Empire 1914–1921* (Boulder: Westview Press, 1987).

6. Alexis de Tocqueville, 'Travail sur l'Algérie' (1841), in Alexis de Tocqueville, *Oeuvres Complètes*, tome 1, ed. A. Jardin (Paris: Gallimard, 1991), p. 696.

7. In a liberal spirit Tocqueville added: 'it is not in the path of our European civilisation that we must hasten them today, but in the path of their own civilisation ... Let us not force the indigenous people into our schools but let us help them rebuild their own schools, increase the number of their teachers, train judges and men of religion who are as necessary to the Islamic civilisation as they are to our own.' Alexis de Tocqueville, 'Rapport sur l'Algérie' (1847), in *Oeuvres Complètes*, tome 1, pp. 815–16.

8. See Elie Kedourie, *Politics in the Middle East* (Oxford: Oxford University Press, 1992); Albert Hourani, *The Emergence of Modern Middle East* (Berkeley: University of California Press, 1981).

9. Even colonialist latecomers such as the Italian fascist regime still hoped in the 1930s that the political, economic, cultural and military achievements of Italy would awake in the Libyan population 'the consciousness and dignity of a Mediterranean people'. Libya's governor, Italo Balbo, demanded, therefore, that the Italian colonial administration copy the policies implemented by the French in neighbouring Algeria. See Claudio G. Segre, *Italo Balbo: A Fascist Life* (Berkeley: University of California Press, 1987), p. 323.

10. Edward W. Said, *Orientalism* (London: Routledge and Kegan Paul, 1978).

11. About Algeria see, particularly, Charles-Robert Agéron, *Les Algériens Musulmans et la France 1871–1919*, 2 vols (Paris: PUF, 1968); *Du Mythe Kabyle aux Politiques Berbères* (Paris: Bourgeois, 1976).

12. Berque, *French North Africa*. See also Julia A. Clancy-Smith, *Rebel and Saint: Muslim Notables, Populist Protests, Colonial Encounters (Algeria and Tunisia, 1800–1904)* (Berkeley: University of California Press, 1994).

13. Frantz Fanon, *Studies in a Dying Colonialism*, tr. H. Chevalier (New York: Monthly Review Press, 1965); *The Wretched of the Earth*, tr. C. Farrington (London: MacGibbon & Kee, 1965).

14. See Nazih N. Ayubi, *Over-Stating the Arab State: Politics and Society in the Middle East* (London: I.B. Tauris, 1995).

15. See William Zartman, 'The military in the politics of succession: Algeria', in J.W. Harbeson (ed.) *The Military in African Politics* (New York: Praeger, 1987).

16. For an appraisal of 'Algerian socialism', see Mahfoud Bennoune, *The Making of Contemporary Algeria, 1830–1987: Colonial Upheavals and Post-Independence Development* (Cambridge: Cambridge University Press, 1988).

17. See Lahouari Addi, *L'Algérie et la Démocratie: Pouvoir et Crise du Politique dans l'Algérie Contemporaine* (Paris: La Découverte, 1994).

18. Ibn Khaldun, *The Muqaddimah: An Introduction to History*, tr. F. Rosenthal (London: Routledge and Kegan Paul, 1958). For an appraisal of Ibn Khaldun's political philosophy see Ernest Gellner, *Muslim Society* (Cambridge: Cambridge University Press, 1981).

19. For Ibn Khaldun this egalitarian type of leadership is the exception rather than the norm, and 'as a rule, man must by necessity be dominated by someone else'. Ibn Khaldun, *The Muqaddimah*, vol. 1, pp. 258, 306.

20. *Ibid.* p. 262.

21. A tribal group is united by an *esprit de corps*, or *assabiyya* in Ibn Khaldun's terminology, which is an intimate, kinship-like relationship of loyalty based on shared life experiences, especially of a military kind. The group so constituted is often called *assabiyya* itself, especially when contrasted with other clans or the rest of the tribe. *Ibid.* p. 263.

22. See Olivier Roy, 'Patronage and solidarity groups: survival or reformation', in Ghassan Salamé (ed.), *Democracy without Democrats* (London: I.B. Tauris, 1994); Ghassan Salamé, '"Strong" and "weak" states: a qualified return to the Muqaddimah', in Giacomo Luciani (ed.), *The Arab State* (London: Routledge, 1990); Sami Zubaida. *Islam, the People and the State: Essays on Political Ideas and Movements in the Middle East* (London: Routledge, 1989).

23. Muammar al-Qaddafi, *The Green Book*, 10th edn (The World Centre for Studies and Research of the Green Book, 1987), p. 97.

24. For an attempt to analyse fundamentalists movements using the Wittgensteinian notion of 'family resemblance', see Martyn E. Marty and R. Scott Appleby, 'Introduction' in M.E. Marty and R.S. Appleby (eds), *Accounting for Fundamentalisms: The Dynamic Character of Movements* (Chicago: University of Chicago Press, 1994).

25. Compare Martyn E. Marty and R. Scott Appleby's 'Remaking the State: The Limits of the Fundamentalist Imagination', in M.E. Marty and R.S. Appleby (eds), *Fundamentalisms and the State: Remaking Polities, Economies and Militance* (Chicago: University of Chicago Press, 1993) with John L. Esposito's *Islam and Politics*, 3rd edn (Syracuse NY: Syracuse University Press, 1991).

26. See John Esposito and John Voll, *Islam and Democracy* (Oxford: Oxford University Press, 1996); Hamid Enayat, *Modern Islamic Political Thought* (Austin: University of Texas Press, 1982); Albert Hourani, *Arabic Thought in the Liberal Age 1798–1939* (Oxford: Oxford University Press, 1962).

27. Interesting biographical accounts can be found in Nikkie R. Keddie, *Sayyid Jamal ad-Din 'al-Afghani': A Political Biography* (Berkeley: University of California Press, 1972); Ibrahim Abu Rabi, *Intellectual Origins of Islamic Resurgence in the Muslim Arab World* (Albany: SUNY Press, 1996).

28. François Guizot, *The History of Civilisation in Europe* (1828), tr. W. Hazlitt (London: Penguin, 1997). About Guizot's philosophy see Larry Siedentop, 'Introduction', in *ibid.*; Pierre Rosanvallon, *Le Moment Guizot* (Paris: Edition Seuil, 1985).

29. Guizot, *The History of Civilisation*, p. 16.

30. Muhammad Abduh and Jamal al-Afghani, 'La prédestination' (*Al-Urwa al-Wuthqa* 1 May 1884), tr. M. Colombe, *Orient*, 21, 1962, p. 121.

31. Muhammad Abduh and Jamal al-Afghani, 'Des causes de la décadence des musulmans et de leur inertie' (*Al-Urwa al-Wuthqa* 10 April 1884), tr. M. Colombe, *Orient*, 22, 1962, p. 76.

32. At first they suggested that the Islamic leadership reorganise itself more rationally by establishing 'the grades of a scientific hierarchy among the Ulama and the function of each', but Abduh later renounced to this contentious idea when his religious and educational reforms gained momentum in the Egyptian establishment. *Ibid.* p. 81.

33. This is one of the main themes of the lectures that Abduh delivered in Beirut in the late 1880s and it constitutes the basis for his main scholarly work. See Muhammad

Abduh, *The Theology of Unity* (1897), tr. I. Musaad and K. Cragg (London: Allen and Unwin, 1966).

34. *Ibid.* pp. 107–8.

35. *Ibid.* pp. 105–6.

36. See Ali Merad, 'L'enseignement politique de Mohammed Abduh aux Algériens', *Orient*, 4, 1963.

37. Quoted in Ali Merad, *Le Réformisme Musulman en Algérie de 1925 à 1940* (Paris: Mouton, 1967).

38. Hamid Enayat, who sees in the works of Rashid Rida the radical break between traditional religious reformers and modern Islamic fundamentalist ideologues, provides a sharp analysis of Rida's views. See Enayat, *Modern Islamic Political Thought*. See also Rashid Rida, *Al-Khilafa aw al-Imama al-Uzma* [The caliphate or the great imamate] (Cairo: Matba'at al-Manar al-Misr, 1934).

39. The best socio-political and historical analysis of the movement is still Richard P. Mitchell's *The Society of the Muslim Brothers* (Oxford: Oxford University Press, 1969). For more recent analyses see, Brynjar Lia, *The Society of the Muslim Brothers in Egypt: The Rise of an Islamic Mass Movement 1928–1942* (London: Ithaca, 1998); Tariq Ramadan, *Aux Sources du Renouveau Musulman: D'al-Afghani à Hassan al Banna, un Siècle de Réformisme Islamique* (Paris: Bayard, 1998).

40. As Gilles Kepel also indicates, by appropriating the economic resources and instrumentalising the independent decision making capacities of the traditional religious centres like the al-Azhar University and the Sufi brotherhoods, the state indirectly undermined the authority of their interpretations of the Islamic doctrine. Gilles Kepel, *The Revenge of God: The Resurgence of Islam, Christianity and Judaism in the Modern World*, tr. A. Bradley (Cambridge: Polity Press, 1994).

41. The Michel's decree, specifying the functions of official imams, was issued in 1933. In 1934, the French *Conseil d'État* declared Arabic a foreign language and restricted its use in the press. In 1938 the French administration started closing down all the Islamic schools not approved by the colonial Board of Education. See Berque, *French North Africa*.

42. See Luc-Willy Deheuvels, *Islam et Pensée Contemporaine en Algérie: La Revue Al-Asala (1971–1981)* (Paris: CNRS, 1991).

43. On the position of Qutb in the Islamic fundamentalist movement see Abu Rabi, *Intellectual Origins of Islamic Resurgence in the Muslim Arab World;* Youssef M. Choueiri, *Islamic Fundamentalism* (London: Pinter, 1990); Gilles Kepel, *Le Prophète et le Pharaon: Les Mouvements Islamistes dans l'Égypte Contemporaine* (Paris: La Découverte, 1984).

44. Sayyid Qutb, *Milestones* (Delhi: Markazi Maktaba Islami, 1995).

45. There is also a more direct copying of the method of organisation of these European movements by the Brotherhood in the 1930s and 1940s. See Mitchell, *The Society of the Muslim Brothers*.

46. Concerning the influence of Carrel on Qutb's political thought, see Choueiri, *Islamic Fundamentalism*.

47. Carrel's obsession with healthy individuals in a healthy society was given greater credibility by the fact that he was a Nobel Prize winner in medicine. Alexis Carrel, *Man the Unknown* (New York: Harper and Brothers, 1935); Henri Bergson, *The Two Sources of Morality and Religion*, tr. R. Audra, C. Brereton and W.H. Carter (London: Macmillan, 1935).

48. Bergson argued that 'there are behind reason the men who have made mankind divine, and who have thus stamped a divine character on reason, which is the essential attribute of man. It is these men who draw us towards an ideal society, while we yield to the pressure of the real one.' Bergson, *The Two Sources of Morality and Religion*, p. 40.

144   Islam and Democracy

49. Qutb insists that, although scientific laws and moral rules are subject to different logics, 'the laws which govern human nature are no different from the laws governing the universe', and they are therefore 'as compelling as scientific laws'. Qutb, *Milestones*, p. 162.
50. For Qutb, 'a society which places the highest value on the "humanity" of man and honours the noble "human" characteristics is truly civilised. If materialism, no matter in what form, is given the highest value, whether it be in the form of a "theory", as in the Marxist interpretation of history, or in the form of material production, as in the case of the United States and European countries, and all other human values are sacrificed on its altar, then such a society is a backward one, or, in Islamic terminology, a *jahili* society.' *Ibid.* pp. 179–80.
51. Qutb argues that Islam 'abhors being reduced to pure thought' but 'loves to appear personified in human beings, in a living organisation and in a practical movement'. *Ibid.* pp. 69–70.
52. *Ibid.* p. 193.
53. Carrel professes that 'an ascetic and mystic minority would rapidly acquire an irresistible power over the dissolute and degraded majority', and that 'such a minority would be in a position to impose by persuasion or perhaps by force, other ways of life upon the majority' (Carrel, *Man the Unknown*, p. 296). Although Carrel was obviously referring to an order of a Christian medieval kind, Qutb could easily transpose this into an evocation of the time of the Prophet.
54. Qutb, *Milestones*, pp. 98–9.
55. *Ibid.* p. 239.

3   THE ALGERIAN POLITICAL TRANSITION: DEMOCRATIC SYMBOLS AND AUTHORITARIAN PRACTICES (1988–91)

1. François Burgat, *L'Islamisme au Maghreb* (Paris: Karthala, 1988). See also Ahmed Rouadjia, *Les Frères et la Mosquée* (Paris: Karthala, 1989).
2. In fact, many Algerians had turned away from the official Islamic institutions precisely because they viewed them as crude instruments of state propaganda. Mohamed Merzouk noted that for these people, the politicised 'fundamentalist' discourse produced within these associations was generally viewed as a rhetorical response to the politicisation and misappropriation of Islam by the state. Hence, they did not necessarily consider that this discourse applied to them specifically and that they should change their unorthodox behaviour, such as their involvement in the Sufi brotherhoods. Mohamed Merzouk, 'Notes sur les Pratiques et Représentations Religieuses en Milieu Populaire' (Oran: URASC, 1991).
3. See Augustus Richard Norton, 'Introduction', in A.R. Norton (ed.) *Civil Society in the Middle East*, 2 vols (Leiden: E.J. Brill, 1995).
4. See Economist Intelligence Unit, 'Algeria: country risk' (London: 1988). For a general assessment see John Ruedy, *Modern Algeria: The Origins and Development of a Nation* (Bloomington: Indiana University Press, 1992); see also the volume edited by Mokhtar Lakehal, *Algérie: De l'Indépendance à l'État d'Urgence* (Paris: L'Harmattan, 1992).
5. See Amar Benamrouche, 'État, conflits sociaux et mouvement syndical en Algérie (1962–1995)', *Monde Arabe Maghreb-Mashrek*, No. 148, 1995.
6. In practice, the 'financial speculators' were usually well connected with the civil servants who regulated the official distribution networks. In the mid-1980s the black-market economy became quasi-institutionalised in the country and periods of scarcity were often engineered by members of the administration who had invested in private business ventures. See Ahmed Henni, *Essai sur l'Économie Parallèle: Cas de l'Algérie* (Alger: ENAG, 1991); Djillali Hadjadj, *Corruption et Démocratie en Algérie* (Paris: Éditions La Dispute, 1998).

7. Some observers invoked a political manipulation of the rioters by some factions within the regime. See Mahfoud Bennoune, 'Algeria's facade of democracy', *Middle East Report*, March–April 1990. See also the well-informed account of the October riots in Abed Charef, *Algérie: Le Grand Dérapage* (Paris: Éditions de l'Aube, 1994).

8. See *Le Monde*, 7 October 1988.

9. In neighbouring Tunisia and Morocco there had also been a wave of food riots in 1984, triggered by the same combination of economic hardships and liberal reforms of the economy. For a comparative perspective, see John Walton and David Seddon, *Free Markets and Food Riots: The Politics of Global Adjustment* (Oxford: Blackwell, 1994).

10. Quoted in *Le Monde*, 9 October 1988.

11. The rumours of massacres might have been exaggerated, but some army units' overkill techniques are now well documented. See Pierre Dévoluy and Mireille Duteil, *La Poudrière Algérienne: Histoire Secrète d'une République sous Influence* (Paris: Calmann-Levy, 1994); Charef, *Algérie: Le Grand Dérapage*. See also the volume edited by the newspaper *Le Matin*, 'Octobre: ils parlent' (Algiers, 1998).

12. Quoted in *Le Monde*, 10 October 1988.

13. Quoted in *Le Monde*, 12 October 1988.

14. Author's interview with Abdelhamid Brahimi, London, January 1997. Brahami was *de facto* exiled from Algeria for denouncing organised corruption inside the Algerian regime when he left office, as well as for siding with the pro-Islamic opposition.

15. See Adam Przeworski, *Democracy and the Market: Political and Economic Reforms in Eastern Europe and Latin America* (Cambridge: Cambridge University Press, 1991).

16. See Fawzi Rouzeik, 'Chronique Algérie', *Annuaire de l'Afrique du Nord, XXVIII, 1989*.

17. See Fawzi Rouzeik, 'Chronique Algérie', *Annuaire de l'Afrique du Nord, XXVIII, 1991*.

18. Author's' interview with senior *Ennahda* cadres, London, March 1997.

19. The participation rate was 65 per cent. See Jacques Fontaine, 'Les élections locales algériennes du 12 juin 1990: Approche statistique et géographique', *Monde Arabe Maghreb-Machreck*, No. 129, 1990. For a more detailed analysis of the socio-economic trends underpinning these electoral results, see Jacques Fontaine, 'Quartiers défavorisés et vote islamique à Alger', *Revue du Monde Musulman et de la Méditerranée*, No. 65, 1993; Said Belguidoum, 'Citadins en attente de la ville: logement et politique à Sétif', *Monde Arabe Maghreb-Machreck*, No. 143, 1994.

20. In particular, the Algerian regime resisted the idea of a debt-rescheduling plan, which it felt would have handed over too great an amount of the state authority to the International Monetary Fund. See Economist Intelligence Unit, 'Algeria: country risk' (London, 1990).

21. See Rouzeik, 'Chronique Algérie', 1991.

22. For an account of the 'strike' and of its outcomes that stresses the calculated aspect of the political violence, see Hugh Roberts, 'From radical mission to equivocal ambition: the expansion and manipulation of Algerian Islamism', in M.E. Marty and R.S. Appleby (eds), *Accounting for Fundamentalisms: The Dynamic Character of Movements* (Chicago: University of Chicago Press, 1994).

23. Later on, at the trial of Madani and Belhadj, the Prime Minister declared that he had not authorised the military intervention of June 1991. See *El Watan*, 9 May 1992.

24. Author's interview with Abdelkader Hachani, Algiers, October 1998.

25. For a journalistic account of the electoral campaign, see particularly *Algérie-actualité*, 2–8 January 1992.

26. Jacques Fontaine, 'Les élections législative algériennes: Résultats du premier tour, 26 décembre 1991', *Monde Arabe Maghreb-Machreck*, No. 135, 1992.

27. Quoted in *El Watan*, 31 December 1991.

28. Cited in *Algérie-actualité*, 9–15 January 1992.

29. Quoted in *L'Évenèment*, 4 January 1992.

30. *Le Monde*, 1 January 1992; and *Le Monde*, 10 January 1992.
31. *Algérie-actualité*, 2–8 January 1992.
32. Quoted in *Le Monde*, 16 January 1992.

4   THE 1992 COUP D'ÉTAT AND BEYOND: WAR AS POLITICS THROUGH OTHER
     MEANS (1992–94)

1. The French version of Chadli's discourse is reprinted in *Le Monde*, 14 January 1992.
2. For a well-informed account of how the military establishment convinced Chadli
   to step down and chose the provisional government, see Pierre Dévoluy and Mireille
   Duteil, *La Poudrière Algérienne: Histoire Secrète d'une République sous Influence* (Paris:
   Calmann-Levy, 1994).
3. Chadli had appointed Khaled Nezzar Defence Minister in July 1990 and Larbi
   Belkheir Interior Minister in October 1991. These two generals were meant to be
   close political allies of the President.
4. Hachani's communiqué is reprinted in *Le Monde*, 15 January 1992.
5. Quoted in *El Forkane*, 22–28 January 1992.
6. *Le Monde*, 16 January 1992.
7. Quoted in *Le Monde*, 25 January 1992; and *Le Monde*, 28 January 1992.
8. Boudiaf's discourse is reprinted in *Algérie-actualité*, 13–19 February 1992.
9. See Luis Martinez, 'L'enivrement de la violence: "Djihad" dans la banlieue d'Alger'
   and Meriem Verges, 'Les héros n'ont pas de préoccupation de ce monde', in R.
   Leveau (ed.), *L'Algérie dans la Guerre* (Bruxelle: Éditions Complexes, 1995).
10. Author's interview with Abdelkader Hachani, Algiers, October 1998.
11. The Algerian government negotiated a $1.5 billion financing deal with a group of
    private creditors led by the Crédit Lyonnais, a bank owned principally by the French
    State. See *Financial Times* 27 February 1992; Economist Intelligence Unit, 'Algeria:
    country risk' (London, 1992).
12. See Dévoluy and Duteil, *La Poudrière Algérienne*.
13. At the end of 1992 the Defence Ministry revealed that some 90 members of the
    armed forced had been court-martialled in connection with the Islamic rebellion.
    Without doubt, many more soldiers' desertions were dealt with more discreetly and
    ruthlessly. In addition, a major problem that the army faced at that time – and has
    continued to face since – was the slump in the number of conscripts joining its ranks.
14. Author's interview with Qamreddine Kerbane, London, June 1997. Kerbane was
    excluded from the FIS executive committee at the 1991 Batna congress for
    advocating a more aggressive stance towards the regime. He later re-integrated the
    executive committee of the FIS which was re-formed abroad by the exiled cadres.
15. Author's interview with Abelkader Hachani, Algiers, October 1998.
16. Chebouti was a former lieutenant of Mustapha Bouyali, a former ALN officer, who
    had launched a very private *jihad* against the Algerian regime in 1982, in response
    to the execution of his brother. For nearly five years, before being killed in an
    ambush, Bouyali had kept the police and the army at bay, and had impressed the
    pro-Islamic youth. During this period, about 200 people were involved in his organ-
    isation at one time or another, including Ali Belhadj. They were all amnestied by
    1990. See Omar Carlier, *Entre Nation et Jihad: Histoire Sociale des Radicalismes Algériens*
    (Paris: Presses de Science Po, 1995); Séverine Labat, *Les Islamistes Algériens: Entre les
    Urnes et le Maquis* (Paris: Éditions du Seuil, 1995).
17. See Labat, *Les Islamistes Algériens*.
18. Martinez attributed the slow start of the Islamic insurrection to the incapacity and
    unwillingness of the MIA to absorb in its ranks all the disgruntled FIS supporters
    fleeing the police. Luis Martinez, *La Guerre Civile en Algérie, 1990–1998* (Paris:
    Éditions Karthala, 1998).

19. See Jocelyne Césari, 'Algérie: chronique intérieure', *Annuaire de l'Afrique du Nord XXXI, 1992*.
20. Extracts from Belhadj's letter are reprinted in *Jeune Afrique*, 8–14 January 1993.
21. On the rifts inside the guerrilla movement, see Michael Willis, *The Islamist Challenge in Algeria: a Political History* (London: Ithaca, 1996); Martinez, *La Guerre Civile*.
22. On the rise of the urban guerrilla movement, see Dévoluy and Duteil, *La Poudrière Algérienne*.
23. As Lahouari Addi pointed out, the regime's utilisation of the assassinations of secular personalities for its own propaganda purposes and the simultaneous media blackout of the army's reprisals reinforced the popular perception that the individuals assassinated were indeed fully on the regime's side, and more generally it demonstrated the existence of a two-speed system of justice. See, Lahouari Addi, 'Les intellectuels qu'on assassine', *Esprit*, January–February 1995.
24. See *Financial Times*, 29 October 1993.
25. At the same time, the FIS could not totally condemn the activities of armed groups that were often the only source of Islamic resistance in the country at that time. See Willis, *The Islamist Challenge*.
26. See François Burgat, 'Algérie: l'AIS et le GIA, itinéraires de constitution et relations', *Monde Arabe Maghreb-Machrek*, No. 149, 1995.
27. On the international implications of these attacks, see Jocelyne Césari, 'L'Effet Airbus', *Les Cahiers de l'Orient*, No. 36–37, 1994–95.

5   A NEW AUTHORITARIANISM: GUIDED DEMOCRACY VERSUS RADICAL ISLAM (1995–2000)

1. Author's interview with Ali Djeddi, Algiers, October 1998.
2. Author's interview with Abdelkader Hachani, Algiers, October 1998.
3. The main points of the Rome accords are reprinted in Slaheddine Bariki, 'Algérie: chronique intérieure', *Annuaire de l'Afrique du Nord, XXXV, 1995*.
4. The decree stated that these measures of clemency applied to 'individuals wanted for terrorism or subversion who surrender voluntarily to the appropriate authorities and who make the pledge to end all form of terrorist or subversive activities', *Journal Officiel de la République Algérienne Démocratique et Populaire*, No. 11, 1 March 1995.
5. Jacques Fontaine, 'Les résultats de l'élection présidentielle du 16 novembre 1995', *Monde Arabe Maghreb-Machrek*, No. 151, 1996.
6. Some leaked reports from the French secret services also mentioned this rigging operation. See *The European*, 21 March 1996; Bariki, 'Algérie', 1995.
7. The text of the Algerian Constitution is published in the *Journal Officiel de la République Algérienne Démocratique et Populaire* (JORA), No. 61, 16 November 1996.
8. Jacques Fontaine, 'Résultats et évolution des forces politiques', *Monde Arabe Maghreb-Machrek*, No. 157, 1997. Although the abstention rate was officially 33 per cent nationwide, it was monitored at over 50 per cent in Algiers, the Mitidja and Kabylia.
9. 'Chronologie: Algérie', *Monde Arabe Maghreb-Machrek*, No. 159, 1998.
10. The RND was granted 80 seats, the FLN 10, the FFS 4 and the MSP 2. 'Chronologie: Algérie', *Monde Arabe Maghreb-Machrek*, No. 159, 1998.
11. The communiqué from Ibrahimi, Ait Ahmed, Hamrouche, Djaballah, Sifi and Khatib read: '1. We take note of regime's determination to deny the citizens the right to take their destiny into their own hands and choose their President. We render it responsible for the consequences of these acts. 2. We confirm that the commitments made by the President of the Republic and the Chief of Staff guaranteeing a free and honest election have not been followed by acts. 3. We decide collectively to retire from the presidential election and deny the legitimate character of the election.' Cited in *El Watan*, 15 April 1999.

12. See *El Watan*, 17 April 1999; and *El Watan*, 19 April 1999.
13. See *La Tribune*, 6 June 1999.
14. Cited in *El Watan*, 7 June 1999. The communiqué of the AIS commander was reprinted in nearly all the Algerian newspapers on 7 June 1999.
15. See *La Tribune*, 7 June 1999.
16. At a press conference organised for a visit by the Egyptian President, Bouteflika declared that Algeria faced 'a complex situation caused by problems of regionalism, tribalism and intolerance, and worsened by political pluralism' (quoted in *La Tribune*, 13 June 1999). In another interview Bouteflika declared that Algeria had not learned much from the conflict and that he was confident that 'she would not learn' (quoted in *El Watan*, 23 July 1999).
17. Independent estimates where somewhat lower but in line with the official ones. The referendum question was: 'are you for or against the initiative of the President of the Republic to establish peace and civil concord?' Even in the habitually sceptical Kabyle community, an estimated 40 per cent of the population turned out to endorse it. See *Le Monde*, 18 September 1999.
18. In practice these officers tended to rule their military regions as personal fiefdoms. See Abdelkader Yefsah, 'L'armée sans hidjab', *Les Temps Modernes*, January–February 1995; Khadidja Abada, 'Armée: La fin d'un mythe', *Les Cahiers de l'Orient*, Nos 36–7, 1994–95. This clannish organisation of the army also explains, in part, why the Islamic fundamentalists were unable to make rapid inroads into officers' circles.
19. Chadli's mandate ran for three more years, and the President could dissolve the Parliament at will. Had Chadli decided to go against the will of the newly elected parliamentarians, he could have dissolved Parliament and ruled by decree until new elections were organised.
20. Paramilitary forces included 2,313 communal guard units and 5,000 'patriots' or 'self-defence groups' (*Groupes de Légitime Défense*, GLD). See Bariki, 'Algérie', 1995.
21. Quoted in *Jane's Defence Weekly*, 25 February 1998.
22. From the war of liberation onwards the army leaders had used a traditional patronage system to increase their political weight and assert their military authority. This reinforced or led to the formation of clans inside the military institution. Boumediene had been the leader of the Oujda clan – from the name of the Moroccan border town where the HQ of the Algerian Liberation Army was located during the war of independence – while the leaders of the post-Chadli period were from the TBS clan – TBS being the first letters of three towns, Tebessa, Batna, Souk-Akhras, that defined their region of origin. See Abada, 'Armée'; Yefsah, 'L'armée sans hidjab'.
23. Cited in *El Moudjahid*, 20 September 1998. It was originally published in the army newspaper *El Djeich*.
24. Quoted in *El Watan*, 12 September 1998.
25. See Amnesty International, 'Algeria: fear and silence' (London: November 1996).
26. See Martinez, *La Guerre Civile*.
27. See François Burgat, 'Algérie: l'AIS et le GIA, itinéraires de constitution et relations', *Monde Arabe Maghreb-Machrek*, No. 149, 1995.
28. Self-defence groups had been formed a year earlier in Kabylia, where they grew out of traditional self-help networks centred on village assemblies. In this region they had had a positive impact, because support for the Islamic fundamentalists was historically low. (In the 1991 parliamentary elections, in the district of Tizi-Ouzou, the regional capital of Kabylia, the FIS received less than 10,000 votes while the FFS scored nearer 150,000.) Such a situation did not occur elsewhere in Algeria where the formation of militias proved to be far more detrimental for local people, as it reduced the possibility of remaining neutral.
29. See Bariki, 'Algérie', 1995.

30. See Amnesty International, 'Algeria: fear and silence'. Slitting throats and cutting heads off had been a traditional war practice in North Africa well before the colonial period, and it became particularly fashionable during the war of independence (despite the FLN officially condemning the practice). See Alistair Horne, *A Savage War of Peace: Algeria 1954–1962* (London: Papermac, 1987).

31. See Habib Souaidia, *La Sale Guerre* (Paris: Éditions La Decouverte, 2001).

32. The GIA tactics did not differ significantly from the non-Islamic forms of guerrilla warfare and insurgency tactics employed in other civil conflicts throughout the world. In Algeria itself, during the war of independence, the French Special Forces and the FLN themselves did not recoil from using these forms of religious–ethnic cleansing. See Horne, *A Savage War of Peace*.

33. See 'Chronologie: Algérie', *Monde Arabe Maghreb-Machrek*, No. 160, 1998, p. 69.

34. This estimate is based on the reports of Algerian newspapers during that period. Most newspapers report thoroughly on civilian casualties (including off-duty policemen and soldiers), but information on military operations and casualties are covered by a law on 'terrorism' that prevents newspapers from disclosing anything but the official body count (usually highly conservative in the case of army losses and optimistic in that of the guerrillas). Journalists usually circumvent this law by quoting the 'personal opinion' of people living near the theatre of operations.

35. See Martinez, *La Guerre Civile*.

36. Hattab's group retained the same uncompromising stance vis-à-vis the regime and, in a communiqué published at the start of 1999, declared that that there would be 'no dialogue nor truce with apostates' – i.e. no agreement with the actual ruling elite. See Jean-Michel Salgon, 'Le groupe salafite pour la prédication et le Combat (GSPC)', *Les Cahiers de l'Orient*, No. 62, 2001. In August 1999, the newspaper *La Tribune* estimated that Hattab's group had 600 armed members. *La Tribune*, 9 August 1999.

37. See Jean-Michel Salgon, 'Évaluation statistique et cartographique: la situation sécuritaire en Algérie 1999–2000', *Les Cahiers de l'Orient*, No. 62, 2001.

38. Nearly 100 civilians were killed in a week in the country in the last week of Ramadan in December 2000. See *Le Monde*, 22 December 2000.

6   A CIVIL SOCIETY IN TRANSITION: SURVIVALIST STRATEGIES AND SOCIAL PROTEST

1. Luis Martinez, *La Guerre Civile en Algérie, 1990–1998* (Paris: Éditions Karthala, 1998).

2. The first law on privatisation of state lands was approved in 1990. However, the quagmire that followed the coup postponed its implementation until 1995. In practice, by 1998, little had been clarified due to the practical and administrative obstacles encountered by the land surveyors. (The main difficulty was that many tenants had sold their lands unofficially, thereby seriously complicating the state planners' task of identifying the 'true' owners when confronted with multiple claims.) See Conseil National Économique et Social (CNES), *Sur le Foncier Agricole* (Algiers, 1998).

3. For small farmers and agricultural workers, farming alone did not suffice to earn a living, as they could not work for several summer and winter months. In the western highlands, where guerrilla activity was high in the 1990s, they used to earn about a third of their income outside the agricultural sector before the war, usually in state-sponsored projects of rural development. See Bureau National d'Étude et de Dévelopment Rural (BNEDER), *Projet de Dévelopement Rural des Montagnes de l'Ouest Algérien* (Algiers, 1996).

4. See *El Watan*, 15 April 1997; *La Tribune*, 18 April 1997. See also, *passim*, Amnesty International, 'Algeria: fear and silence' (London, November 1996).

5. Author's interviews with civil servants from the Agriculture and Forestry Department, Mascara and Sidi-bel-Abbès, September 1998.
6. Author's interviews with civil servants from the Agriculture and Forestry Department, Mascara and Sidi-bel-Abbès, September 1998.
7. Devoluy and Duteil indicate that similar agreements were in place in the early years of the conflict in the suburban areas. Urban guerrilla groups only targeted the police forces outside of the area where they themselves lived, while local policemen did not arrest these local guerrillas but only those coming from outside their district. See Pierre Dévoluy and Mireille Duteil, *La Poudrière Algérienne: Histoire Secrète d'une République sous Influence* (Paris: Calmann-Levy, 1994).
8. On this occasion the militiamen involved were put on trial and received jail sentences. Usually these incidents were treated more discreetly by local army commanders and military tribunals. In this case the extensive coverage of the trial in the press, after an initial information blackout by the official media, was a belated attempt by the government to show the fairness of its justice system at a time when the exactions of the security forces had damaged the regime's image. See *El Watan*, 8 June 1998; and *El Watan*, 11 June 1998. See also, *passim*, Amnesty International, 'Algeria: fear and silence'.
9. See Martinez, *La Guerre Civile en Algérie*.
10. The informal economy of the border town of Maghnia has been particularly well described in the press. See, for example, *El Watan*, 23 July 1998. The activities of Hattab's Group for Preaching and Combat are also detailed in Jean-Michel Salgon, 'Le groupe salafite pour la prédication et le Combat (GSPC)', *Les Cahiers de l'Orient*, No. 62, 2001.
11. In the early years of the conflict goods were simply stolen and partially redistributed by the urban guerrilla groups. Once the state regained control of the towns and began to implement its programme of economic liberalisation, commercial opportunities were linked to more subtle protection rackets and to the re-investment of the spoils of war. See Martinez, *La Guerre Civile en Algérie*.
12. In the first half of the 1990s, the annual growth rate of the urban population (4.5 per cent) was twice the national average. Housing shortages were a problem well before the beginning of the civil war. On these urban conditions and the social violence it generated, see Slimane Medhar, *La Violence Sociale en Algérie* (Algiers: Éditions Thala, 1997).
13. In Algeria, as in the rest of the region, the observation that social tensions and political Islam are both reinforced by the arrival of successive waves of rural migrants describes a long-term phenomenon. Already in the late 1970s Von Sivers noted that in urban areas the surge in Islamic 'traditionalism' – as he then described the phenomenon – was a consequence of an increased rural emigration. Peter Von Sivers, 'National integration and traditional rural organisation in Algeria, 1970–1980: background for Islamic traditionalism?' in S.A. Arjomand (ed.), *From Nationalism to Revolutionary Islam* (Oxford: Macmillan, 1984).
14. In 1996 the population of Oran was estimated at between 800,000 and 900,000 inhabitants. About 100,000 inhabitants constituted the shantytowns' population. See Bureau d'Étude et de Réalisation en Urbanisme de Saida (URSA), *Plan Directeur d'Aménagement et d'Urbanisme du Groupement d'Oran, Phase III* (Oran, 1997).
15. Between 1988 and 1995, some of Oran's suburban districts had had a population increase of up to 20 per cent – the town proper having a population increase of only 1 per cent. See URSA, *Plan Directeur d'Aménagement et d'Urbanisme du Groupement d'Oran*.
16. Cited in *El Watan*, 28 December 1998.
17. Significantly, the migrant workers' remittances, the country's second source of foreign currency (after oil), also evaded the official banking system to a similar degree. See CNES, *Rapport de la Sixième Session Plénière* (Algiers, 1996); *Situation de la*

Communauté Algérienne à l'Étranger (Algiers, 1997); *Le Système des Relations de Travail dans le Contexte de l'Ajustement Structurel* (Algiers, 1998).

18. See Clement M. Henry, *The Mediterranean Debt Crescent: Money and Power in Algeria, Egypt, Morocco, Tunisia and Turkey* (Gainesville: University Press of Florida, 1996). And compare Henni's earlier analysis, in which he pointed out that the Algerian informal economy was a consequence of the state management of the banking sector – particularly the fact that it was practically impossible to invest without personal connections in the administration. Ahmed Henni, *Essai sur l'Économie Parallèle: Cas de l'Algérie* (Alger: ENAG, 1991).

19. In the region religious and ethnic ties are always crucial in organising solidarity networks and social protest. See Guilain Denoeux, *Urban Unrest in the Middle East: A Comparative Study of Informal Networks in Egypt, Iran and Lebanon* (Albany: State University of New York Press, 1993); and see the two volumes edited by A.R. Norton, *Civil Society in the Middle East* (Leiden: E.J. Brill, 1995).

20. The best account of the rise of the 'Islamic fundamentalist' associative movement and of the 'free mosques' in Algeria in the 1980s is Ahmed Rouadjia, *Les Frères et la Mosquée* (Paris: Karthala, 1989). See also François Burgat, *L'Islamisme au Maghreb* (Paris: Karthala, 1988).

21. See Hassan Remaoun, 'École, histoire, et enjeux institutionels', *Les Temps Modernes*, No. 580, 1995.

22. Author's interview with Sheikh Shamseddine, Algiers, October 1998.

23. In Belcourt, most cadres of this association were either university educated or had an extensive experience as social workers. Their computerised monitoring system of the association's social projects and funds was also clearly more efficient than that of the local administration, which seriously lacked qualified personnel, modern material and funds.

24. James C. Scott, *Domination and the Arts of Resistance: Hidden Transcripts* (New Haven: Yale University Press, 1990). In the present context, because of the conceptual instability of the categories of 'dominant' and 'dominated', it would be difficult to explain why a young, urban dwelling, university educated, French-speaking cadre of an Islamic association would rather identify himself with an old Muslim peasant from the Highlands with unorthodox religious views than with a secular-minded young townsperson working as government employee – that is unless one posits specific criteria, such as religion, as the foundations of these 'hidden transcripts'.

25. See Pierre Bourdieu, *Outline of a Theory of Practice*, tr. R. Nice (Cambridge: Cambridge University Press, 1977); and see also the volume edited by J.B. Thompson, *Pierre Bourdieu: Language and Symbolic Power* (Oxford: Polity Press, 1991).

26. Author's interview with Sheikh Shamseddine, Algiers, October 1998.

27. Author's interview with Ali Djeddi, Algiers, October 1998.

28. See Ali Belhadj, *El-Munquid*, Nos 23–4, 1991.

29. See Lahouari Addi, 'Les intellectuels qu'on assassine', *Esprit*, January–February 1995.

30. Quoted in *El Watan*, 30 June 1998. Unsurprisingly in Tizi-Ouzou the following day the Culture Secretary and the Health Minister had to run for their lives to escape an angry crowd, which had gathered after they attempted to visit to the hospital where Lounes' body was kept.

31. Lounes had also been kidnapped once by local Islamic guerrillas, but was then released unharmed after a few weeks of negotiations between the guerrillas and the local Kabyle community.

32. The government had linked the linguistic issue to the pro-democracy critique most strongly expressed in the press written in the minorities' languages, *Tamazigh* and French. Commenting on the French-language Algerian press, the Culture Secretary (responsible for implementing the law on Arabicisation) had argued that 'the newspapers using the language of the injurious colonialist are at the source of all the ills and misery that affect the country ... This press is French in its form and

content ... It has nothing to do with the Algerian people and their culture.' Quoted in *El Watan*, 30 May 1998.

33. Quoted in *El Watan*, 1 July 1998.

34. The commission of inquiry, led by a well-respected Kabyle judge, later showed that the *gendarmerie* had used live ammunition against the demonstrators – allegedly in contravention of the orders issued in Algiers. Extracts from the commission report are reprinted in *Le Monde*, 1 August 2001.

35. Significantly, the witnesses to Lounes' murder, and particularly his wife, retracted the declarations they made in 1998, which implicated the Islamic guerrillas in the assassination. See *Le Monde*, 30 April 2001.

7   THE INTERNATIONAL ARENA: STRENGTHS AND WEAKNESSES OF THE NEW WORLD ORDER

1. See Giacomo Luciani, 'The oil rent, the fiscal crisis of the state and democratization', in Ghassan Salamé (ed.), *Democracy without Democrats* (London: I.B. Tauris, 1994).

2. See *Financial Times*, 2 April 1992, and *Financial Times*, 9 April 1992.

3. *Financial Times*, 12 September 1992.

4. See *Financial Times*, 27 October 1992, and *Financial Times*, 3 November 1992.

5. Economist Intelligence Unit, 'Algeria: Country Risk' (London, 1992).

6. Quoted in Jocelyne Césari, 'L'Effet Airbus', *Les Cahiers de l'Orient*, Nos 36–7, 1994–95, p. 179.

7. See Economist Intelligence Unit, 'Algeria: Country Risk' (London, 1995).

8. See Fawzi Rouzeik, 'Algérie: chronique intérieure', and Edouard Van Buu, 'Algérie, chronique juridique', *Annuaire de l'Afrique du Nord, XXXIII, 1994*. This spectacular increase in military expenditure was partly attributable to the depreciation of the Algerian Dinar. In constant prices, these expenditures rose from $926 million in 1991 (1.3 per cent of the GDP) to $1,355 million in 1992 (GDP 2.1 per cent), to $1,666 million in 1993 (GDP 2.7 per cent) and attained $2,027 million in 1994 (GDP 3.3 per cent). See P. George, A. Courade Allebeck, E. Loose-Weintraub, 'Tables of military expenditures', in Stockholm International Peace Research Institute (SIPRI), *Armament, Disarmament and International Security*, 1996–97.

9. See Slaheddine Bariki, 'Algérie: chronique intérieure', *Annuaire de l'Afrique du Nord, XXXIV, 1995*.

10. Quoted in Bariki, 'Algérie: chronique intérieure'.

11. Eric Gobe, 'Note sur l'économie de l'Algérie en 1995', *Annuaire de l'Afrique du Nord, XXXIV, 1995*.

12. Edouard Van Buu, 'Algérie, chronique juridique', *Annuaire de l'Afrique du Nord, XXXIV, 1995*.

13. See *Financial Times*, 29 October 1993.

14. Between 1991 and 1995, foreign oil companies invested $5.5 billion in Algeria. See Ahmed Bouyacoub, 'Les investissements étrangers en Algérie 1990–1996: quelles perspectives?', *Annuaire de l'Afrique du Nord, XXXV, 1996*.

15. 'Chronologie: Algérie', *Monde Arabe Maghreb-Machrek*, Nos 159–60, 1998.

16. See *El Watan*, 10 March 1999.

17. See Robert Jackson, *Quasi-States: Sovereignty, International Relations, and the Third World* (Cambridge: Cambridge University Press, 1990); Fred Halliday, *Rethinking International Relations* (London: Macmillan, 1994).

18. The most contentious aspect of this debate is probably the responsibility of the United States in playing the Islamic card in the Muslim world during the Cold War, in order to contain potential communist or nationalistic influences. See Fawaz A. Gerges, *America and Political Islam: Clash of Cultures or Clash of Interests?*

(Cambridge: Cambridge University Press, 1999); Maria do Céu Pinto, *Political Islam and the United States: A Study of US Policy towards Islamic Movements in the Middle East* (London: Ithaca, 1999). See also the slightly older but highly topical volume edited by Leo E. Rose and Kamal Matinuddin, *Beyond Afghanistan: The Emerging US–Pakistan Relations* (Berkeley: University of California Press, 1989).

19. Samuel P. Huntington, *The Third Wave: Democratization in the Late Twentieth Century* (Norman: University of Oklahoma Press, 1991); Francis Fukuyama, *The End of History and the Last Man* (New York: Free Press, 1992).

20. On closer inspection, however, this support proved to be more ambiguous and contingent on each polity's domestic situation. See James Piscatori, 'Religion and realpolitik: Islamic responses to the Gulf War', in J. Piscatori (ed.), *Islamic Fundamentalisms and the Gulf Crisis* (Chicago: The American Academy of Arts and Sciences, 1991).

21. See, for example, *International Herald Tribune*, 8 January 1992.

22. For a didactic attempt to assuage these fears see particularly, John L. Esposito, *The Islamic Threat: Myth or Reality?* (Oxford: Oxford University Press, 1992).

23. Quoted in *The Middle East*, No. 272 (November 1997), p. 10.

24. In practice, the only positive outcome of this mission was to highlight the problem of the 'disappeared', the persons gone missing whilst in the custody of the state. Their number was estimated at 1,735 since the beginning of the conflict by the Algerian Interior Ministry – the Algerian League for Human Rights considering for its part that this number was near 18,000. See 'Chronologie: Algérie', *Monde Arabe Maghreb-Machrek*, No. 160, 1998.

25. About the patterns of military and economic aid in the region during the Cold War, see Alan Richards and John Waterbury, *A Political Economy of the Middle East: State, Class and Economic Development* (Boulder: Westview Press, 1990).

26. A perverse effect of the IMF reforms was to make the state administration even more the leading employer in the country with over 25 per cent of the total workforce in 1998. See Conseil National Économique et Social, *Le Système des Relations de Travail dans le Contexte de l'Ajustement Structurel* (Algiers, 1998). More generally at the regional level, see Clement M. Henry, *The Mediterranean Debt Crescent: Money and Power in Algeria, Egypt, Morocco, Tunisia and Turkey* (Gainesville: University Press of Florida, 1996).

27. The main drawback of a model of economic development guided by a distributive rationale is that the population constitutes an economic burden rather than an asset. (And for a country with a rapidly growing population, it is obvious that the expansion of the distributive networks cannot always keep up with the socio-economic demands/needs of the citizenry.) Still, Giacomo Luciani is right to remark that, for a while, in this region these 'allocation states' did no worse than more conventional 'production states'. Algeria, in particular, had in 1988 a Gross Domestic Product per capita superior to that of its two 'liberal' neighbours Morocco and Tunisia – $2,400 compared to $1,000 and $1,300 respectively – because of its oil-financed 'socialist' policy of industrialisation. (By 1995, however, Morocco and Tunisia had increased their GDP per capita to $1,300 and $2,000 respectively, while that of Algeria had fallen to $1,500 – partly because of the civil war, partly because of the programme of structural adjustment of the IMF.) See Giacomo Luciani, 'Allocation vs. production states: a theoretical framework', in Luciani (ed.), *The Arab State*; United Nations, *Statistical Yearbook 1997* (New York: United Nations, 1998).

28. See John Walton and David Seddon, *Free Markets and Food Riots: The Politics of Global Adjustment* (Oxford: Blackwell, 1994).

29. See Ahmed Henni, *Essai sur l'Économie Parallèle: Cas de l'Algérie* (Algiers: ENAG, 1991).

30. See Djillali Hadjadj, *Corruption et Démocratie en Algérie* (Paris: Éditions La Dispute, 1998).

31. Metin Heper, 'Islam and democracy in Turkey: towards a reconciliation?', *The Middle East Journal*, 51 (1), 1997.
32. In analytical terms this predicament remains what Michael Hudson identified some 25 years ago as these regimes' inability to generate structural legitimacy. See Michael C. Hudson, *Arab Politics: The Search for Legitimacy* (New Haven: Yale University Press, 1977).
33. In 1993, as the GIA began to target French nationals in Algeria, Charles Pasqua, the French Interior Minister, even deflected the media criticism against Sheikh Sahraoui by arguing that he had always had a good reputation and that he had helped the French authorities by unequivocally condemning the actions of the GIA. Cited in *Le Monde*, 17 November 1993.
34. See Richard Labévière, 'Les réseaux européens des islamistes algériens: entre déshérence et reconversion' *Les Cahiers de l'Orient*, No. 62, 2001.
35. Extracts from the declarations of one of the ringleader, Boualem Bensaid, made during his 1999 trial are reprinted in *Le Monde*, 3 June 1999.
36. Richard Labévière, 'Les réseaux européens des islamistes algériens'.
37. An interview of Kelkal made by a sociologist during a routine survey of youth culture in poor suburban areas three years before these events showed clearly the evolution of Kelkal's views. The interview is reprinted in *Le Monde*, 7 October 1995.
38. The grand jury of Virginia later indicted Moussaoui for conspiracy with bin Laden and al-Qaida and accused him of having prepared acts of terrorism, of air piracy, of destruction of aircraft, of utilisation of weapons of mass destruction and of murder. About Moussaoui's Islamic conversion and itinerary see *Le Monde*, 27 September 2001.
39. *Le Monde*, 26 September 2001.
40. *Le Monde*, 4 December 2001. In April, however, the Italian police had already arrested the Tunisian Ben Kemais, the leader of a GSPC cell whom they suspected of planning an attack on the American embassy in Rome. In August, Djamel Beghal, a dual French-Algerian citizen, was presented by the French police as an important organiser of the al-Qaida network in Europe. On the basis of the declaration he made to United Arab Emirate police, the French also suspected his group of plotting to bomb the American embassy in Paris.

8   CONCLUSION: LEARNING AND UNLEARNING TO BE DEMOCRATIC

1. Tocqueville concluded that 'only a great genius can save a ruler who tries to help his subjects after a long oppression'. Alexis de Tocqueville, *The Old Regime and the Revolution*, tr. A.S. Kahan (Chicago, Chicago University Press, 1998), p. 222.
2. For a political analysis that highlights the failure of the democratic pole to build such a liberal consensus in Algeria, see Robert Mortimer, 'Islamists, soldiers, and democrats: the second Algerian war', *Middle East Journal*, 50 (1), 1996. The classic exploration of the opposition between democracy and liberalism is Carl Schmitt, *The Crisis of Parliamentary Democracy*, tr. E. Kennedy (Cambridge MA: MIT Press, 1985). If it is clear by now that Schmitt's conclusions are a little overstated, it is far less clear exactly why many contemporary liberal democracies function just as well as they do – and even less clear how this could be reproduced elsewhere. On this last point see John Dunn, 'How democracies succeed', *Economy and Society*, 25 (4), 1996.
3. See Barry Buzan and Richard Little, *International Systems in World History* (Oxford: Oxford University Press, 2000); Andrew Linklater, *The Transformation of Political Community: Ethical Foundations of the post-Westphalian Era* (Cambridge: Polity Press, 1998).
4. See Jean L. Cohen and Andrew Arato, *Civil Society and Political Theory* (Cambridge MA: MIT Press, 1992); and compare the practical observations made by the con-

tributors to Augustus Richard Norton's *Civil Society in the Middle East*, 2 vols (Leiden: E.J. Brill, 1995).

5. Quoted in *El-Munquid*, No. 9, 1991. In his 1991 pamphlet on 'apostasy and reconciliation', written before the FIS faced state repression, Ali Belhadj had concluded that 'Islam' still needed the 'areas of specialisation' that were perfected by armed Islamic movements. However, he warned would-be freedom fighters that 'an Islamic group whose activities are specific to the place it operates ought not to undermine someone else's activities because what is a priority in the present might be a secondary objective in the future'. Ali Belhadj, *Al-Irchad wal-Nosho fi Bayani Ahkam al-Riddat wa Suluh* [*Guidance and Advice in Understanding the Judgements on Apostasy and Reconciliation*], FIS pamphlet, 1991, p. 172.

6. Quoted in *Le Monde*, 12 January 2002.

7. For an account of democratic success that emphasises this didactic aspect of politics, see Dunn, 'How democracies succeed'.

8. See Frédéric Volpi, 'Language, practices and the formation of a transnational liberal-democratic ethos', *Global Society*, 16 (1), 2002.

9. On the limited reach of foreign (US) civic education efforts see Clement M. Henry, 'Promoting democracy: USAID at sea or off to cyberspace', *Middle East Policy*, V (1), 1997.

References

Abada, Khadidja. 'Armée: la fin d'un mythe', *Les Cahiers de l'Orient*, Nos 36–7, 1994–95.

Abduh, Muhammad. *The Theology of Unity* (1897), tr. I. Musaad and K. Cragg (London: Allen and Unwin, 1966).

Abduh, Muhammad and Jamal al-Afghani. 'Des causes de la décadence des musulmans et de leur inertie', (*Al-Urwa al-Wuthqa*, 10 April 1884), tr. M. Colombe, *Orient*, No. 22, 1962.

Abduh, Muhammad and Jamal al-Afghani. 'La prédestination', (*Al-Urwa al-Wuthqa*, 1 May 1884), tr. M. Colombe, *Orient*, No. 21, 1962.

Abu Rabi, Ibrahim. *Intellectual Origins of Islamic Resurgence in the Muslim Arab World* (Albany: SUNY Press, 1996).

Addi, Lahouari. *L'Algérie et la Démocratie: Pouvoir et Crise du Politique dans l'Algérie Contemporaine* (Paris: La Découverte, 1994).

Addi, Lahouari. 'Les intellectuels qu'on assassine', *Esprit*, January–February 1995.

Agéron, Charles-Robert. *Les Algériens Musulmans et la France 1871–1919*, 2 vols (Paris: PUF, 1968).

Agéron, Charles-Robert. *Du Mythe Kabyle aux Politiques Berbères* (Paris: Bourgeois, 1976).

Althusser, Louis. 'Ideology and ideological states apparatuses', in *Lenin and Philosophy, and other essays*, tr. B. Brewster (London: New Left Books, 1971).

Amnesty International, 'Algeria: fear and silence' (London, November 1996).

Amnesty International, 'United Nations General Assembly, 56th session 2001, draft comprehensive convention on international terrorism: a threat to human rights standards' (London, October 2001).

Armstrong, David. *Revolution and World Order: The Revolutionary State in International Society* (Oxford: Clarendon Press, 1993).

Ayubi, Nazih N. *Over-Stating the Arab State: Politics and Society in the Middle East* (London: I.B. Tauris, 1995).

Bariki, Slaheddine. 'Algérie: chronique intérieure', *Annuaire de l'Afrique du Nord, XXXV, 1995*.

Belguidoum, Said. 'Citadins en attente de la ville: logement et politique à Sétif', *Monde Arabe Maghreb-Machreck*, No. 143, 1994.

Belhadj, Ali. *Al-Irchad wal-Nosho fi Bayani Ahkam al-Riddat wa Suluh* [Guidance and Advice in Understanding the Judgements on Apostasy and Reconciliation], FIS pamphlet, 1991.

Benamrouche, Amar. 'État, conflits sociaux et mouvement syndical en Algérie (1962–1995)', *Monde Arabe Maghreb-Mashreck*, No. 148, 1995.

Bennoune, Mahfoud. *The Making of Contemporary Algeria, 1830–1987: Colonial Upheavals and Post-Independence Development* (Cambridge: Cambridge University Press, 1988).

Bennoune, Mahfoud. 'Algeria's facade of democracy', *Middle East Report*, March–April 1990.

Bergson, Henri. *The Two Sources of Morality and Religion*, tr. R. Audra, C. Brereton and W.H. Carter (London: Macmillan, 1935).

Berque, Jacques. *French North Africa: the Maghrib Between Two World Wars*, tr. J. Stewart (London: Faber and Faber, 1967).

Bourdieu, Pierre. *Outline of a Theory of Practice*, tr. R. Nice (Cambridge: Cambridge University Press, 1977).

Bourdieu, Pierre. 'Political representation: elements for a theory of the political field', tr. G. Raymond and M. Adamson, in J.B Thompson (ed.), *Pierre Bourdieu: Language and Symbolic Power* (Oxford: Polity Press, 1991).

Bouyacoub, Ahmed. 'Les investissements étrangers en Algérie 1990–1996: quelles perspectives?', *Annuaire de l'Afrique du Nord, XXXV, 1996.*

Bratton, Michael and Nicholas van de Walle. *Democratic Experiments in Africa: Regime Transitions in Comparative Perspective* (Cambridge: Cambridge University Press, 1997).

Bureau d'Étude et de Réalisation en Urbanisme de Saida (URSA), *Plan Directeur d'Aménagement et d'Urbanisme du Groupement d'Oran, Phase III* (Oran, 1997).

Bureau National d'Étude et de Dévelopment Rural (BNEDER), *Projet de Dévelopement Rural des Montagnes de l'Ouest Algérien* (Algiers, 1996).

Burgat, François. *L'Islamisme au Maghreb* (Paris: Karthala, 1988).

Burgat, François. 'Algérie: l'AIS et le GIA, itinéraires de constitution et relations', *Monde Arabe Maghreb-Machrek,* No. 149, 1995.

Burgat, Francois. 'De l'islamisme au postislamisme, vie et mort d'un concept', *Esprit,* No. 277, August–September 2001.

Burns, Gene. 'Ideology, Culture, and Ambiguity: The Revolutionary Process in Iran', *Theory and Society,* 25 (3), 1996.

Buu, Edouard Van. 'Algérie, chronique juridique', *Annuaire de l'Afrique du Nord, XXXIII, 1994.*

Buu, Edouard Van. 'Algérie, chronique juridique', *Annuaire de l'Afrique du Nord, XXXIV, 1995.*

Buzan, Barry and Richard Little. *International Systems in World History* (Oxford: Oxford University Press, 2000).

Carlier, Omar. *Entre Nation et Jihad: Histoire Sociale des Radicalismes Algériens* (Paris: Presses de Science Po, 1995).

Carrel, Alexis. *Man the Unknown* (New York: Harper and Brothers, 1935).

Césari, Jocelyne. 'Algérie: chronique intérieure', *Annuaire de l'Afrique du Nord XXXI, 1992.*

Césari, Jocelyne. 'L'Effet Airbus', *Les Cahiers de l'Orient,* Nos 36–7, 1994–95.

Céu Pinto, Maria do. *Political Islam and the United States: A Study of US Policy towards Islamic Movements in the Middle East* (London: Ithaca, 1999).

Charef, Abed. *Algérie: Le Grand Dérapage* (Paris: Éditions de l'Aube, 1994).

Choueiri, Youssef M. *Islamic Fundamentalism* (London: Pinter, 1990).

Clancy-Smith, Julia A. *Rebel and Saint: Muslim Notables, Populist Protests, Colonial Encounters (Algeria and Tunisia, 1800–1904)* (Berkeley: University of California Press, 1994).

Cohen, Jean L. and Andrew Arato. *Civil Society and Political Theory* (Cambridge MA: MIT Press, 1992).

Colburn, Forrest D. *The Vogue of Revolutions in Poor Countries* (Princeton: Princeton University Press, 1994).

Conseil National Économique et Social, *Rapport de la Sixième Session Plénière* (Algiers, 1996).

Conseil National Économique et Social, *Situation de la Communauté Algérienne à l'Étranger* (Algiers, 1997).

Conseil National Économique et Social, *Sur le Foncier Agricole* (Algiers, 1998).

Conseil National Économique et Social, *Le Système des Relations de Travail dans le Contexte de l'Ajustement Structurel* (Algiers, 1998).

Deheuvels, Luc-Willy. *Islam et Pensée Contemporaine en Algérie: La Revue Al-Asala (1971–1981)* (Paris: CNRS, 1991).

Denoeux, Guilain. *Urban Unrest in the Middle East: A Comparative Study of Informal Networks in Egypt, Iran and Lebanon* (Albany: State University of New York Press, 1993).

Dévoluy, Pierre and Mireille Duteil. *La Poudrière Algérienne: Histoire Secrète d'une République sous Influence* (Paris: Calmann-Levy, 1994).

Diamond, Larry. 'Is Pakistan the (reverse) wave of the future?' *Journal of Democracy* Vol. 11 (July 2000).

Dunn, John. 'Practising history and social science on 'realist' assumptions', in *Political Obligation in its Historical Context* (Cambridge: Cambridge University Press, 1980).

Dunn, John. *Modern Revolutions* (Cambridge: Cambridge University Press, 1989).

Dunn, John. 'Revolution', in T. Ball, J. Farr and R. Hanson (eds), *Political Innovation and Conceptual Change* (Cambridge: Cambridge University Press, 1989).

Dunn, John. 'Responsibility without power: states and the incoherence of the modern conception of the political good', in *Interpreting Political Responsibility* (Cambridge: Polity Press, 1990).

Dunn, John. 'How democracies succeed', *Economy and Society*, 25 (4), 1996.

Economist Intelligence Unit, 'Algeria: country risk' (London: 1988).

Economist Intelligence Unit, 'Algeria: country risk' (London, 1990).

Economist Intelligence Unit, 'Algeria: country risk' (London, 1992).

Economist Intelligence Unit, 'Algeria: country risk' (London, 1995).

Eickelman, Dale F. and James Piscatori. *Muslim Politics* (Princeton: Princeton University Press, 1996).

Enayat, Hamid. *Modern Islamic Political Thought* (Austin: University of Texas Press, 1982).

Entelis, John P. 'State-society relations: Algeria as a case study', in M. Tessler, J. Nachtwey and A. Banda (eds), *Area Studies and Social Sciences: Strategies for Understanding Middle East Politics* (Bloomington: Indiana University Press, 1999).

Esposito, John. *Islam and Politics*, 3rd edn (Syracuse NY: Syracuse University Press, 1991).

Esposito, John. *The Islamic Threat: Myth or Reality* (Oxford: Oxford University Press, 1992).

Esposito, John and John Voll. *Islam and Democracy* (Oxford: Oxford University Press, 1996).

Fanon, Frantz. *Studies in a Dying Colonialism*, tr. H. Chevalier (New York: Monthly Review Press, 1965).

Fanon, Frantz. *The Wretched of the Earth*, tr. C. Farrington (London: MacGibbon & Kee, 1965).

Fontaine, Jacques. 'Les élections locales algériennes du 12 juin 1990: Approche statistique et géographique', *Monde Arabe Maghreb-Machreck*, No. 129, 1990.

Fontaine, Jacques. 'Les élections législative algériennes: Résultats du premier tour, 26 décembre 1991', *Monde Arabe Maghreb-Machreck*, No. 135, 1992.

Fontaine, Jacques. 'Quartiers défavorisés et vote islamique à Alger', *Revue du Monde Musulman et de la Méditerranée*, No. 65, 1993.

Fontaine, Jacques. 'Les résultats de l'élection présidentielle du 16 novembre 1995', *Monde Arabe Maghreb-Machrek*, No. 151, 1996.

Fontaine, Jacques. 'Résultats et évolution des forces politiques', *Monde Arabe Maghreb-Machrek*, No. 157, 1997.

Fukuyama, Francis. *The End of History and the Last Man* (New York: Free Press, 1992).

Gellner, Ernest. *Muslim Society* (Cambridge: Cambridge University Press, 1981).

Gellner, Ernest. *Conditions of Liberty: Civil Society and its Rivals* (London: Hamish Hamilton, 1994).

George, P., A. Courade Allebeck, E. Loose-Weintraub, 'Tables of military expenditures', in Stockholm International Peace Research Institute (SIPRI), *Armament, Disarmament and International Security*, 1996–97.

Gerges, Fawaz A. *America and Political Islam: Clash of Cultures or Clash of Interests?* (Cambridge: Cambridge University Press, 1999).

Geuss, Raymond. *The Idea of a Critical Theory* (Cambridge: Cambridge University Press, 1981).

Gobe, Eric. 'Note sur l'économie de l'Algérie en 1995', *Annuaire de l'Afrique du Nord*, XXXIV, 1995.

Goldstone, Jack A. *Revolution and Rebellion in the Early Modern World* (Berkeley: University of California Press, 1991).

Goldstone, Jack A. 'Predicting revolutions: why we could (and should) have foreseen the revolutions of 1989–1991 in the USSR and Eastern Europe', *Contention*, 2 (2), 1993.

Gramsci, Antonio. *Selections from the Prison Notebooks*, ed. and tr. Q. Hoare and G.N. Smith (London: Lawrence and Wishart, 1971).

Guizot, Francois. *The History of Civilisation in Europe* (1828), tr. W. Hazlitt, (London: Penguin, 1997).

Hadjadj, Djillali. *Corruption et Démocratie en Algérie* (Paris: Éditions La Dispute, 1998).

Halliday, Fred. *Rethinking International Relations* (London: Macmillan, 1994).

Henni, Ahmed. *Essai sur l'Économie Parallèle: Cas de l'Algérie* (Alger: ENAG, 1991).

Henry, Clement M. *The Mediterranean Debt Crescent: Money and Power in Algeria, Egypt, Morocco, Tunisia and Turkey* (Gainesville: University Press of Florida, 1996).

Henry, Clement M. 'Promoting democracy: USAID at sea or off to cyberspace', *Middle East Policy*, V (1), 1997.

Heper, Metin. 'Islam and democracy in Turkey: towards a reconciliation?', *The Middle East Journal*, 51 (1), 1997.

Horne, Alistair. *A Savage War of Peace: Algeria 1954–1962* (London: Papermac, 1987).

Hourani, Albert. *Arabic Thought in the Liberal Age 1798–1939* (Oxford: Oxford University Press, 1962).

Hourani, Albert. *The Emergence of Modern Middle East* (Berkeley: University of California Press, 1981).

Hudson, Michael C. *Arab Politics: The Search for Legitimacy* (New Haven: Yale University Press, 1977).

Huntington, Samuel P. *Political Order in Changing Societies* (New Haven: Yale University Press, 1968).

Huntington, Samuel P. *The Third Wave: Democratization in the Late Twentieth Century* (Norman: University of Oklahoma Press, 1991).

Huntington, Samuel P. *The Clash of Civilisations and the Remaking of the World Order* (New York: Simon and Schuster, 1996).

Ibn Khaldun, *The Muqaddimah: An Introduction to History*, tr. F. Rosenthal (London: Routledge and Kegan Paul, 1958).

Jackson, Robert. *Quasi-States: Sovereignty, International Relations, and the Third World* (Cambridge: Cambridge University Press, 1990).

Keddie, Nikkie R. *Sayyid Jamal ad-Din 'al-Afghani': A Political Biography* (Berkeley: University of California Press, 1972).

Kedourie, Elie. *England and the Middle East: The Destruction of the Ottoman Empire 1914–1921* (Boulder: Westview Press, 1987).

Kedourie, Elie. *Politics in the Middle East* (Oxford: Oxford University Press, 1992).

Kepel, Gilles. *Le Prophète et le Pharaon: Les Mouvements Islamistes dans l'Égypte Contemporaine* (Paris: La Découverte, 1984).

Kepel, Gilles. *The Revenge of God: The Resurgence of Islam, Christianity and Judaism in the Modern World*, tr. A. Bradley (Cambridge: Polity Press, 1994).

Kepel, Gilles. *Jihad: Expansion et Déclin de l'Islamisme* (Paris: Gallimard, 2000).

Khoury, Philip. *Syria and the French Mandate: The Politics of Arab Nationalism 1920–1945* (London: I.B. Tauris, 1987).

Kurzman, Charles. 'Structural opportunity and perceived opportunity in social movement theory: the Iranian Revolution of 1979', *American Sociological Review*, 61 (1), 1996.

Labat, Séverine. *Les Islamistes Algériens: Entre les Urnes et le Maquis* (Paris, Éditions du Seuil, 1995).

Labévière, Richard. 'Les réseaux européens des islamistes algériens: entre déshérence et reconversion', *Les Cahiers de l'Orient*, No. 62, 2001.

Lakehal, Mokhtar (ed.). *Algérie: De l'Indépendance à l'État d'Urgence* (Paris: L'Harmattan, 1992).

Lewis, Bernard. *The Political Language of Islam* (Chicago: University of Chicago Press, 1988).

Lia, Brynjar. *The Society of the Muslim Brothers in Egypt: The Rise of an Islamic Mass Movement 1928–1942* (London: Ithaca, 1998).

Linklater, Andrew. *The Transformation of Political Community: Ethical Foundations of the post-Westphalian Era* (Cambridge: Polity Press, 1998).

Luciani, Giacomo. 'Allocation vs. production states: a theoretical framework', in Giacomo Luciani (ed.), *The Arab State* (London: Routledge, 1990).

Luciani, Giacomo. 'The oil rent, the fiscal crisis of the state and democratization', in Ghassan Salamé (ed.), *Democracy without Democrats* (London: I.B. Tauris, 1994).

Martinez, Luis. 'L'enivrement de la violence: 'djihad' dans la banlieue d'Alger', in R. Leveau (ed.), *L'Algérie dans la Guerre* (Bruxelle: Éditions Complexes, 1995).

Martinez, Luis. *La Guerre Civile en Algérie, 1990–1998* (Paris: Éditions Karthala, 1998).

Marty, Martyn E. and R. Scott Appleby. 'Remaking the State: The Limits of the Fundamentalist Imagination', in M.E. Marty and R.S. Appleby (eds), *Fundamentalisms and the State: Remaking Polities, Economies and Militance* (Chicago: University of Chicago Press, 1993).

Marty, Martyn E. and R. Scott Appleby. 'Introduction' in M.E. Marty and R.S. Appleby (eds), *Accounting for Fundamentalisms: The Dynamic Character of Movements* (Chicago: University of Chicago Press, 1994).

Medhar, Slimane. *La Violence Sociale en Algérie* (Algiers: Éditions Thala, 1997).

Merad, Ali. 'L'enseignement politique de Mohammed Abduh aux Algériens', *Orient*, No. 4, 1963.

Merad, Ali. *Le Réformisme Musulman en Algérie de 1925 à 1940* (Paris: Mouton, 1967).

Merzouk, Mohamed. 'Notes sur les Pratiques et Représentations Religieuses en Milieu Populaire' (Oran: URASC, 1991).

Migdal, Joel S. *Strong Societies and Weak States: State–Society Relations and State Capabilities in the Third World* (Princeton: Princeton University Press, 1988).

Mitchell, Richard P. *The Society of the Muslim Brothers* (Oxford: Oxford University Press, 1969).

Moaddel, Mansoor. 'Ideology as episodic discourse: the case of the Iranian revolution', *American Sociology Review*, 57, 1992.

Mortimer, Robert. 'Islamists, soldiers, and democrats: the second Algerian war', *Middle East Journal*, 50 (1), 1996.

Norton, Augustus Richard. 'Introduction', in A.R. Norton (ed.), *Civil Society in the Middle East*, 2 vol. (Leiden: E.J. Brill, 1995).

O'Donnell, Guillermo. 'Illusions about consolidation', in L. Diamond, M. Plattner, Y. Chu and H. Tien (eds), *Consolidating the Third Wave Democracies* (Baltimore: Johns Hopkins University Press, 1997).

O'Donnell, Guillermo and Phillipe Schmitter. 'Tentative conclusions about uncertain democracies', in Guillermo O'Donnell, Phillipe Schmitter and Lawrence Whitehead (eds), *Transitions from Authoritarian Rule: Prospects for Democracy*, 3 vols (Baltimore: Johns Hopkins University Press, 1986).

Piscatori, James. 'Religion and realpolitik: Islamic responses to the Gulf War', in J. Piscatori (ed.), *Islamic Fundamentalisms and the Gulf Crisis* (Chicago: The American Academy of Arts and Sciences, 1991).

Prochaska, David. *Making Algeria French: Colonialism in Bône 1870–1920* (Cambridge: Cambridge University Press, 1990).

Przeworski, Adam. *Democracy and the Market: Political and Economic Reforms in Eastern Europe and Latin America* (Cambridge: Cambridge University Press, 1991).

Przeworski, Adam. 'Minimalist conception of democracy: a defence', in I. Shapiro and C. Hacker-Cordon (eds), *Democracy's Value* (Cambridge: Cambridge University Press, 1999).

Putnam, Robert D. *Making Democracy Works: Civic Traditions in Modern Italy* (Princeton: Princeton University Press, 1993).

Qaddafi, Muammar al. *The Green Book*, 10th edn (The World Centre for Studies and Research of the Green Book, 1987).

Quandt, William B. *Between Ballots and Bullets* (Washington: Brookings Institution Press, 1998).

Qutb, Sayyid. *Milestones* (Delhi: Markazi Maktaba Islami, 1995).

Ramadan, Tariq. *Aux Sources du Renouveau Musulman: D'al-Afghani à Hassan al Banna, un Siècle de Réformisme Islamique* (Paris: Bayard, 1998).

Remaoun, Hassan. 'École, histoire, et enjeux institutionels', *Les Temps Modernes*, No. 580, 1995.

Richard, Yan. *Shi'ite Islam: Polity, Ideology and Creed*, tr. A. Nevill (Oxford: Blackwell, 1995).

Richards, Alan and John Waterbury. *A Political Economy of the Middle East: State, Class and Economic Development* (Boulder: Westview Press, 1990).

Rida, Rashid. *Al-Khilafa aw al-Imama al-Uzma* [The caliphate or the great imamate] (Cairo: Matba'at al-Manar al-Misr, 1934).

Roberts, Hugh. 'From radical mission to equivocal ambition: the expansion and manipulation of Algerian Islamism', in M.E. Marty and R.S. Appleby (eds), *Accounting for Fundamentalisms: The Dynamic Character of Movements* (Chicago: University of Chicago Press, 1994).

Roeder, Philip G. *Red Sunset: The Failure of the Soviet Union* (Princeton: Princeton University Press, 1993).

Rosanvallon, Pierre. *Le Moment Guizot* (Paris: Edition Seuil, 1985).

Rose, Leo E. and Kamal Matinuddin, *Beyond Afghanistan: The Emerging US–Pakistan Relations* (Berkeley: University of California Press, 1989).

Rouadjia, Ahmed. *Les Frères et la Mosquée* (Paris: Karthala, 1989).

Rouzeik, Fawzi 'Chronique Algérie', *Annuaire de l'Afrique du Nord, XXVIII, 1989*.

Rouzeik, Fawzi 'Chronique Algérie', *Annuaire de l'Afrique du Nord, XXVIII, 1991*.

Rouzeik, Fawzi. 'Algérie: chronique intérieure', *Annuaire de l'Afrique du Nord, XXXIII, 1994*.

Roy, Olivier. 'Patronage and solidarity groups: survival or reformation', in Ghassan Salamé (ed.), *Democracy without Democrats* (London: I.B. Tauris, 1994).

Roy, Olivier. 'Les islamologues ont-ils inventés l'islamisme', *Esprit*, No. 277 (August–September 2001).

Ruedy, John. *Modern Algeria: The Origins and Development of a Nation* (Bloomington: Indiana University Press, 1992).

Rustow, Dankwart. 'Transitions to democracy: toward a dynamic model', *Comparative Politics*, 2 (3), 1970.

Said, Edward W. *Orientalism* (London: Routledge and Kegan Paul, 1978).

Salamé, Ghassan. '"Strong" and "weak" states: a qualified return to the Muqaddimah', in Giacomo Luciani (ed.), *The Arab State* (London: Routledge, 1990).

Salgon, Jean-Michel. 'Le groupe salafite pour la prédication et le Combat (GSPC)', *Les Cahiers de l'Orient*, No. 62, 2001.

Salgon, Jean-Michel. 'Évaluation statistique et cartographique: la situation sécuritaire en Algérie 1999–2000', *Les Cahiers de l'Orient*, No. 62, 2001.

Schmitt, Carl. *The Crisis of Parliamentary Democracy*, tr. E. Kennedy (Cambridge MA: MIT Press, 1985).

Schmitt, Carl. *The Concept of the Political*, tr. G. Schwab (Chicago: University of Chicago Press, 1996).

Schmitter, Phillipe. 'Interest systems and the consolidation of democracies', in L. Diamond and G. Marks (eds), *Reexamining Democracy: Essays in Honour of Seymour Martin Lipset* (London: Sage, 1992).

Scott, James C. *Domination and the Arts of Resistance: Hidden Transcripts* (New Haven: Yale University Press, 1990).

Segre, Claudio G. *Italo Balbo: A Fascist Life* (Berkeley: University of California Press, 1987).

Shils, Edward. 'The virtue of civil society', *Government and Opposition*, 26 (1), 1991.

Siedentop, Larry. 'Introduction', in Francois Guizot, *The History of Civilisation in Europe* (1828), tr. W. Hazlitt, (London: Penguin, 1997).

Sivan, Emmanuel. 'Arabs and democracy: Illusions of change', *Journal of Democracy*, Vol.11 (July 2000).

Sivers, Peter Von. 'National integration and traditional rural organisation in Algeria, 1970–1980: background for Islamic traditionalism?' in S.A. Arjomand (ed.), *From Nationalism to Revolutionary Islam* (Oxford: Macmillan, 1984).

Skocpol, Theda. *States and Social Revolutions* (Cambridge: Cambridge University Press, 1979).

Skocpol, Theda. 'Rentier state and Shi'a Islam in the Iranian revolution', *Theory and Society*, 11 (3), 1982.

Spencer, Claire. 'Algeria: France's Disarray and Europe's Conundrum', in B.A. Roberson (ed.), *The Middle East and Europe: The Power Deficit* (London: Routledge, 1998).

Souaidia, Habib. *La Sale Guerre* (Paris: Éditions La Decouverte, 2001).

Stone, Martin. *The Agony of Algeria* (London: Hurst and Company, 1997).

Taylor, Michael. 'Rationality and revolutionary collective action', in M. Taylor (ed.), *Rationality and Revolution* (Cambridge: Cambridge University Press, 1988).

Taylor, Michael. 'Structure, culture and action in the explanation of social change' *Politics and Society*, 17, 1989.

Taylor, Michael. 'When rationality fails', in J. Friedman (ed.), *The Rational Choice Controversy: Economic Models of Politics Reconsidered*, (New Haven: Yale University Press, 1996).

Tismaneanu, Vladimir. *Fantasies of Salvation: Democracy, Nationalism, and Myth in Post-Communist Europe* (Princeton: Princeton University Press, 1998).

Tocqueville, Alexis de. *Democracy in America*, tr. G. Lawrence (Chicago: Encyclopaedia Britannica, 1990).

Tocqueville, Alexis de. 'Travail sur l'Algérie' (1841), in Alexis de Tocqueville, *Oeuvres Complètes*, tome 1, ed. A. Jardin (Paris: Gallimard, 1991).

Tocqueville, Alexis de. 'Rapport sur l'Algérie' (1847), in Alexis de Tocqueville, *Oeuvres Complètes*, tome 1, ed. A. Jardin (Paris: Gallimard, 1991).

Tocqueville, Alexis de. *The Old Regime and the Revolution*, tr. A.S. Kahan (Chicago, Chicago University Press, 1998).

United Nations. *Statistical Yearbook 1997* (New York: United Nations, 1998).

United States Department of State. '2001 report on foreign terrorist organisations' (Washington, October 2001).

Verges, Meriem. 'Les héros n'ont pas de préoccupation de ce monde', in R. Leveau (ed.), *L'Algérie dans la Guerre* (Bruxelle: Éditions Complexes, 1995).

Volpi, Frédéric. 'Democracy in Algeria: continuity and change in the organisation of political representation', *Journal of North African Studies*, 5 (2), 2000.

Volpi, Frédéric. 'Understanding the rationale of the Islamic fundamentalists' political strategies', *Totalitarian Movements and Political Religions*, 1 (3), 2000.

Volpi, Frédéric. 'Democratisation and its enemies: the Algerian transition to authoritarianism 1988–2001', in Robin Luckham and Gavin Cawthra (eds), *Governing Security: Democratic Control of Military and Security Establishments in Transitional Democracies* (London: Zed Books, 2003).

Volpi, Frédéric. 'Language, practices and the formation of a transnational liberal-democratic ethos', *Global Society*, 16 (1), 2002.

Walton, John and David Seddon. *Free Markets and Food Riots: The Politics of Global Adjustment* (Oxford: Blackwell, 1994).

Weber, Max. *Economy and Society*, eds G. Roth and C. Wittich (New York: Bedminter Press, 1968).

Wickham-Crowley, Timothy P. *Guerrillas and Revolution in Latin America: A Comparative Study of Insurgents and Regimes since 1956* (Princeton: Princeton University Press, 1992).

Willis, Michael. *The Islamist Challenge in Algeria: a Political History* (London: Ithaca, 1996).

Yack, Bernard. *The Longing for Total Revolution: Philosophical Sources of Social Discontent from Rousseau to Marx* (Princeton: Princeton University Press, 1985).

Yefsah, Abdelkader. 'L'armée sans hidjab', *Les Temps Modernes*, January–February 1995.

Zartman, William. 'The military in the politics of succession: Algeria', in J.W. Harbeson (ed.) *The Military in African Politics* (New York: Praeger, 1987).

Zubaida, Sami. *Islam, the People and the State: Essays on Political Ideas and Movements in the Middle East* (London: Routledge, 1989).

Index

Abdelkader, Emir, 20
Abdessallam, Belaid, 64, 111–12
Abduh, Muhammad, 27–31, 33–4
Afghanistan, 15, 17, 68, 124, 126
Afghani, Djaffar al-, 69
Afghani, Jamal al-, 27–8, 30, 33–4
AIS *see* Islamic Salvation Army
Ait Ahmed, Hocine, 23, 52, 79
Algeria, locations in,
    Ain Hamra, 96
    Algiers, 20, 39–42, 46, 48, 50, 52,
        58–60, 64–5, 68, 73, 78, 80, 89–91,
        100, 103–5, 107
    Bab-el-Oued, 46, 90
    Batna, 51, 59, 67
    Bejaia, 80, 106
    Belcourt, 41, 90, 100, 102
    Constantine, 39–40, 48, 97
    Mitidja, 89–90
    Oran, 41,48, 80, 97, 99, 105
    Tizi-Ouzou, 41, 80, 104, 106–7
Al-Qaida, 14–15, 124, 126
Althusser, Louis, 6
Amnesty laws, 74, 82, 91, 136
Anarchism, 8, 15, 35, 108, 129
Annan, Kofi, 118
Arab Socialism, 13, 23, 37, 49, 64
Armed Islamic Groups / *Groupements
    Islamiques Armés* (GIA), 14–16,
    69–75, 88–92, 96, 101, 104, 112,
    114, 124–5
Armed Islamic Movement / *Mouvement
    Islamique Armé* (MIA), 68–71
Armstrong, David, 13
Assabiyya, 24–5
Assassination campaigns, 69–70, 75,
    89–90, 104, 112, 114
Association of Mujahidin (*also* associa-
    tion of war veterans), 57, 62–3, 79
Authoritarianism, 12, 15, 19, 25, 62, 66,
    72–82, 117, 119

Banna, Hassan al-, 31
Belhadj, Ali, 41, 43, 46, 50–1, 73, 78, 82,
    102–3, 132
Belkheir, Gen. Larbi, 55
Belloucif, Gen. Mustapha, 63
Ben Ali, President Zine El Abidine, 57

Ben Badis, Sheikh Abdelhamid, 30, 32
Ben Bella, Ahmed, 23
Benaicha, Ahmed, 77
Benhabiles, Abdelmélik, 55
Benkhelil, H., 55
Bergson, Henri, 33
Benhamouda, Abdelhak, 52
Bensaid, Boualem, 125
Berber minority, 23, 46, 60
    aarch movement 107, 134
    Berber Cultural Movement /
        Mouvement Culturel Berbère (MCB),
        105–6, 108
    Berber Spring, 37, 104, 106
    insurrection of 1988, 104–6
    insurrection of 2001, 106–8
    see also civil society
Berque, Jacques, 22
Betchine, Col. Mohammed, 86
Bin Laden, Osama, 14, 92, 124
Blood feuds, 94–6
Boudiaf, Mohammed, 23, 53–4, 57,
    59–60, 62–4, 111
Boukhamkham, Abdelkader, 72
Boukrouh, Noureddine, 79
Boumediene, Houari, 83–4
Bourdieu, Pierre, 10, 102
Bourgeoisie, 120–1
Bouteflika, Abdelaziz, 79–82, 107, 115
Brahimi, Abdelhamid, 44
Brahimi, Lakhdar, 55
Burgat, François, 37
Bush, George W., 14, 17, 126

Carrel, Alexis, 33
Chadli Benjedid, 53, 59–60, 66, 78
    and the military, 83–4
    and the October riots, 39–42
    and the strike of 1991, 50–1
    Chadli's reforms, 43–49
    Chadli's resignation, 55, 62
Chebouti, Abdelkader, 68
Chirac, Jacques, 74
Civil society, 16, 38, 98–9, 120, 130, 137
    Islamic charities & associations, 37–8,
        61, 70, 98–104, 107
    Berber & Kabyle associations, 37, 98,
        103–8

Moussaoui, Zacarias. 126
Movement for a Peaceful Society (MSP),
    77–8, 107, see also Hamas
Mubarak, Hosni, 57
Mujahidin (also mujahid), 89, 92
Multipartyism, 46, 122
Musharaf, Pervez, 18
Muslim Brotherhood, 31–3, 125
Myths, 9–11

Nannah, Mahfoud, 43, 74–5, 79, 81, 105,
    135
Nasser, Col. Gamal Abdel, 32–3, 61
National Commission for Dialogue /
    Commission Nationale de Dialogue
    (CND), 65–6
National Liberation Front / Front de
    Libération Nationale (FLN), 37, 40–1,
    45–6, 48–52, 54, 57–9, 61–2, 66,
    73–81, 84, 104, 107, 109, 133
National Rally for Democracy / Rassem-
    blement National pour la Démocratie
    (RND), 76–8, 80–1, 105
Nepotism, 23, 60, 76
New World Order, 4, 9, 56, 110, 116–18
Nezzar, Gen. Khaled, 55, 57, 62, 65, 83–5
North Africa, 5–6, 19–21, 23–5, 32, 37,
    117–18, 121, 125–6, 128, 131–2, 136

October 1988 riots, 38–46, 59, 83, 86, 98,
    128
O'Donnell, Guillermo, 3, 7
Oil, 70, 130
    companies, 70, 111, 114
    price, 110, 115
    revenues, 38, 96, 98, 115, 120
Organised crime, 93, 95–6

Pakistan, 14–5, 17–18, 68
Palestine, 17, 127
Patronage, 63, 86, 95, 131, 133
Philippines, The, 14
Political pluralism, 46, 48, 122
Political violence, 64, 76–7, 82, 93
Poor, the, 38, 69, 100–1, 131
Press, see media
Privatisation, 97–8, 113–14
Przeworski, Adam, 4
Putnam, Robert, 12

Qaddafi, Col. Muammar al-, 25, 57
Qutb, Sayyid, 27, 32–6

Raissi, Lofti, 126

Rally for Culture and Democracy /
    Rassemblement pour la Culture et la
    Démocratie (RCD), 52, 74, 76–8,
    104–5, 107, 134
Ramda, Rachid, 124
Realpolitik, 3, 21
Reform movement, 27–32, 80
Redjam, Abderrazak, 69, 89
Revolution, 1–3, 5, 8, 13, 35
Rida, Rashid, 30–1

Sadi, Said, 52, 74–5
Sahraoui, sheikh Abdelbaki, 123–4
Said, Edward, 21
Said, Mohammed, 67, 69, 88–9
Salafiyya, 27, 30–2, 34
San Egidio conference, 73
Saudi Arabia, 13–14, 49
Schmitt, Carl, 9
Schmitter, Phillipe, 3–4, 7
Scott, James, 101–2
September 2001, 8, 14, 115, 125–6
Shamseddine, sheikh, 100–2
Shanoun, sheikh Ahmed, 43
Shi'ism, 11, 132
Sifi, Mokdad, 79
Skocpol, Theda, 5
Socialist Forces Front / Front des Forces
    Socialistes (FFS), 52, 57–8, 61–2, 66,
    73–4, 77–8, 104–5, 107–8, 134
Solana, Javier, 111
Somalia, 14, 118
South Africa, 86
Soviet Union, 2, 6, 117
Spain, 111, 126
Spencer, Herbert, 29
State administration, 39, 45, 49, 63,
    100–2, 107
State building, 19–23, 109
State High Committee / Haut Comité
    d'État (HCE), 56–8, 60, 62, 64–6
Sudan, The, 65
Supreme Court / Conseil Constitutionnel,
    53, 55, 79
Syria, 3, 121
Structuralism, 5–6

Taleb Ibrahimi, Ahmed, 32, 79–80, 91
Taylor, Michael, 4
Terrorism
    inside Algeria, 88–92, 124–5
    International, 13, 92, 125–7
    'Islamic', 14–16, 115